The Leader

Second Edition

Charles B. Strozier · Daniel Offer · Oliger Abdyli
Editors

The Leader

Psychological Essays

Second Edition

 Springer

Editors
Charles B. Strozier
John Jay College
Center on Terrorism
Brooklyn, NY 10019, USA
charlesbstrozier@yahoo.com

Daniel Offer
Northwestern University
Northbrook, IL 60062, USA
dmo@northwestern.edu

Oliger Abdyli
John Jay College
Center on Terrorism
New York, NY 10019, USA
oliger.abdyli@jjay.cuny.edu

ISBN 978-1-4419-8385-5   e-ISBN 978-1-4419-8387-9
DOI 10.1007/978-1-4419-8387-9
Springer New York Dordrecht Heidelberg London

Library of Congress Control Number: 2011928059

Printed on acid-free paper

Springer is part of Springer Science+Business Media (www.springer.com)

Preface

The study of leadership has long occupied a central place in popular imagination. People want to understand the figures they admire (or despise), how and why they come to power, and what is the nature of the ideals leaders carry forward for the group. In the university, the study of leadership occupies the attention of scholars in many fields, especially history and political science, but also in psychology and psychoanalysis and increasingly as well as in more distant parts of the campus such as business schools. Interest in leadership, however, antedates the modern academy, as it can be truly said to have originated in the Bible, and with Plato and the Greek philosophers. This widespread and interdisciplinary concern has resulted in all kinds of overlapping studies that are sometimes descriptive and phenomenological and at other times more analytical and comparative.

Our contribution to this burgeoning field is to examine the psychology of leadership from a psychoanalytic point of view. The book spends a good deal of time noting the evolution of the ideas about leadership from the Greeks through Sigmund Freud and his followers to the extensive literature on the subject in the last half century. There is much to be gained by carefully studying this literature. Some studies, for example, such as Erik Erikson's biographies of Martin Luther and Mohandas Gandhi, are exquisite in their intelligence, insight, and beauty of expression, although we may raise concerns about his theories. In fact, for the most part, we are more impressed with the limitations of most of the work done on the psychology of leadership in the twentieth century than with its enduring quality.

The problem, we suggest, is conceptual. In the early years of the century, writers stumbled about under the weight of Freudian drive theory on their shoulders. Ideas about sexuality and early conflicts had some relevance in the clinic but were especially cumbersome in dealing with leaders in the historical or political realms. There never seemed to be sufficient evidence to prove what observers were trying to argue. As psychological theory evolved, supple thinkers such Erikson, Robert Jay Lifton, and others found more creative approaches to understanding leaders in a variety of fields. Things began to open up intellectually.

However, no one in psychoanalysis made more of a contribution to the ideas that are relevant for understanding leadership than Heinz Kohut (1913–1981). Most of the important contemporary workers in the vineyard of psychoanalysis are children of Kohut. He refashioned the theory in ways that unlinked it from dependence on stale ideas that have little relevance in the real world that leaders inhabit. He showed the depth of our subtle interdependencies with others in ways that can be described with actual leaders. He suggested ways of thinking about group behavior and the relation between leaders and followers. And, perhaps most of all, Kohut jettisoned drive theory, saving psychoanalysis from itself, and making it available for a profound understanding of the psychology of leadership without compromising the needs of scholarship for evidence that is available for others to locate, study, and replicate.

If that is the argument of the book, we try also to be ecumenical in our approach. There is nothing to be gained by narrow-mindedness, and no single thinker can possibly be said to solve all the conceptual complexities of the psychology of leadership. The discussion of the literature highlights much valuable early work that merits revisiting. Some of the studies, then, in the second part of the book—Thomas A. Kohut, for example—assume a Kohutian perspective, while others reflect the writer's own concerns, as with Dan McAdams's discussion of "narrative theory" in his analysis of George W. Bush. All, however, are attentive to larger issues of theory and meaning for future writers on the psychology of leadership.

New York, USA   Charles B. Strozier

Acknowledgments

This book has come to fruition in two incarnations and over many years. Charles B. Strozier and Daniel Offer began thinking about it seriously in 1979 after Arnold Goldberg came to them with the suggestion that they consider a conference on the implications of the work of Heinz Kohut regarding leadership. The conference that resulted at Michael Reese Hospital in June 1979 was a remarkable event, and it included participants as diverse as Heinz Kohut, Peter Gay, Bruce Mazlish, Robert Jay Lifton, Fred Weinstein, Michael Franz Basch, and others. Strozier and Offer worked with the papers from that conference, elicited other contributions, and, over four years, researched the topic of leadership on their own. A first edition of the book, *The Leader: Psychohistorical Essays*, was published in 1985 by Plenum Press.

Over the years, new scholarly developments in the field and, of course, the appearance of a whole new slate of important political leaders caused Strozier and Offer to feel it would pay to revisit the earlier volume and even to reconceptualize it. They were particularly pleased that the reconsideration of the themes in the earlier volume coincided with a major conference on "The Psychology of Leadership," sponsored by the Chicago Institute for Psychoanalysis, on December 5, 2009. The second conference provided several of the papers in the completely revised second section of the volume. Strozier and Offer were also pleased to have Oliger Abdyli join them as a coeditor at this stage of the work. Everything in the first section was brought up-to-date and much content was added as a result of further research and reflection.

A number of research assistants have assisted in the work over the years, including Michael Creany, Patricia Michaelson, and Linnea Larson. We are grateful to the many psychiatric residents and fellows of the Michael Reese Hospital for participating in seminars on this topic and sharing with us their ideas about leadership. We are particularly grateful to our friend, Herman Sinaiko, for his stimulating suggestions at an early period in our own work.

We are indebted to the Illinois Humanities Council for its partial support of the project, which has also been supported by the Adolescent Research Fund: In Memory of Judith Offer, of the Department of Psychiatry of Michael Reese Hospital.

New York, USA   Charles B. Strozier
Seattle, Washington, USA   Daniel Offer
New York, USA   Oliger Abdyli

Contents

Part I   The Past

1   Leaders in Ancient Times: Joseph, Plato, and Alcibiades   3
Charles B. Strozier, Daniel Offer, and Oliger Abdyli

2   Freud and His Followers   13
Charles B. Strozier and Daniel Offer

**3   From Erik H. Erikson to Heinz Kohut: Expanding Theories
of Leadership**   31
Charles B. Strozier and Oliger Abdyli

Part II   Studies

4   Lincoln and the Crisis of the 1850s: Thoughts on the Group Self . .   57
Charles B. Strozier

**5   Mirror Image of the Nation: An Investigation of Kaiser
Wilhelm II's Leadership of the Germans**   77
Thomas A. Kohut

6   Osama Bin Laden: The Man and the Myth 119
Bruce B. Lawrence

**7   Redemptive Narratives in the Life and the Presidency
of George W. Bush** 135
Dan P. McAdams

8   Paranoid Leadership 153
David M. Terman

Subject Index 171

Contributors

Oliger Abdyli John Jay College, Center on Terrorism, New York, NY 10019, USA, oliger.abdyli@jjay.cuny.edu

Thomas A. Kohut Sue and Edgar Wachenheim III Professor of History, Williams College, Williamstown, MA, USA, thomas.a.kohut@williams.edu

Bruce B. Lawrence Duke University, Durham NC, USA, bruce.bbl@gmail.com

Dan P. McAdams Department of Psychology, Northwestern University, 2120 Campus Drive, Evanston, IL 60208, USA, dmca@northwestern.edu

Daniel Offer Northwestern University, Northbrook, IL 60062, USA, dmo@northwestern.edu

Charles B. Strozier John Jay College, Center on Terrorism, New York, NY 10019, USA, charlesbstrozier@yahoo.com

David M. Terman Training and Supervising Analyst, former Director, Chicago Institute for Psychoanalysis, dmterman@comcast.net

About the Editors

Charles B. Strozier has a Harvard B.A., and an M.A. and a PhD from the University of Chicago. He received training as a research candidate at the Chicago Institute for Psychoanalysis and clinical psychoanalytic training at TRISP in New York City. He is a Professor of History and the Founding Director of the Center on Terrorism, John Jay College, City University of New York, and a practicing psychoanalyst in New York City. Strozier's most recent book, edited with several colleagues, is *The Fundamentalist Mindset: Psychological Perspectives on Religion, Violence, and History* (Oxford, 2010), and in 2011 has his forthcoming interview study, *Until the Fires Stopped Burning: 9/11 and New York City*. His earlier books include a prize-winning psychological study of Abraham Lincoln (*Lincoln's Quest for Union: A Psychological Portrait*, 1982, revised edition in paper 2001) and *Heinz Kohut: The Making of a Psychoanalyst* (2001), which won the Gradiva Award from the National Association for the Advancement of Psychoanalysis, the Goethe Prize from the Canadian Psychoanalytic Association, and was nominated for a Pulitzer Prize. He is also the author of *Apocalypse: On the Psychology of Fundamentalism in America* (1994, new edition 2002) and has edited, with Michael Flynn, *Trauma and Self* (1996), *Genocide, War, and Human Survival* (1996), and *The Year 2000* (1997). Strozier was the founding editor (until 1986) of *The Psychohistory Review*, and has published scores of articles and book chapters on aspects of history and psychoanalysis.

Daniel Offer, M.D., received his B.S. from the University of Rochester and his M.D. from the University of Chicago. He interned at the University of Illinois's Research and Educational Hospital. He received his psychiatric training at Michael Reese Hospital and Medical Center, Chicago, Illinois. He is also a graduate of the Chicago Institute for Psychoanalysis. Offer is currently Professor Emeritus of Psychiatry and Behavioral Sciences at the Feinberg School of Medicine of Northwestern University. He has spent his whole career in academic psychiatry. He has published 17 books and has written more than 200 articles. He has also developed an original psychological test (The Offer Self-Image Questionnaire), which has been translated into 26 languages. Offer was a Fellow at The Center for Advanced Studies in the

Behavioral Sciences at Stanford University, 1973–1974. He was the founding editor of and served as editor-in-chief for 35 years of Springer's *Journal of Youth and Adolescence*.

Oliger Abdyli holds an M.A. in Public Administration, Inspector General Track—International Inspection and Oversight and a B.A. in Government—Political Science from John Jay College. He is also the recipient of the Certificate in Terrorism Studies offered by the Center on Terrorism. In the near future, Mr. Abdyli intends to pursue a Ph.D. in Political Science. His research interests include politically motivated terrorism and state response to terrorist activities, political utilization of fear and paranoia to induce groupthink and social compliance, as well as corruption and larger governance issues.

About the Authors

Thomas A. Kohut received a B.A. from Oberlin College and a Ph.D. in history from the University of Minnesota. He is also a graduate of the Cincinnati Psychoanalytic Institute. He is currently Sue and Edgar Wachenheim III Professor of History at Williams College in Williamstown, Massachusetts. Kohut is a member of the Board of Trustees of the Austen Riggs Center in Stockbridge, Massachusetts, and is Chair of the Council of Scholars of the Erik Erikson Institute at Austen Riggs. From 2000 to 2006, Kohut served as Dean of the Faculty at Williams College. Kohut has written two books: *A German Generation: An Experiential History of the Twentieth Century* (New Haven: Yale University Press; in press); *Wilhelm II and the Germans: A Study in Leadership* (New York: Oxford University Press, 1991). He has also published articles on a number of historical and psychological topics, including the German humorist, Wilhelm Busch, letters from German soldiers at Stalingrad, and psychohistory, history, and psychoanalysis.

Bruce B. Lawrence is a 1962 magna cum laude graduate of Princeton in History and Middle East Studies. After a tour of duty with the US Navy, he earned a Masters of Divinity from Episcopal Divinity School (Cambridge) in 1967, and then in 1972 received his Ph.D. from Yale, specializing in History of Religions, with emphasis on Islam and Hinduism. He joined the Duke faculty in 1971 and continues to teach at Duke, though he has also taught abroad (first at Aligarh Muslim University and later Oxford), while also enjoying brief stints at Dartmouth and also at the University of Chicago. Since 2000, he has been the Marcus Family Professor of the Humanities, and since 2006 Inaugural Director of the Duke Islamic Studies Center. He has authored, coauthored, edited, or coedited fifteen books, many of which have won prizes. His research focuses on Islam in all phases and all disciplines, with special attention to institutional Islam in Asia, Indo-Persian Sufism, the religious masks of violence, and contemporary Islam as both Abrahamic faith and religious ideology. In 2008, he was awarded a Carnegie Scholarship on Islam, in order to pursue his current project on minority citizenship in Africa as well as Asia.

Dan P. McAdams is Professor of Psychology and of Human Development and Social Policy, and Chair of the Psychology Department, at Northwestern University. He received his B.S. degree from Valparaiso University in 1976 and his Ph.D. in Psychology and Social Relations from Harvard University in 1979. Author of nearly 200 scientific articles and chapters, numerous edited volumes, and six books, Professor McAdams works in the areas of personality and life span developmental psychology. His theoretical and empirical writings focus on concepts of self and identity in contemporary American society and on themes of power, intimacy, redemption, and generativity across the adult life course. Professor McAdams has authored *The Redemptive Self: Stories Americans Live By* (Oxford University Press, 2006) by integrating research he and his students have conducted over the past 15 years. *The Redemptive Self* charts a new psychology of American identity as expressed in cultural and historical American texts and images and in the life stories of caring and productive American adults in their midlife years. The book won the 2006 William James Award from the American Psychological Association for best general-interest book in psychology, across all subfields, and the 2007 Association of American Publishers Award for excellence in professional and scholarly publishing. Professor McAdams is also the 1989 winner of the Henry A. Murray Award from the American Psychological Association, for his research and writings on personality and the study of lives, and the 2006 Theodore Sarbin Award for contributions to theoretical and philosophical psychology. He is a Fellow of the American Psychological Association (Division 8) and the American Psychological Society, has served on the Executive Committee of the Society for Personality and Social Psychology, and is a Founding Member of the Association for Research in Personality.

David M. Terman has a B.A., B.S., and an M.D. from the University of Chicago. He received his psychiatric training at Michael Reese Hospital, P and P I and his psychoanalytic training from the Chicago Institute for Psychoanalysis. He is the former Director of the Chicago Institute where he remains a Faculty Member and a Training and Supervising Analyst. He has published extensive clinical and theoretical papers on Self Psychology, and he is a member of the International Council of Self Psychology. He is coauthor and editor with Charles Strozier and James Jones of *The Fundamentalist Mindset: Psychological Perspectives on Religion, Violence, and History.*

Part I
The Past

Chapter 1
Leaders in Ancient Times:
Joseph, Plato, and Alcibiades

Charles B. Strozier, Daniel Offer, and Oliger Abdyli

Joseph

The story of Joseph is one of the most fascinating, detailed, and complex stories in the Bible. Although there is no direct archeological evidence that relates the Israelites to Egypt, it is assumed that the Israelites who emigrated from Canaan (Palestine) to Egypt in search of a more fruitful land were the Hyksos, Semitic tribes who invaded Egypt in 1730 BC and ruled Egypt for 150 years.

It is likely that the story of Joseph is that of a leader who belonged to a marginal group (a nomadic tribe) that ruled a stable society which had been in existence for over a thousand years.

According to the Bible, in his adolescence, Joseph was his father's favorite child because "he was the son of his old age" (Genesis 37:3). Jacob, his *father,* made him a coat of many colors, which caused much envy and jealousy among his brothers. They developed strong hateful feelings toward Joseph, though he did not understand why. Joseph was apparently pleased with himself and his position in the family. He had two blatantly self-centered dreams in which everyone was to serve Joseph. This annoyed even his father.

Later, Joseph was sent by his father to see whether everything was all right with his brothers. As he approached them, they said to each other, "Behold, this dreamer cometh" (Genesis 37:19). Not only did he stand out as the favorite, he also fantasized about his superior place in the world. The brothers considered killing him, but did not, and in the end sold Joseph as a slave to a passing tribe for twenty pieces of silver. They went back home and told their father that Joseph had been killed by a beast.

Joseph was sold to an Egyptian officer named Potiphar. Joseph was a loyal servant and worked his way up to become the overseer of Potiphar's household. Here Joseph's story in the Bible makes a detour, and we are told that Joseph was "of beautiful form and fair to look upon" (Genesis 39:6; we might wonder whether we

C.B. Strozier (✉)
John Jay College, Center on Terrorism, New York, NY 10019, USA
e-mail: charlesbstrozier@yahoo.com

C.B. Strozier et al. (eds.), *The Leader*, 2nd ed., DOI 10.1007/978-1-4419-8387-9_1,
© Springer Science+Business Media, LLC 2011

see here the influence of the Greeks). The wife of his master took to him and tried to seduce him. Joseph, ever loyal, refused, and she became infuriated with him and accused him of trying to rape her. The consequence was that Joseph ended up in jail.

The above story is amazingly similar to the "The Tale of the Two Brothers" found in the "Ordinary Papyrus" from the Nineteenth Dynasty (ca. 1300 BC), which states:

> Once upon a time there were two brothers....The name of the elder one was Anubis, the younger was called Bata. Anubis owned a house and a wife and his younger brother lived with him as if he were his own son. He drove the cattle out to the fields and brought them home at night and slept with them in the cowshed. When ploughing time came round, the two brothers were ploughing the land together. They had been a few days in the fields when they ran out of corn. The elder brother therefore sent the younger one off: "Hurry and bring us corn from the city." The younger brother found his elder brother's wife having a hairdo. "Up," he said, "and give me some corn, for I have to hurry back to the field. My brother said: 'Quick, don't waste any time.' " He loaded up with corn and wheat and went out with his burden....Then said she to him: "You have so much energy! Every day I see how strong you are....Come! Let us lie down for an hour!—It may give you pleasure, and I shall also make you fine clothes." Then the young man was as angry as a southern panther at this wicked suggestion that had been made to him. He said to her: "What a disgraceful proposal you have just made....Never do it again and I shall say nothing to anyone." So saying, he slung his load on his back and went out to the fields. The wife began to be frightened about what she had said. She got hold of some grease paint and made herself up to look like someone who had been violently assaulted. Her husband...found his wife lying prostrate as a result of the [pretended] outrage. Her husband said to her: "Who has been with you?" She replied: "No one...apart from your younger brother. When he came to fetch the corn he found me sitting alone and said to me: 'Come, let us lie down for an hour! Do up your hair.' But I paid no attention to him. 'Am I not your mother! and is your elder brother not like a father to *you!*' I said to him. But he was afraid and struck me to stop me telling you about it. If you leave him alive now I shall die." Then his brother grew as wild as a southern panther. He sharpened his knife...to kill his younger brother. (Keller, 99–100)

In jail, Joseph's talents helped him again as he ran the prison for its keeper. Through brilliant dream interpretation, he was able to leave the prison. Joseph understood people well and was able to present himself as a natural leader of men. Hence, Pharaoh turned to him and, when Joseph was 30 years old, Pharaoh appointed him vizier of Egypt. Joseph was a most able leader and guided the Egyptian people through tense and difficult times.

The biblical story goes on in detail to describe how Joseph and his brothers resolved their past conflicts. When famine reigned over the Middle East, the Israelites needed food and Joseph's brothers went to Egypt to obtain it. Since Joseph had planned well ahead of the famine, there was food in Egypt and therefore people from all over the Middle East went to Egypt to buy food. When Joseph encountered his brothers, he recognized them, but they did not recognize him. Joseph remembered his adolescent dreams and what his brothers had done to him. He accused them of spying and jailed them. Through a number of complex transactions, Joseph instilled panic in his brothers to avenge himself, driving them to desperation and hopelessness. Only after they were completely at his mercy and totally powerless did he reveal to them that he was their brother. In the end, Joseph, the leader among his brothers, turned out to be the noble, powerful, all-giving, and forgiving person.

Jacob joined with the whole tribe as they migrated to Egypt, where with Joseph as their leader they began the formation of a new and great nation, Israel. Joseph arranged for the Israelites to settle down in Goshen, a land that was extremely fertile and particularly well suited for raising cattle. His brothers and their kin settled there comfortably and multiplied.

Meanwhile, Joseph had consolidated his power over Egypt. He had exchanged the food that he had stored during the years of plenty for money, cattle, horses, and, finally, rights to the land. He then arranged a new system of taxation, under which 20% of the gross income of the people went to Pharaoh and the rest was retained by the people. The Egyptians, as the Bible tells us, despised cattle breeders, and it is unlikely that under ordinary circumstances such a person as Joseph would have risen to such prominence. As Keller (1969) put it:

> Only *under* the *foreign* overlords, the Hyksos, would an "Asiatic" have [had] the chance to rise to the highest office in the state. Under the Hyksos we repeatedly find officials with Semitic names. On scarabs dating from the Hyksos period the name "Jacob-Her" has been clearly deciphered. "And it is not impossible," concludes the great American Egyptologist James Henry Breasted, "that a leader of the Israelite tribe of Jacob gained control for a time in the Nile valley in this obscure period. Such an occurrence would fit in surprisingly well with the migration to Egypt of Israelite tribes which in any case must have taken place about this time."

After Jacob's death, Joseph's brothers were afraid that "Joseph will hate us, and will fully requite us all the evil which we did unto *him*" (Genesis 50:15). They went to him, treated him with tremendous admiration, and asked for his forgiveness. As a matter of fact, they treated Joseph as if he were their God—a far cry from the way they had treated him in the past. Joseph was embarrassed by the way his brothers revered him, and told them, "Fear not; for am I in the place of God?" (Genesis 50:19). He comforted his brothers and assured them that he would not avenge their past wrongdoings. Joseph went on to live to a ripe old age without any problems that we know about.

Joseph's story, like all biblical stories, has been studied for over 3,000 years by a vast number of scholars. We do not intend to discuss the story of Joseph, except from a very limited psychohistorical perspective. There is no information about Joseph as a child, except that he had lost his mother at a young age and that he was his father's favorite. Joseph's adolescent self-centeredness so irritated his brothers that they considered killing him. The story of Joseph, as we have pointed out, is mixed with earlier myths, and it is very hard to separate one myth from another. The use and abuse of power, the place of revenge and violence, spying, cheating, stealing, forgiveness, graciousness, reverence, and dreams of grandeur are all part of the story of Joseph, which even describes a new system of taxation that is organized particularly to help those in power. The story's components are not that different from what we see among leaders today: money, power, sex, violence, and wisdom. Finally, Joseph was an outsider to Egypt, and, because he saw it more clearly as such, he was able to undertake certain programs which produced newer systems of government. The insiders, as wise as they were, could not comprehend what was necessary to do in Egypt under a crisis. In this case, only an outsider, Joseph, was able to understand

Pharaoh's dreams (his internal problems) and offer new solutions for them. The new leader integrated tradition with a revamped system. For Joseph and the Egyptians, this worked exceedingly well.

Plato

Plato was perhaps the first systematic theorist of the psychological basis of leadership. The remarkable insights of the *Republic* probe the varieties of leadership styles, how these styles respond to the needs of followers, the relationship between childrearing and adulthood, and political behavior, and offer an astute psychobiographical analysis of the tyrant.

These ideas are spelled out most clearly in Books VIII and IX of the *Republic*. In the dialogue between Socrates and Glaucon, Socrates describes the different forms of government: the aristocratic, the oligarchic, the democratic, and the tyrannical. Most of the earlier sections of the *Republic* develop in detail Plato's sense of a good and just man and how he rules in an aristocratic republic that rewards the good. In these two books of the *Republic,* Plato analyzes the forms of government that depart from this ideal. It is not a historical model, which describes the evolution of governmental form over time, but an abstract study of how the state can diverge from the ideal. Plato acknowledges exceptions—for example, a purchased kingdom or a mixed form of government—but he argues that the principal competing types of the state are the oligarchic, the democratic, and the tyrannical.

Plato argues that what mediates the movement from one form of government to another is the changed collective experience of childhood. For example, the aristocracy of the good and just cannot last. "Not only for plants that grow from the earth," states Socrates,

> but also for animals that live upon it there is a cycle of bearing and barrenness for soul and body as often as the revolutions of their orbs come full circle, in brief courses for the short-lived and oppositely for the opposite; by the laws of prosperous birth or infertility for your race, the men you have bred to be your rulers will not for all their wisdom ascertain by reasoning combined with sensation, but they will escape them, and there will be a time when they will beget children out of season.[1]

These children come to neglect their elders, their music, their gymnastics, and their culture. They become adults avid for wealth and all the sensual pleasures; their homes (as adults) will be "literal love nests."[2] Money comes to occupy the center of their existence and they strive only to acquire wealth. This characterizes an oligarchy, a form of government in which the rich control and the poor are excluded. The citizens in such a state never turn their thoughts to true culture.[3]

---

[1] Plato, *Republic,* trans. Paul Shorey, 2 volumes (Cambridge: Harvard University Press, 1963), II, 245–246.

[2] Ibid., 251.

[3] Ibid., 255.

And where do you look, asks Socrates, to explain the emergence of such citizens? "To guardianships of orphans, and any such opportunities of doing injustice with impunity."[4]

Oligarchy, *however, contains the* seeds of its own destruction, for among the huddled, poor, and disenfranchised masses are youth of vigor and strength. They observe in battle, for example, the cowardice and weakness of the pampered rich. They talk to each other and learn that all the poor are in the same situation. Resentment builds and eventually the poor band together and kill the rich by force of arms or by some form of terrorism. Then the masses appropriate the wealth and take control of the government. Thus, democracy ensues.

In democracy, each person leads his or her life as one pleases. Possibly, "this is the most beautiful of all politics; as a garment of many colors, embroidered with all kinds of hues, so this, decked and diversified with every type of character, would appear the most beautiful."[5] However, such a form of government tramples underfoot the good person who from childhood has pursued truth and beauty. Such humans get lost in the shuffle, for in a democracy, everyone is equal, there is no discrimination, and equality is granted equally *to* equals and unequals alike.[6] The common youth tastes the pleasures of wealth and indulges all his appetites; he drinks or plays the flute or exercises or seemingly occupies himself with philosophy as whim or the moment dictate.[7]

The very lack of discrimination inherent in democracy opens the way to despotism, by which people are held in the grip of the "most cruel and bitter servile servitude."[8] The problem, essentially, is one of pleasure: "Of our necessary pleasures and appetites," Socrates tells Glaucon,

"there are some lawless ones, I think, which probably are to be found in us all, but which, when controlled by the laws and the better desires in alliance with reason, can in some men be altogether got rid of, or so nearly so that only a few weak ones remain, while in others the remnant is stronger and more numerous." "What desires do *you* mean?" he [Glauconi] said. "Those," said I, "that are awakened in sleep when the rest of the soul, the rational, gentle and dominant part, slumbers, but the beastly and savage part, replete with food and wine, gambols and, repelling sleep, endeavors to sally forth and satisfy its own instincts. You are aware that in such case there is nothing it will not venture to undertake as being released from all sense of shame and all reason. It does not shrink from attempting to lie with a mother in fancy or with anyone else, man, God, or brute. It is ready for any foul deed of blood; it abstains from no food, and, in a word, falls short of no extreme of folly and shamelessness."[9]

The tyrant lives out these fantasies; that is, he enacts what must be restrained by good law but which, Plato recognizes, is all too human: "There exists in every *one*

---

[4]Ibid., 275.
[5]Ibid., 287.
[6]Ibid., 291.
[7]Ibid., 301–303.
[8]Ibid., 333.
[9]Ibid., 335–337.

of us, even in some reputed most respectable, a terrible, fierce and lawless brood of desires, which it seems are revealed in our sleep."[10]

The tyrant's hubris lies in his excesses and in his lack of control: "Then a man becomes tyrannical in the full sense of the word, my friend, 'I said,' when either by nature or by habits or by both he has become even as the drunken, the erotid, the maniacal."[11] The tyrant is in his waking life "what he rarely became in sleep."[12] And again: "He [the tyrant] is, I presume, the man who, in his waking hours, has the qualities we found in his dream state."[13]

Plato's theory of leadership thus describes a movement along a continuum of control, from the prevalence of the good and virtuous (controlled and adaptive ego strengths) in an aristocracy, to the dissolute and wanton pursuit of pleasure (the emergence of normally repressed impulses and the breakdown of creative sublimations) in oligarchies and democracies, to the lawless and unbridled passions (pure id) of despotism. His argument is psychologically astute, for it recognizes the place of the tyrant's passions in the dream of the good and the just. Hubris is excess or, in our terms, enactment. Just laws build in control so that virtue can flourish. But the good is fragile. Children, especially, can be born out of season and mediate the unraveling of the controls of the inner demons.

Alcibiades

Plutarch (AD 46–120) was a historian who discussed the leading political figures of ancient times in his monumental work entitled *The Lives of the Noble Grecians and Romans*,[14] which encompasses biographies of 51 of the noblest Greeks and Romans of the five centuries before Christ. Each *Life* gives a detailed description of the military, political, and personal achievements of its subject and devotes attention to his style of leadership, his motivation(s), and the interplay of his personality with the character of his followers. Plutarch, who seems to have had a strong platonic conviction of right and wrong, discussed the leaders of ancient times from a moralistic point of view and was quick to add his own impression of how good or bad each leader was as a human being. He often attributed the success or failure of a particular leader to how good, virtuous, or respectful of laws that leader was. The *Lives* shows Plutarch's great awareness of how an individual leader's psychodynamics, or even psychopathology, organizes his style of leadership. Personal characteristics, such as ambition, virtue, cruelty, revenge, commitment, and innate talent, all played a major part in the success or failure of leaders of ancient times. Plutarch described

---

[10] Ibid., 339.

[11] Ibid., 343–345.

[12] Ibid., 349.

[13] Ibid., 353.

[14] Plutarch, *The Lives of The Noble Grecians and Romans*, trans. John Dryden (New York: Modern Library, 1964).

every conceivable psychological characteristic known to human, blending narration of achievements with a discussion of psychological traits in his own personal style. We regard Plutarch as the first psychohistorian in the Western world.

In terms of modern psychology, it is of interest that the only factors which Plutarch clearly omits from his discussions are those concerning childhood. He says little about the childhoods of the political figures he treats in the *Lives,* making only general statements concerning their lineage. Although unconscious factors are not discussed as such, Plutarch often offers dreams or other psychological mechanisms to illustrate the complexities of the phenomena he discusses.

Although Freud lived eighteen centuries later, Plutarch's psychology is definitely a conflict psychology, in terms of his examination of the human situation. He presents his heroes as continually struggling with two conflicting emotions or states, of which one is usually good and the other evil. Humans struggle not only between the virtues, but also between two different and conflicting emotional states.

In order to illustrate Plutarch's method, we shall use his discussion of Alcibiades, surely one of the most interesting political leaders of ancient times. He illustrates, in our opinion, a controversial yet brilliant leader.

Alcibiades was born in Athens in 450 BC and died in Phrygia (now Turkey) in 404 BC He was born with "a silver spoon in his mouth," of noble origin (he was distantly related to the famed Pericles), a most promising, intellectually brilliant, physically strong, extremely handsome, and very courageous young man, who was a marvelous orator with an excellent sense of humor, but also a self-centered and impulsive individual. The only known fact about his childhood is that his father, Clinias, was killed in the battle of Coronae when Alcibiades was only 3 or 4 years old. Pericles, who was busy in Athenian politics, became his guardian, and one wonders how much time he had for Alcibiades. Considering the kind of outstanding qualities that nature had bestowed on Alcibiades, it was not surprising that the famed Socrates took a keen interest in him and took him under his wing early in Alcibiades's youth.

There is no question that Alcibiades was an extremely gifted leader. He was a military genius, who never lost a battle regardless of whose side he was on. It seems, however, that whenever he had achieved an ambition and become revered by his fellow men, he would do something impulsive which gratified his immediate needs but which was self-destructive in the long run. One can only wonder what would have happened to Athens if the military had followed Alcibiades's advice in the war with Sparta. But by that time his reputation had become so tarnished that even though his military genius was intact, the Athenians no longer believed in him.

Let us examine his life in more detail. In his youth, according to Plutarch's account, Alcibiades possessed a thirst for knowledge, yet he was easily caught by pleasure and overcome by temperamental feelings. While in grammar school, he was known to have struck a teacher. When, as a child, Alcibiades once wanted to speak to his guardian, Pericles, and was told that he could not because Pericles was busy counseling how to give his accounts to the Athenians, Alcibiades said as he went away, "Were better for him to consider how he might avoid giving up his accounts at all."[15] He once gave a box on the ear to a wealthy and noble man, Hipponides. He had no quarrel with Hipponides; he did it only as a jest, because he had told his peers he would do it. He later felt ashamed of his action and went to the nobleman's home, took off his clothes, and asked Hipponides to beat him up as much as he pleased. Hipponides laughed and forgave him; as a matter of fact, Alcibiades later married his daughter. To use current terminology, it seems that Alcibiades was an impulsive youngster who was looking for love and acceptance, and was without consistent adult guidance.

Alcibiades's vanity and ambition made him an easy prey for those who wanted to use him. He would get inflated ideas about his political strength, and it took the patience of Socrates to humble and correct him and to show him how far from perfection in virtue he was.

As Plutarch said, "He possessed the people with great hopes, and he himself entertained yet greater".[16] When Alcibiades entered public life, he was thought to have great advantages; his noble birth, wealth, courage, and charisma were unmistakable. In 420 BC he became a general and opposed the aristocrat Nicias. He led an Athenian armada to Sicily and won the first battle easily. However, he was accused by his enemies of profaning the busts of Hermes throughout the city. He was recalled to Athens for trial. He escaped to Sparta, where he was highly regarded, and helped the Spartans win the war against Athens. He changed his personal habits to conform to the Spartan way of life, giving up "high living" and easily gaining the Spartans' respect and affection. However, Alcibiades could not leave well enough alone. While the Spartan king Agis II was away on a military expedition, Alcibiades had an affair with the king's wife and had a son by her. As a result, he had to flee Sparta. He joined the archenemy of the Greeks, the Persians. He charmed the Persian king, who hated Greeks passionately, and helped the Persians in their wars with the Greeks.

Later, in 411 BC, Alcibiades returned to Athens and helped her in some dramatic military victories. Forgiven by the Athenians for his past activities, he was welcomed in Athens as a hero. "Nevertheless," says Plutarch, "this public joy was mixed with some tears, and the present happiness was allayed by the remembrance of the miseries they [the Athenians] had endured."[17] There remained much suspicion of Alcibiades, and upon the first opportunity his enemies invented a malicious story about him which, according to Plutarch, was factually incorrect. Alcibiades had to flee again, this time to Turkey, where he was later assassinated, supposedly by the Spartans. Sparta conquered Athens, and the one leader who might have prevented this had to escape shamefully. As Plutarch said,

If ever a man was ruined by his own glory, it was Alcibiades. For his continual success had produced such an idea of his courage and conduct, that if he failed in anything he undertook, it was imputed to his neglect, and no one would believe it was through want of power.[18]

---

[15] Ibid., 237.

[16] Ibid., 244.

[17] Ibid., 257.

[18] Ibid., 259.

Alcibiades was probably the most gifted Athenian leader of his generation, during an era which is considered the golden age of Athens. He was, however, an impulsive, self-centered man and a pleasure-seeker who lived from moment to moment during peacetime. He showed his courage and talent best during crisis periods. He was not a cruel person; although a traitor to his homeland, he nonetheless came to Athens's help when he believed her survival was at stake. He was a man who could be quite generous at times, but his unpredictability made people mistrust him. In addition, his numerous talents created intense jealousy and hatred among some. He believed in his own right to succeed without modulating and moderating his own fantasies. Were his seeds of self-destruction too strong for him to overcome? Or would he have succeeded under different circumstances? It is possible that he was simply too gifted for his own good, as well as for that of his fellow men, and that his inordinate talent did not allow him to develop a sense of proportion. Things came so easily for him that he might have believed that it was his divine right to lead and govern. All this may have prevented him from dealing with failures which were of his own making. The crises which he did create did not seem to teach him anything, but rather only strengthened his sense of superiority over others. His childlike belief in his own invulnerability caused him to exaggerate his capacities as well as to underestimate his personal enemies. His continuous search for glory, together with his unmasked ambition, formed a deadly combination which allowed for no compromise with his followers. Nothing seemed impossible for him, but in the end, he simply ran out of impossible tasks and was assassinated.

Chapter 2
Freud and His Followers

Charles B. Strozier and Daniel Offer

It is said that Freud and his circle put so much emphasis on understanding history, art, literature, religion, and culture generally because, in that early period, they lacked sufficient numbers of patients to discuss psychoanalytic issues among themselves with any degree of scientific rigor. Their real interests were clinical and theoretical, but the only "cases" at hand lay in history, politics, and art and literature.[1] While true, the early Freudians were deeply committed to gaining an understanding of the hidden motives and deeper meanings of everything human. The world of the consulting room mattered in special ways (it was the laboratory), but the data it yielded lacked broad theoretical significance unless also applied to culture in the broadest sense. Applied psychoanalysis for the early Freudians was not the frosting on the cake it that it became in later years; everything hung on it.

Freud's own decade of splendid isolation and his break with Wilhelm Fliess merged into the conscious shaping of a movement in 1902. It was then that he first asked a number of colleagues influenced by his work to attend meetings in his house on Wednesday evenings. For the first 4 years, no record exists of the proceedings. From 1906 on, however, Otto Rank dutifully kept thorough notes on the discussions, which continued on a regular basis until 1911 and after that fitfully until 1933 (after 1918there is no record of the scientific discussions). Rank's notes, amazingly enough, were saved from the Nazis by Paul Federn. Paul's son, Ernst, and Herman Nunberg later transcribed, translated, edited, and published the notes in four volumes. These *Minutes of the Vienna Psychoanalytic Society* provide a unique glimpse into the first group for applied psychoanalysis.

The discussions were diverse and often heated. On December 4, 1907, Isidor Sadger presented some psychoanalytic thoughts on the poetry of Konrad Ferdinand Meyer. Max Graf led the discussion by dismissing Meyer as an insignificant poet and Sadger as "quite careless in supporting his hypotheses and theses." Wilhelm

---

C.B. Strozier (✉)
John Jay College, Center on Terrorism, New York, NY 10019, USA
e-mail: charlesbstrozier@yahoo.com

[1] *Minutes of the Vienna Psychoanalytic Society,* ed. Herman Numberg and Ernst Federn, 4 volumes (New York: International Universities Press, 1962), I, xxviii.

C.B. Strozier et al. (eds.), *The Leader*, 2nd ed., DOI 10.1007/978-1-4419-8387-9_2,
© Springer Science+Business Media, LLC 2011

Stekel labeled Sadger's work as "surface psychology" and expressed his fear by saying that his work would "harm our cause"; according to Stekel, Sadger's presentation was "nonsense," not to mention inelegant: "the relationship to his mother should have been indicated just once and discretely, not emphasized in such an obtrusive manner." Otto Rank tried to find some redeeming virtues in Sadger's presentation but was quickly drowned out by Paul Federn, who was indignant about Sadger's failure to discuss Meyer's sexual development. "Sadger has not said a single word about the poet's sexual development," Federn opined,

> because one just does not know anything about it; therefore, one cannot write a pathography. Meyer must have had significant sexual experiences. A neurotic person [that is, Sadger] has recognized from Meyer's work the incestuous relationship to his sister. Meyer was probably an onanist and was ashamed of this before his mother.

Fritz Wittels, sensing that things were getting out of hand, expressed chagrin at "the personal outburst of rage and indignation on the part of Stekel and Federn." Freud also advised moderation but went on to express the view that "Sadger's investigation has not clarified anything." Freud then gave his own thumbnail sketch of Meyer's personality, his development, and the meanings of his poetry. A chastened Sadger had the last word. He had hoped for more than invective and insult, he said. Furthermore, he had learned nothing from the substantive criticisms. "It is not possible accurately to deduce a poet's real experiences from his works because there is nothing to distinguish the real from the illusory; one does not know where truth ends and poetic imagination begins."[2]

A little less than a year later—on October 14, 1908—it was Stekel's turn to be chastised. His presentation dealt with a play by Franz Grillparzer, *Der Traum, em Leben* ("A Dream Is Life"). We learn from Rank's notes that Stekel apparently approached the play as a source of data from understanding the suffering and neurosis of Grillparzer himself. Stekel concluded that Grillparzer was a compulsive neurotic. The discussion was, at first, gentle, by the standards of this group. Federn saw in the presentation "the whole Stekel, with all his faults and his merits. With his customary lack of critical judgment, Stekel jumbles up everything, and is utterly arbitrary about details." Reitler, however, liked the presentation and mentioned several interesting aspects of it. He was echoed by Wittels, Steiner, Rie, Sadger, and Rank.

Then Freud spoke. Not only did he disagree with the diagnosis, he also felt there was "not the slightest evidence that Grillparzer was an obsessional neurotic." Furthermore, Freud felt Stekel had "misunderstood" the question of Grillparzer's sexuality and his method was too "radical" and wildly indiscriminate. Freud's critical views seemed to influence the remaining commentators—Albert Joachim, Adolph Deutsch, Edward Hitschmann, and Alfred Adler—who were all, except for Deutsch, quite outspoken in their dislike for the paper. Joachim doubted Stekel's method, on the grounds that "an artist's creating resembles only in part that of

---

[2]Ibid., 254–258.

the neurotic." Hitschmann sarcastically criticized Stekel's argument. How, he wondered, could Grillparzer feel constrained in love as an adult because he had not possessed his mother as a child, when "very many men do not possess their mother, and yet do not become sexually impotent"? Adler ended the attack by charging that Stekel had arbitrarily lined up single elements in the Grillparzer play and then completely botched the interpretation. Stekel, in his "last word," thanked only "the professor" and noted that the paper had fulfilled its purpose because it had served as the occasion for Freud's reply.[3]

And there was that urn. Until 1908, the name of each member of the group was written on a piece of paper and placed in an urn. After the presentation, everyone present was obliged to comment in the order in which his name was randomly drawn from the urn. The idea was Freud's, though it was an old Rabbinic tradition that was intended to prevent the teacher from monopolizing discussion and encourage the students to speak up and find their own voice. The urn, however, gave "the professor" a subtle power to grade his pupils/followers on a weekly basis specifically in relation to their understanding of his theories. It is no wonder the members of the group spoke of the "tyranny of the urn." Federn even reported later that many members of the group were sneaking out of the meetings after the presentation and before discussion to avoid having their name drawn.[4] The first proposal in the 1908 "Motions Concerning the Reorganization of the Meetings" was to abolish the urn. In the meeting during which the motions were discussed, February 5, 1908, there was some sharp exchange on most of the proposals. The first motion (to abolish the urn), however, was carried unanimously.[5]

From our comfortable perspective, it is rather easy to see the underlying tension in the Vienna group and, as is often done in the biographies of Freud, to unmask the leader of psychoanalysis for imperiously imposing his personality on the group and forcing submission to his ideas. This aspect of the early psychoanalytic group lent it the quality of a religious, or at least an ideological, movement. Strenuous disagreement was allowed, even encouraged, but real dissent required a complete split and separation from Freud. There was a clear and forceful leader in this group, a leader, furthermore, who manipulated his followers and enforced submission. The followers psychologically bought into this process as they idealized Freud the man and the exciting new ideas of psychoanalysis. In Freud's own subsequent formulation of such relationships, the followers came to share a common ego ideal in Freud and in this sense blended their differing and contentious personalities into a group that was given psychological coherence by the leadership of Freud.

Nevertheless, it is worth remembering that Freud was the one with original ideas in this group. There was also the reality of external derision for psychoanalytic theory. It took, perhaps, a measure of enforced group cohesion to keep things moving forward and to remain focused on relevant topics of research and discussion.

---

[3] Ibid., II, 2–12.
[4] Ibid., 299.
[5] Ibid., 298–303.

Nor were the members of the group wholly naive regarding the tyranny of Freud's leadership role. They rebelled against the urn. The meetings even moved out of Freud's home in 1908. Many presentations sharply diverged from Freud's ideas, and so much remained unexplored that neither Freud nor his followers could easily define a single, orthodox line to follow. Stekel, for example, in these early years, was always refreshingly odd. The group process, whatever else it did, also fostered a remarkable creativity in the group.[6]

Discussion of leaders, while not the central theme in the group, did occur. On April 10, 1907, Fritz Wittels presented a paper on Tatjana Leontiev, a Russian revolutionary figure who had tried to assassinate a top Czarist figure. Wittels compared Leontiev to a long list of female assassins, beginning with biblical figures (including Jael, who killed Sisera by driving a nail through his temple, and Judith, who beheaded Holofernes) and proceeding through, oddly enough, Joan of Arc. The choice of antecedent, however, is a little clearer in light of Wittels's interpretation that Jael's nail, for Wittels, "is a penis symbol." The case of Judith, who used a sword to behead Holofernes in anticipation of his raping her, is similar: This act liberated

> the cry of the flesh to accomplish also a praiseworthy deed. What gratification under the cloak of an idealistic motive... She may also be a virgin because blood must flow during the deed which she plans to commit. When her father was leading her to her wedding, she looked up to him and said, "Surely, Mannasseh looks quite different." Here, for the first time, the importance of the father is indicated. We can readily assume that in all these cases the girl's first sexual affection for her father plays its role; for this love is indeed always rejected.[7]

The discussion indicated that the group had a more reasonable sensitivity to political reality than Wittels's presentation would suggest. Both Adler and Freud were disturbed at Wittels's failure to assess adequately the political context of a revolutionary figure. Adler stressed that ideology cannot be divorced from emotional life; ideology, he continued, cannot explain everything, though ideology itself can be analyzed. Freud was concerned with the harshness of Wittels's condemnation of assassins and noted the limits of such unmasking of unconscious motives. A sound interpretation, he said, requires a certain tolerance for such hidden emotions. Nevertheless, Freud had begun his comments affirming the basic line of thought in Wittels's interpretation. "It is the suppressed erotism," he said, "which puts the weapon in the hand of these women. Every act of hate issues from erotic tendencies. Repudiated love, in particular, renders this transformation possible.[8]

The content of the Vienna group's discussion thus ranged far and wide, though the purpose was always focused—to apply Freud's thought to culture, art, literature, and history. From the very beginning, it was apparent to the members of the group

---

[6]Heinz Kohut, "Creativeness, Charisma, Group Psychology: Reflections on the Self-Analysis of Freud," in *The Search for the Self: Selected Writings of Heinz Kohut, 1950–1978*, ed. Paul H. Ornstein, 4 volumes (New York: International Universities Press, 1978), II, 793–843.

[7]Ibid., I, 160–161.

[8]Ibid., 164.

that they faced special problems of method. The term that emerged early on to des-
ignate the way that they were approaching the study of the individual poet, artist,
or historical figure was "pathography," or, as the editors of the *Minutes* put it, "a
biography written from a medical point of view with particular attention to psychic
anomalies."[9] The term "pathography" was in common intellectual coinage then, but
it clearly captured the assumptions and method of the Vienna group with particular
accuracy. Isidor Sadger, for example, made a number of presentations in the early
years on the sexual and emotional pathology of poets as part of his larger medical
study of hereditary predisposition.[10] Freud, as usual, set the tone. In his presentation
near the end of 1909 on Leonardo da Vinci, he noted parenthetically but obviously
(for this group) that: "We shall, of course, first inquire into the man's sexual life in
order, on that basis, to understand the peculiarities of his character."[11]

The idea is that the rules of the clinic spill over to culture. Sadger noted
unabashedly that he wrote pathographies "purely out of medical interest, not for
the purpose of throwing light on the process of artistic creation, which, by the
way, remains unexplained even by psychoanalytic interpretation."[12] Freud guarded
against any mechanistic applications of his ideas on the neuroses to classify culture
material, but he never questioned that psychoanalytic theory can be used to illumi-
nate "pathographic material."[13] The only one of the Vienna group ever to raise a
serious methodological objection to the group's approach to psychobiography was
Max Graf, who once distinguished a case history from a psychological portrayal.
"The case history," he said, "is a pathography and it is only possible where the
sources are rich *and* when pathology exists. Pathography, however, tells little of the
creative process." To understand that, he noted, gilding the lily, "requires the artistic
sensitivity of Freud himself."[14]

Nevertheless, there was some sensitivity to the limits of applying psychoanalytic
theory. The group knew they were searching for clinical relevance in the nonclinical
world. If they were not exactly humble about that, they were often cautious. No one
could get away unscathed in talking about repression in reference to a nation's psychic life.[15] Furthermore, Freud recognized a fundamental distinction between his
enterprise and that of what we should now call the social sciences and humanities.
Freud believed that psychology was ultimately grounded in biology and chemistry.
He had abandoned his "Project for a Scientific Psychology" only because he knew
too little of brain function and neurological processes at the cellular level to carry
forward his investigations fully. Instead, he turned to a world of metaphors in psychology. His life's work, as he said later with a degree of false humility, was only a

---

[9] Ibid., I, 169.
[10] Ibid., 98.
[11] Ibid., II, 338–352.
[12] Ibid., I, 267–268.
[13] Ibid., 179–180.
[14] Ibid., 259–269.
[15] Ibid., 8, for example.

detour. History and literature, however, are not way stations to a deeper, more fundamental reality in the natural sciences. Freud knew that, although he sometimes acted otherwise, and whether or not the group seemed to realize it at all.

II

After the early period of meeting in Freud's home, his followers for the most part directed their energies in the area of applied analysis and leadership into *Imago,* which was founded in 1912 and published continuously until 1937. The editor (until 1927) was Otto Rank, the secretary of the earlier group. *Imago,* subtitled *Zeitschrift für der Psychoanalyze auf der Geisteswissenschaften,* deserves special consideration.

Imago dealt mostly with literary topics, with frequent mention of religion and only occasional forays into history and issues of leadership. In this respect, *Imago* closely reflected the orientation of the early group (of which, most of the authors represented in *Imago* had been members). Thus, in the first decade of publication, *Imago* published only five articles (out of a total of 138) that dealt with issues directly relating to leadership. This figure would be approximately tripled if one were to include articles on religion and anthropology. Freud, for example, published *Totem and Taboo* in several parts in *Imago* as it emerged. Alice Balint submitted *Der Familienvater* in 1913, arguing that the prairie Indians were unable to resolve their Oedipus complex successfully and were therefore stuck, as a culture, in early adolescence. For the most part, however, *Imago* continued in its publication of formal articles in contrast with what had been looser and more wide-ranging in the Vienna discussion group. Isidor Sadger wrote for it a series of articles on poets that reflected his long-standing interest in pathographies. Ernest Jones wrote a two-part article on the psychology of salt. Theodor Reik analyzed humor. Lou Andreas-Salomé wrote on the "female type." The few gems we have in these years merit close scrutiny.

In the very first issue of the *Imago* in 1912, Carl Abraham wrote a psychoanalytic study of Amenhotep IV in which he focused attention on Amenhotep's religious activities, which, he argued, can be seen as the successful sublimation of the Egyptian monarch's aggression toward his father.[16] Like that of many dynasties, Abraham wrote, Amenhotep's family history showed increasing decadence after initial strength. His forefathers were warriors who established a great Egyptian empire. His father, Amenhotep III, was a weak ruler whose prowess was as a hunter. The physically weak Amenhotep IV, last in the direct line, was a dreamer, whose history resembled that of Freud's neurotics.

Amenhotep IV's mother, Teje, surpassed his father in intelligence, energy, and beauty, and she managed the government as Amenhotep III grew old, and was active as regent after he died. Abraham argues that Amenhotep IV's libido was clearly

---

[16] Karl Abraham, "Amenhotep IV. Psychoanalytische Beitrage zurn Verständis seiner PersOnlichkeit und des monotheistischen Aton-Kultes," *Imago,* 1 (1912), 334–360.

fixated on his mother and that, as in many such cases, the mother was substituted for by an adored wife, Nefertiti. Amenhotep IV never took a harem, contrary to custom, even when Nefertiti bore only daughters, and in surviving inscriptions and artwork he emphasized monogamous love. After Amenhotep III's death, Teje had begun to favor the worship of Aton over the traditional high god Amon. Amenhotep IV carried this further, completely replacing the god of his fathers with a new, single god: Aton. Typically, the father was rejected and replaced by an even more powerful figure. Aton was created by Amenhotep IV as a spiritual (not anthropomorphic) god of peace and was accompanied by an ethos of peace and the sublimation of sadistic human offerings. He was represented as a sun whose rays ended in hands embracing the king. Amenhotep IV changed his name to Ikhnaton and called himself the son of Aton, just as neurotics often fantasize that they really have highborn fathers.

The only aggression in Amenhotep's reign, Abraham continues, was that against his father. He persecuted the priests of Amon and had Amon's name erased from all inscriptions—which, of course, included inscriptions naming his father. When Teje died, Amenhotep buried her not beside his father, but in the tomb in which he expected to be buried himself. In fact, Amenhotep IV rejected much of the tradition his father had supported, even moving the capital city north toward the old Lower Egypt.

Abraham concludes that Amenhotep IV religion of one god (to replace one father), a peaceful god of love (a father sharing his own personality), represents a successful sublimation. His choice of Aton in particular is significant: The sun is often a father figure (it is a single one, unlike the myriad stars, and its warmth represents love), and Aton was related to Adonis, who like Amenhotep IV, was young, died young, and preferred beauty to war. And, like the neurotic, Amenhotep IV lived in a dream world, ignoring the reality of evil and the necessity of protecting his empire.

Two years later, Ludwig Jekels produced another psychobiographical sketch in the pages of *Imago*.[17] This one dealt with the turning point in the life of Napoleon I. Jekels's concern in his article is to explain Napoleon's abrupt shift from being a Corsican to Frenchman. As a child, Napoleon had hated the French conquerors and invented schemes to overthrow them. He idealized Paoli, an older patriot who had been regent of Corsica before the French Occupation. But Napoleon returned to Corsica in 1793, when the king of France was out of power and the French had declared war on England. At that time, Paoli was dishonored for his connections with England. Then, Napoleon abruptly accused Paoli of treason, took the side of his rival Saliceti, and, since the populace still supported Paoli, had his house burned and left Corsica. Jekels expressed disagreement with the traditional political explanation for this sudden shift of loyalties on the part of Napoleon. He claimed, instead, that a purely political explanation fails to explain the speed or intensity of the change in Napoleon's loyalties.

---

[17]Ludwig Jekels, "Der Wendepunkt im Leben Napoleons I," *Imago*, 3 (1914), 313–381.

In this regard, Jekels argued that Napoleon's patriotism resulted from his bond with his mother, and that the earth itself, for Napoleon, was a mother figure. Thus, Napoleon's ideal was the patriotic woman of Sparta (his own mother was a Corsican patriot), and he insisted that it was wrong for sexual love to replace patriotism in the modern era. In general, the women in Napoleon's life were often mother substitutes, women who were older than himself and often widows. Napoleon's mother was rumored to have had an affair with Marbeuf, the French governor who had befriended the family. As in both family and politics, outsiders conquered. Jekels notes that Napoleon in general hated women, with the great exception of Josephine, whose infidelity he accepted, although he demanded chastity in other women. While Napoleon was ambivalent toward his own father, he identified especially with Charlemagne, who also founded a dynasty and planned to conquer Spain and Italy. (Jekels notes that Napoleon's father's name was "Charles Marie.") Also, after the death of his father, Napoleon took his father's role in the family and supported the family, even though he was the second son.

Jekels concluded that Napoleon's fixation on his mother and ambivalence toward his father are clear. The ambivalence led him to have two kinds of father figures—those of love and those of hate—Paoli, on the one hand, and Marbeuf and the king, on the other. After the king was executed in January 1793, Napoleon was much more a Frenchman. The father who had kept him from his mother but had shared her with foreigners was now gone; now his Oedipus complex urged him to possess that mother. France before had symbolized Marbeuf (a rival) to Napoleon; now it meant his mother. Paoli had been the idealized father who protected his mother (Corsica) from a stranger. But after Louis was killed, Napoleon wanted all his father figures to fall, especially since Paoli supported the English, who had played the role of bringing foreigners to the mother. Napoleon thus turned against Paoli, thereby imitating his own father, who had abandoned Paoli when he (the father) worked with the French occupiers. From then on, Napoleon had no more patriotism for Corsica but had a series of mother substitutes (Italy, the Near East) he was driven to possess and authority figures he was driven to defeat. Thus, Jekels neatly links an event in Napoleon's personal history with significant large-scale political developments of the French Revolution. That the connections in Jekels's article are arbitrary and superficial go without saying.

It was six more years before *Imago* published another psychological study of leadership. This one, in 1920, was by Emil Lorenz and dealt with the question of political mythology.[18] Lorenz's concern was the psychology, or inner dynamics, of politics, and how in the quest for power rational and irrational motives mix.

A state, Lorenz argued, is founded both upon a sense of community among its citizens and upon a set hierarchy with a leader at its apex. Lorenz saw two forces at work, both of which mirrored the Oedipus complex: ambivalence toward the leader, who is a father figure, and love for the nurturing "motherland." In this regard, Lorenz cited Livy's description of Brutus, who recognized that "the mother" mentioned in

---

[18]Emil Lorenz, "Der Politische Mythos. Probleme und Vorarbeiten," *Imago,* 6 (1920), 402–421.

an oracle was the land, and proceeded to kill the tyrant ruler and to take his place, so that the ruler became the son and husband of the earth.

Then, oddly, Lorenz examined a series of plays by Schiller to develop his argument. These plays dealt with regicide, revolution, and freedom fighting. In general, Lorenz saw the freedom fighter as the son of the land, fighting the father-tyrant and taking his place. He notes the frequency with which the freedom fighter is also an idiot figure (Brutus, Tell, Don Carlos), just as the hero of fairy tales is often the youngest or dumbest of the group. Lorenz believed that this relates to the child's game of pretended ignorance.

Lorenz went on to repeat that all rulers, priests, and magicians are father figures, and that the earth is the "mother" of all people, who are thus brothers. During revolutionary times, there is a return to the potency of the mother. If the people have a strong relationship to the land, libido freed by revolution can end up as loyalty or have other positive qualities. Where is no such strong relationship between the people and "mother" earth, however, the hatred directed at the ruler/father can lead to horrors like the barbarism of the French Revolution. Lorenz also argued that the negativism and the misogyny of assassins and revolutionaries are caused by their overpowering bond with their mothers.

Finally, Lorenz delineated three historical phases in the development of political realities. At first, monastic tribes had male leaders, but females were also worshipped. In time, cultures came to be characterized by bonds to both the land/mother and the leader/father. Finally, mass movements arose when there was overpopulation and land could be bought and sold. These developments could lead to socialism and a new, leaderless, "female" community.

The scope of Lorenz's comments on politics was not to be repeated for some time in the pages of *Imago*. In the next couple of years, there was a return to the more familiar and comfortable use of psychoanalytic theory in interpreting individual leaders. Thus, in 1921 J. C. Flügel wrote an interesting study of the character and life of Henry VIII.[19] According to Flügel, the marital problems of Henry VIII were caused by three powerful and conflicting desires, all derived from the Oedipal complex: First, he required and hated rivals in love affairs; second, he desired and was repulsed by incestuous relationships; and third, he demanded that his women be chaste. Henry's Oedipal complex was particularly powerful because he was the son of a king and had seen his father neglect a beautiful wife; also, his mother's Yorkish relatives viewed her offspring as more legitimate rulers than the Tudor Henry VII. Henry VIII's feelings were transferred to his older brother, Arthur, whose widow, he married. Henry's father had also considered marrying Katherine of Aragon, thus making Henry, Henry's father, and Henry's brother sexual rivals.

When Henry became king, he achieved a balance between his egotistic and sexual desires, as exemplified by his self-assurance and his need for the pope's approval, respectively. However, the egotistical side of his character became dominant after his first divorce, when, as the head of the Church of England, he became his own

---

[19] J. C. Flügel, "Charakter und Eheleben Heinrichs VIII," *Imago,* 7 (1920), 424–441.

father/pope/God figure. His horror of Katherine seems to have been genuine—she was, after all, his sister—but he chose another sister as his next wife (he had had an affair with Anne Boleyn's sister Mary). Furthermore, while Anne had led Henry on for years, refusing to sleep with him, Henry grew bored with her almost as soon as they were married. He needed some hindrance to keep him interested, which Flügel argues is a fairly obvious Oedipal need. The accusations with which Henry condemned Anne were his own projections: that she had slept with her brother (as Henry had wanted to commit incest) and that she had planned to kill him (as Henry had wanted to kill his father and brother).

His next wife, Jane Seymour, was also a relative, whom Henry had met in her brother's house. While she was probably not a virgin, Henry shut his eyes to her past. Jane died soon after the marriage. His next marriage, to Anne of Cleves, was political and was ended when Henry no longer needed a Protestant alliance. His next wife, Katherine Howard, was also beheaded for infidelity, this time undoubtedly real; Henry had blinded himself to her past sexual relationships and went through a personal crisis when he had to face the truth. Finally, Katherine Parr, twice widowed, was a nearly perfect match, given Henry's Oedipal drives: She had been engaged to Jane Seymour's brother (and was thus a "sister"), and she shared his brother's wife's name.

The next year William Boven published a study of Alexander the Great, which returned to the exaggerated speculation of the earlier period.[20] Boven's goal was to discover the source of Alexander's megalomania, and he argued that Alexander conquered Asia basically as a compensatory effort to conquer his father. Alexander was dose to his mother, Olympias, who was reputedly involved with magic in certain erotic cults. There were rumors that she slept with strange beasts. She also hated her husband, Philip, who was both autocratic and unfaithful to her. Alexander was a promising boy—smart, talented, and brave—and competed actively with his father, taking satisfaction in being a better warrior.

When Philip took a new wife, Alexander's position as heir was threatened, and he and his mother Olympias went into exile. Eventually, Alexander returned and regained his father's graces before the latter was murdered. Alexander began his reign with energy, first murdering any possible pretenders to the throne, and then proceeding with his ambitious conquests.

Boven contends that Alexander was in fact avenging his mother on his father. He notes that Alexander was famed for his kindness to women. On the other hand, he spontaneously murdered an old friend for praising Philip (again "killing his father"). As his megalomania grew, Alexander claimed to be a son of Zeus, which was an obvious rejection of Philip and was perhaps based on Olympias's cult activities. Eventually, Alexander placed himself with Heracles and Dionysius, below no one but Zeus himself, and he wanted his mother also to be given a place among the gods. Alexander's final triumph, then, over his father, Philip, came in the conquest of Asia, which he equated with his father.

---

[20] William Boven, "Alexander der Grosse," *Imago,* 8 (1922), 418–439.

In that same first decade of *Imago's* publication, a number of writers published psychoanalytic studies relating to leadership in other journals and some in full-length books. It was a time of general fertility in applied psychoanalytic work, after the closed period of the Vienna meetings but before the vast expansion of the work after the late 1920s. For example, Hans Sachs wrote a short analysis of a dream that Bismarck had had in 1863. Sachs published his article in the *International Zeitschrift für Psychoanalyse* in 1913.[21] In the dream that Bismarck reported in his journal, he was riding on an Alpine path that got progressively narrower, with a cliff on one side and a gorge on the other, until there was no room to go forward, turn around, or dismount. Bismarck got angry, hit the cliff on his left with his whip, and called on God for help, at which point the whip got infinitely long and the cliff fell away like a curtain to reveal a road, a landscape like Bohemia with Prussian troops. The dream ended with Bismarck wanting to tell the king about it immediately.

On one level, Sachs interprets the dream as a masturbation fantasy: The whip is held in the left hand, meaning something is forbidden, and it grows to enormous length. But on another level, he argues that Bismarck was comparing himself to Moses, for, like Moses, he was trying to free an ungrateful people. The Bible story in which Moses knocked against a rock and water sprang forth is also partly sexual: Moses, acting against God's will, got the water but was punished. Bismarck's wish to tell the king what had happened was like bragging of a sexual conquest or asking for punishment—but he was protected because of the overt political message.

The Napoleons fascinated the early Freudians. Ernest Jones in the *Journal of Abnormal Psychology* in 1913 wrote about Louis Bonaparte, who he argued was worthy of study because he helped cause his brother Napoleon's downfall.[22] Napoleon, intending to bring Holland more completely under his control, had made Louis king of Holland in 1806. When Napoleon wanted a blockade against England, which would have been a great sacrifice for Holland, Louis took an independent, pro-Dutch position. Napoleon eventually absorbed Holland in the greater France, but chronic discontent persisted there until his overthrow.

Jones claims that Louis's incompetent political behavior was the result of introjection, and it mirrored his personal life and his relationship with his brother. Louis, Napoleon's favorite brother, had been educated by him personally, and was on his staff at an early age. When he was twenty, though, an attack of venereal disease led to a character change; from then on, he was a moody hypochondriac and complainer who constantly resigned from positions of leadership to go to spas. Napoleon's attitude toward Louis—first his overestimation, then his increasing annoyance—was in fact reasonable and consistent, but was interpreted by Louis as the vacillation of an overfond, overstern parent.

---

[21] Hanns Sachs, "Em Traum Bismarcks," *Internationale Zeitschrift für Psychoanalyze,* 1 (1913), 80–83.

[22] Ernest Jones, "The Case of Louis Bonaparte, King of Holland," *Journal of Abnormal Psychology,* 8 (1913), 289–301.

Louis's homosexual attraction to Napoleon was his main conflict. He was noticeably effeminate, which he counteracted by sexual exploits. Napoleon married Louis off to Josephine's daughter. The marriage was a failure, for Louis was jealous of Napoleon's fondness for his eldest son, who was rumored to be Napoleon's own. Louis sued for divorce at the same time Napoleon was divorcing Josephine, a decision which Jones sees as an indication of his feelings of identity with Napoleon. He was extremely bitter when Napoleon finally did have a son of his own.

In Jones's view, Louis's jealousy and delusions of persecution stemmed from his repressed homosexuality. In such cases, the original love turns to hate, and the hater then assumes that the love object hates him in return. Louis's alternating love and hatred for Napoleon were consistent with his syndrome, and his tendencies affected his behavior. For example, after having shown jealous suspicion that his wife had slept with Napoleon (which was probably not true), Louis claimed years later that Napoleon had never been unfaithful to Josephine, although that was known to be false. Jones concludes that Louis's obsession with his personal relationship with Napoleon kept him from being a competent leader.

In general, the widening scope of applied psychoanalytic work in this period represented an increase in the quantity of work that was done without significant advances in method or theoretical approaches.[23] In general, the interpretations now read as somewhat wooden, though there is no question the psychological approach to leadership had become its own subfield.

III

Freud's own formal efforts at applied psychoanalytic work covered an enormous range after the early period of incubation. Only music did not interest him. Two of his books touched directly on questions of leadership: *Group Psychology and the Analysis of the Ego* (1921) and, with William Bullitt, *Thomas Woodrow Wilson:*

---

[23] Some additional studies of leadership by the early figures around Freud include the following: Paul Federn, *Zur Psychologie der Revolution* (Vienna: Anzengruber-Verlag, 1919); J. C. Flügel, *Men and Their Motives: Psychoanalytic Studies* (New York: International Universities Press, 1947 (1934)); Eich Fromm, "Politik und Psychoanalyse," *Psychoanalytische Bewegung,* 2 (1930), 305–313; the English version of E. Hitschmann's essays, *Great Men: Psychoanalytic Studies* (New York: International Universities Press, 1956); Ernest Jones, "Psycho-Analyze Roosevelts," *Zentralblatt für Psychoanalyse,* 2 (1912), 675–677; Geza Roheim, "Killing the Divine King," *Man,* 15 (1915), 26–28. By the 1920s, and well into the 1930s, it became quite popular to undertake psychoanalytic studies of leaders. This category includes those influenced by Freud but not in direct contact with him, the early Vienna group, or a part of *Imago.* A few representative authors (this is not a complete listing) include the following: Hill Berkeley, "A Short Study of the Life and Character of Mohammed," *International Journal of Psychoanalysis,* 2 (1921), 31–53; F. Chamberlain, *The Private Character of Queen Elizabeth* (London, 1921); L. Pierce Clark, *Lincoln: A Psycho-Biography* (New York, 1933); R. Behrendt, "Das Problem Fuhres und Mosse und die Psychoanalyse," *Psychoanalytische Benegung,* 1 (1929), 134–154.

A Psychological Study (1966 [1932]).[24] Leadership, if somewhat more broadly considered, however, was a major concern of Freud. His extensive theoretical writings on the Oedipus complex in a sense describe the psychological process of leading and following in a family. A study like his of Leonardo da Vinci in 1910 focuses on a major leader in the world of art. *Totem and Taboo* (1913) argues that the origins of civilization lay in the struggle with the clan leader of primitive cultures. *Civilization and Its Discontents* (1930) explores the complex mechanisms of guilt and repression in modern life that fuel the dynamics of mass behavior. And, finally, in his grand study of Moses, *Moses and Monotheism* (1939), Freud returned at the end of his own life to a leader who helped shape the beginnings of Western civilization.

In terms of leadership, probably the single most important generalization to make about Freud's work is the centrality of the family model for him. The father of the family defines the psychological world of leadership, all else in metaphor. For Freud himself, this had great personal significance in his understanding of his own relationship with his father, Jacob, who died in 1897. It was his father's death that prompted Freud's own self-analysis. Of the many insights that emerged from that experience, none was of greater significance than his own ambivalence toward his father and, by extension, toward figures of authority in general. *The Interpretation of Dreams,* if read as an autobiography, shows Freud's intense unconscious struggle with the multiple meanings of leadership in his own experience.

The extent to which Freud's major dreams in *The interpretation of Dreams* center on the interrelated issues of Freud's own rightness in response to criticism, and his ambitious assertiveness toward figures of authority, for example, is remarkable. In the Irma dream, Freud constructed an elaborate defense for himself in response to his perceived criticism from his friend, Otto, who had reported to Freud on the dream day that Irma, Freud's patient, was "better, but not quite well."[25] Freud's dream blames Irma, because she is recalcitrant; Dr. M., his senior colleague, whom Freud emasculates but who confirms his diagnosis; and Otto, who has really caused the problem anyway because he thoughtlessly gave an injection with a dirty syringe.[26] In the preamble to the Count Thun dream, Freud explains the slight he felt when the Austrian politician marched past him on the railroad platform on the way to an audience with the emperor. Count Thun waved aside the ticket inspector with a curt motion of his hand and without any explanation. Freud then situated himself on the same platform, hummed a rebellious tune from an opera, recalled the French comedy with the line about the great gentleman who had taken the trouble to be born, and pushed the train officials (without success) for a compartment with

---

[24] S. Freud and C. Bullitt, *Thomas Woodrow Wilson: A Psychological Study* (New York: Houghton Mifflin, 1966 [1932]).

[25] Sigmund Freud, "Group Psychology and the Analysis of the Ego," in *The Standard Edition of the Complete Psychological Works of Sigmund Freud,* ed. James Strachey, vol. XVIII. (London: Hogarth Press, 1955).

[26] Sigmund Freud, *The Interpretation of Dreams,* ed. James Strachey, one-volume paperback (New York: Avon Library, 1900), 139.

a lavatory. He also dreamed of revolution and associated to his dream of urinating in his parents' bedroom, to which his father's response was to say, "The boy will come to nothing."[27] As Freud noted, "This must have been a frightful blow to my ambition, for references to this scene are still constantly recurring in my dreams and are always linked with an enumeration of my achievements and success, as though I wanted to say, 'You see, I *have* come to something.'"[28]

Freud, however, argued from his own self-analysis how his—and therefore everyone's—rivalry with the male figure of authority in the family was rooted in his libidinal attachment for his mother. The favored son of a young mother, he was to say, has a special kind of self-confidence. The tension in mediating the young boy's love for his mother and the rivalry with his father are captured in the complex that Freud labeled after the story of Oedipus Rex. In the first formulation of the Oedipus complex (in *The Interpretation of Dreams*), Freud uses Hamlet's story to illustrate the deadening effect of overpowering ambivalence (Hamlet is "sicklied o'er with the pale cast of thought"). Hamlet can act in all ways except one: He cannot take "vengeance on the man who did away with his father and took that father's place with his mother, the man who shows him the repressed wishes of his own childhood realized."[29] The sense one has here, as well as in case histories like Little Hans, Dr. Paul Schreber, and the Rat Man, is that the boy's attraction for the mother has a thin edge of danger, but that the real family source of ambivalence, struggle, and competition lies in the relationship with father. For it is the father, who is everyone's own private leader, who mediates the delicate transition from inner to outer, from psychology to politics, from the family to culture.

Erikson, whose father abandoned his mother before his birth and who later, in his thirties, adopted himself as his own father (Erik, son of Erik), said of fathers, "A man must confront his childhood and, above all, give an account of his conflicts with his father."[30] And, further, leaders, who were once children, *"have* to become their own fathers and in a way their father's fathers while not yet adult. This spells special conflicts and special tasks."[31] If the mother regulates the private sources of the self—love and sex most of all—one can only become something in a public world in relation to the father. A nice clinical expression of this idea in Freud is the case of Little Hans, who literally could not leave home (mother) because of his phobia that the father/horse would bite him for falling down. The world was too dangerous even to enter until Hans could resolve his conflicts with his father.[32]

---

[27] Ibid., 139–154.

[28] Ibid., 241–247.

[29] Ibid., 298–299.

[30] Erik H. Erikson, *Gandhi's Truth: On the Origins of Militant Nonviolence* (New York: Norton, 1969), 123.

[31] Ibid., 102.

[32] Sigmund Freud, "Analysis of a Phobia in a Five-Year-Old Boy," *Standard Edition*, X (1909), 3–149.

Hans was later reincarnated in Woodrow Wilson, whose excruciating ambivalence toward papa led to (disastrously, in the view of Freud and Bullitt) redrafting the map of Europe in the Treaty of Versailles. Wilson thus never worked through the gnawing resentments that lay buried under his intense idealization of his impressive and articulate father; he simply acted them all out, first in the Princeton fight with Dean West, then with the world at Versailles. By then, time and disease had aggravated his own grandiosity and his ambivalence toward his father. He became the Jesus of the world in lieu of God and his dead father. The stage for his theatrical enactments shifted, but the psychological conflicts that cast the play never altered. Whatever indelicacies of exposition justify the attribution of actual authorship to Bullitt, there is equally no question that the ideas expressed in the book belong to Freud. Wilson's behavior was neurotic in Freud's view precisely because it carried the private family issues of the son's ambivalence toward the father directly into the public realm.

In Freud's view, the general family issues with the father cluster around certain core conflicts which can be clearly identified and form the basis for the prediction of one's behavior. For Freud, these conflicts were largely instinctive and drive-related in nature. They cannot be avoided. The libidinal attachment to the mother that generates rivalry with the father is, in a sense, encoded. Because they come so early and are so central, such conflictual beginnings necessarily carry over to the public realm. To paraphrase Lincoln, we cannot escape our own history. Freud's world is, in essence, one of conflict, in which behavior is firmly rooted in pathology. It is a grim, pessimistic view of the world. The hidden and renounced in everyone are the pathological products of an average and expectable family environment. We may grow beyond our origins, but only with difficulty, and we are always subject to regression in the face of difficulties, and to what Freud called the return of the repressed.

As he commented in his introduction to the Wilson book:

> Fools, visionaries, sufferers from delusions, neurotics and lunatics have played great roles at all times in the history of mankind and not merely when the accident of birth had bequeathed them sovereignty. Usually they have wreaked havoc; but not always. Such persons have exercised far-reaching influence upon their own and later times, they have given impetus to important cultural movements and have made great discoveries. They have been able to accomplish such achievements on the one hand through the help of the intact portion of their personalities, that is to say in spite of their abnormalities, but on the other hand it is often precisely the pathological traits of their characters, the one-sidedness of their development, the abnormal strengthening of certain desires, the uncritical and unrestrained abandonment to a single aim, which give them the power to drag others after them and to overcome the resistance of the world.[33]

This pathological model also defined for Freud the misty origins of culture itself. In *Totem and Taboo,* Freud argued that the powerful father dominated the primal horde and retained for himself sole possession of the women while excluding the young males. Resentment and envy eventually drove the other males to band

---

[33] Freud and Bullitt, *Wilson,* xvi.

together and kill the father. This deed required massive repression and atonement, which Freud felt was the basis for religion and civilization. Freud's conclusions to the book stressed that these phylogenetic beginnings of civilization resulted in the neurotic's inhibition of action, in sharp contrast with primitive man, who is uninhibited and whose "thought passes directly into action," according to Freud. In other words, first there is historical reality, which for various reasons requires repression and the creation of new psychological structures. Culture and civilization as we know them evolve from this process. The residue of the historical event, however, appears embedded ontogenetically in everyone's experience. The drives, according to Freud, activate ingrained phylogenetic memories which become, for the individual, fantasies of what the human race once acted out.[34]

Carl Jung pushed these ideas to their ultimate conclusion. But even with Freud, one cannot understand the individual in the family or in civilization generally without close attention to the deeply embedded unconscious memories from the group's collective past. As Heinz Kohut has often argued, Freud's model is an elegant and consistent whole. It all hangs on drives and the notion of pathology as a "normal" part of the soul *(die Seele)*. What is true for the individual is likewise valid for the group. Ontogeny and phylogeny must logically and psychologically be interrelated. The problem is how to define the link. Fathers, presidents, and kings must lead, and individuals and groups follow, largely in response to internal messages from long-lost events. We are free, perhaps, but not quite as free as we might imagine.

Another feature of the family model for leadership in Freud's thinking was that it centered on maleness. For Freud, the leader in the family and politics, not to mention the broader spheres of culture, art, and civilization, is always male. Freud always examines the unfolding of the Oedipus complex from the boy's point of view, adding only parenthetically that the analogue of the boy's conflicts occurs in girls. Only in Lecture 33 of his *New Introductory Lectures* did Freud systematically review the question of femininity, which he considers a "riddle."[35] He argues that the clitoris is an atrophied penis, and that psychologically femininity seeks passive aims.[36] The real dilemma, however, for girls, as opposed to boys, is the task of shifting libidinal excitation from the clitoris to the vagina and the special complications of exchanging the maternal love object for the paternal as the Oedipus complex unfolds. All this, in Freud's view, profoundly affects superego formation in girls, "which cannot attain the strength and independence which give it cultural significance."[37] Basically, it seems from Freud's argument, because psychosexual development is more complicated for females, they are more prone to neurosis. It is not a huge step in logic to assume that they would also be unfit to fill positions of leadership, either in the family or in politics.

---

[34] Sigmund Freud, "Totem and Taboo," *Standard Edition*, XIII (1913): 9–162.

[35] Sigmund Freud, *New Introductory Lectures on Psychoanalysis*, ed. James Strachey, paperback edition (New York: Norton, 1933), 113.

[36] Ibid., 114–115.

[37] Ibid., 129.

Freud's most important and, in fact, his only systematic discussion of leadership per se was the 1921 monograph, *Group Psychology and the Analysis of the Ego.* The opening paragraph makes clear Freud's intention to use clinical psychoanalytic insights to understand group phenomena. It states the assumption that governed the Vienna meetings:

> In the individual's mental life, someone else is invariably involved, as a model, as an object, as a helper, and an opponent; and so from the very first individual psychology, in this extended but entirely justifiable sense of the words, is at the same time social psychology as well.[38]

Freud then dissects at length Gustave Le Bon's *Psychologie de Foules* (1895) as a way of separating his own views from those of the most significant thinker to date on the same issues. What most interested Freud about Le Bon's work was his idea of a primitive group mind. Groups, for Freud, reduce differences to their lowest common denominator, so that the individual seems to be lost in an almost hypnotic way. A group is impulsive, changeable, and irritable. As Freud had noted in *Totem and Taboo,* a group "cannot tolerate any delay between its desire and the fulfillment of what it desires. It has a sense of omnipotence; the notion of impossibility disappears for the individual in a group."[39] Furthermore, a group never doubts its sense of rightness or strength. It is both intolerant of differences and somewhat ironically obedient to authority. It demands leaders who are strong and even violent, seeking domination and oppression from them. "A group," for Freud, "is an obedient herd, which could never live without a master. It has such a thirst for obedience that it submits instinctively to anyone who appoints himself its master."[40] Freud discusses other theorists on the subject—such as W. McDougall, author of the 1920 study, *The Group Mind*—but finds nothing as evocative as Le Bon's study.

In a general sense, the fundamental fact of group behavior for Freud lies in the interrelated ideas of intensification of affect and inhibition of intellect as the psychological influences on individuals in groups.[41] Both these aspects of group behavior are derived from the libidinal ties that bind people together in the mass: ". . . a group is held together by Eros, which holds together everything in the world."[42] To lose one's place in the group is terrifying, precisely because such loss threatens one's basic libidinal organization; group fear is thus directly analogous to anxiety in the individual.

> Fear in an individual is provoked either by the greatness of a danger or by the cessation of emotional ties (libidinal cathexes); the latter is the case of neurotic fear or anxiety. In just the same way panic arises either owing to an increase of the common danger or owing to

---

[38] Sigmund Freud, "Group Psychology," *Standard Edition,* XVIII: 69.

[39] Ibid., 77.

[40] Ibid., 81.

[41] Ibid., 88.

[42] Ibid., 92.

the disappearance of the emotional ties which hold the group together; and the latter case is analogous to that of neurotic anxiety.[43]

The question then becomes how to define more precisely the exact nature of the libidinal ties among individuals in groups. This leads Freud to a discussion of identification, which "endeavors to mould a person's own ego after fashion of one that has been taken as a model."[44] Identification describes both the first form of a tie with an object and a regressive substitute for a libidinal object relation. It may also, however, represent a "new perception of a common quality shared with some other person who is not an object of the sexual instinct."[45] It is in this "new" sense that identification serves as the basis of group cohesion. In this, and indeed in any of the meanings of identification, the loved object is placed within one's own ego as an ideal. In individual psychology, one can observe the force of such developmental structuralization in various breakdown products as homosexuality, depression, hypnosis, and the normal state of being in love (where the object is intensely idealized). In groups, there is a pooling of ego ideals in regard to the figure of the leader: "A primary group of this kind is a number of individuals who have put one and the same object in the place of their ego ideal and have consequently identified themselves with one another in their ego."[46]

The leader of a group is heavily invested by all members of the group, whose attachment provides the raison d'être for their emotional survival. As such, a group revives the primal horde and its psychology is "the oldest human psychology."[47] A group regressively re-creates the original bonds in human affairs. In a phylogenetic sense, individual structuralization that establishes one's own object sources as an inner voice (the ego ideal) represents a differentiation of the primitive relation of group members to the idealized leader. It seems, however, to be a historical process marked by frequent backsliding.[48] We keep forming groups and creating idealized leaders.

In Freudian terms, therefore, leaders are not altogether welcome in human society. We suffer under them and bear the consequence of their actions. Collective pooling of ego ideals in a group forces regressive idealization of the external leader that is primitive and archaic in its form and meanings. Freud never addresses the specific role of the leader in enhancing this process. The leader seems to be created largely out of collective need, an almost accidental by-product of group process. Furthermore, the leader's power is immense, for the psychological bond of groups to him gives license to all peremptory needs of the leader himself. For at least what was to come in Germany, and in some other extreme historical circumstances, Freud's approach was prescient.

---

[43] Ibid., 97.
[44] Ibid., 106.
[45] Ibid., 108.
[46] Ibid., 116.
[47] Ibid., 123.
[48] Ibid., 123.

Chapter 3
From Erik H. Erikson to Heinz Kohut: Expanding Theories of Leadership

Charles B. Strozier and Oliger Abdyli

Of all the people influenced by Freud, Erik Erikson most creatively bridged psychoanalysis and history. He began as an artist, but in the 1920s was drawn into analysis with Anna Freud and eventually graduated from the Vienna Psychoanalytic Society in the portentous year of 1933. On the boat coming to America shortly afterwards, Erikson shared an essay on Hitler with the diplomat and historian George Kennan, who helped him to translate it into English. In America, Erikson soon established his reputation as a child analyst and became acquainted with people like Margaret Mead. In the late 1930s and 1940s, he conducted a series of studies that culminated in his first book, *Childhood and Society* (1950). After that, his interests have always included both the clinical and the historical.[1]

The range, not to mention the depth, of Erik Erikson's work on leadership is remarkable. There are three full-length biographical studies, of Martin Luther, Mohandas Gandhi, and Thomas Jefferson.[2] One is almost tempted to add Sigmund Freud to that list, for surely Erikson's scattered essays on the founder of psychoanalysis make up a monograph (though to pull the essays together would make for a rather disjointed book). In different articles and in parts of various books, Erikson has also dealt with William James, George Bernard Shaw, Albert Einstein, Adolf Hitler, Maxim Gorky, and even Jesus of Nazareth.[3] It is an impressive body of work.

C.B. Strozier (✉)
John Jay College, Center on Terrorism, New York, NY 10019, USA
e-mail: charlesbstrozier@yahoo.com

[1] Lawrence Friedman, *Identity's Architect: A Biography of Erik H. Erikson* (Cambridge, MA: Harvard University Press, 2000); note also Robert Coles, *Erik H. Erikson: The Growth of His Work* (Boston: Little, Brown, 1970).

[2] Erik H. Erikson, *Young Man Luther* (1958); *Gandhi's Truth* (1968); and *Dimensions of a New Identity* (New York: Norton, 1974).

[3] For William James, see *Identity: Youth and Crisis* (New York: Norton, 1968), 150–155; for George Bernard Shaw, ibid., 142–150; for Albert Einstein, "Psychoanalytic Reflections on Einstein's Centenary," in *Albert Einstein: Historical and Cultural Perspectives,* ed. Gerald Holton and Yehuda Elkam (Princeton, NJ: Princeton University Press, 1979), 151–174; for Adolf Hitler, *Childhood and Society* (New York: Norton, 1963 [1950]), 326–358, and *Young Man Luther,* 105–110; for Maxim Gorky, *Childhood and Society,* 359–402; for Jesus, "The Galilean Sayings and the Sense of 'I,'" *Yale Review* 70 (1981): 321–362.

C.B. Strozier et al. (eds.), *The Leader*, 2nd ed., DOI 10.1007/978-1-4419-8387-9_3,
© Springer Science+Business Media, LLC 2011

The sometimes bewildering diversity of Erikson's applied analytic work should not obscure an articulated theory of leadership that emerges in his writings. There is, first of all, the notion that the leader himself—there are no women in Erikson's corpus—is to be understood psychologically in terms of various vicissitudes in the eight stages of the life cycle. In theory, at least, a given life history unfolds epigenetically according to a psychosocial plan, and a hierarchy of "virtues" accrues to those who pass muster at each stage of life. Erikson's famous chart, in which developmental progress is plotted diagonally, attempts to capture the enduring effects of fixation, arrest, and regression as well.

The chart, however, also expresses the essential idea that growth and change occur throughout the life cycle. Nothing is immutable. Erikson's detailed discussion of Gandhi's midlife crisis is perhaps his most complete elaboration of this concept. As a young man in South Africa, Gandhi had perfected his political style in *Satyagraha* (pressure for social and political reform through assertive nonviolent resistance). But he had never used the hunger strike and had not yet developed resonance with the hundreds of millions of Indians yearning for political integrity and freedom from the British. Gandhi's first foray into this market was ambivalent and apparently inconsequential. He chose for his first Indian action a minor textile strike in Ahmedabad in 1918, which he infused with religious zeal and moral purpose by declaring a fast until death unless the workers received a 37% increase in salary. Gandhi doubted the validity of his actions from the outset—he had to agree with the charge that the fast was more blackmail than legitimate—and in the end he reluctantly accepted a purely face-saving compromise to the strike. His personal punishment exceeded anything meted out by the owners, for he shortly suffered what amounted to a nervous breakdown. But like Abraham Lincoln, Gandhi learned from his mistakes. In this great crisis of generativity, Gandhi found a proper voice with which to speak to his followers. He redefined Satyagraha. He discovered his own capacity for political and moral commitment. Neither he nor the British were ever again quite the same.

Most of Erikson's work, however, has focused on adolescence and its concomitant crisis of identity. Some would even say that he helped create the identity crisis as almost a rite of passage for adolescents, who seem to wear their crises on their sleeves, whether Edwardian or leather. But it is worth stressing that the detailed cases Erikson provides to illustrate the precise meaning of the identity crisis are historical. Martin Luther, one of the first examples Erikson cites, remains the most interesting. In 1505, on his way home from college while contemplating the choice of bride and career his father had made for him, Martin heard God call him to the faith during a thunderstorm and fled into the Augustinian order. In the monastery a kindly superior, Father Staupitz, listened patiently to Martin's compulsive confessions, guided him to think critically about the Scriptures, and, it seems, fell in love with him.[4] Martin weathered many emotional storms within himself during his "moratorium" before he posted his 95 theses on the Wittenberg Church door in 1517.

---

[4] Erikson, *Young Man Luther*, 169.

A less well-known, but equally fascinating, case that Erikson discusses to illustrate the identity crisis is that of George Bernard Shaw. At twenty, Shaw broke loose from an oppressive family and a good future in business and left Ireland to avoid the danger of success in business, which would be unequal to the enormity of his unconscious ambition.[5] He went to England, where he spent the next few years filling up five pages a day with turgid prose that led to five unpublished novels. It was, he said, his "professional apprenticeship."[6] As Erikson notes, Shaw managed to abandon unacceptable work without relinquishing the work habit. As Shaw himself noted, he worked as his father drank, and in the process he found a solid anchor in his mastery of the symbolism of paternal impotence.[7] Erikson concludes in one of his best passages on the place of work in identity formation:

> Man, to take his place in society, must acquire a "conflict-free," habitual use of a dominant faculty, to be elaborated in an occupation; a limitless resource, a feedback, as it were, from the immediate exercise of this occupation, from the companionship it provides, and from its tradition; and, finally, an intelligible theory of the processes of life which the old atheist, eager to shock to the last, calls a religion.[8]

Erikson elaborated his thoughts on Hitler in two *works—Childhood and Society* and *Young Man Luther*. The adolescent Hitler was a troubled but intensely creative young man. He had one friend, August Kubizek, with whom he used to walk the streets of Linz. Hitler would talk passionately of art and literature, pausing occasionally to read his friend passages of his poetry from a small black book he always carried with him. But most of all, young Hitler talked of architecture and his dreamy plan to rebuild the city. "That house there was in a wrong position," he told Kubizek; "it would have to be abolished." Kubizek continued:

> "That street needed a correction in order to give a more compact impression. Away with this horrible, completely bungled tenement block Let's have a free vista to the Castle." Thus he was always rebuilding the town. . . . He gave his whole self to his imaginary building and was completely carried away by it. Once he had conceived an idea he was like one possessed. Nothing else existed for him—he was oblivious to time, sleep and hunger. . . He could never walk through the streets without being provoked by what he saw. Usually he carried around in his head, at the same time, half a dozen different building projects, and sometimes I could not help feeling that all the buildings of the town were lined up in his brain like a giant panorama. . . .. He felt responsible for everything that was being built.[9]

Erikson notes, quoting Trevor-Roper, that one of Hitler's last projects in the bunker as his world collapsed around him was to design a new opera house and picture gallery for Linz. And Erikson concludes:

> This account illustrates the eerie balance between destructiveness and constructiveness, between suicidal Nothingness and dictatorial Allness, in a young man who at fifteen "felt responsible for everything that was being built," that is, was dominated by an overwhelming conscience and a kind of premature integrity such as characterizes all ideological leaders;

---

[5] Erikson, *Identity*, 143.
[6] Ibid., 144.
[7] Ibid., 145.
[8] Ibid., 150.
[9] Erikson, *Young Man Luther*, 105–106.

he had selected, with deadly obsessiveness, *his* medium of salvation: architecture. Maybe, maybe, if he had been permitted to build, he would not have destroyed.[10]

There is a good deal more to Erikson's theory of leadership than the psychobiographical account of great men's conflicts. Pathology, where it exists, must be confronted. But the capacity to lead, create, and inspire has sources that lie outside conflict. One important source of the leader's effectiveness is his manipulation of symbolism. For example, in his book on Thomas Jefferson, *Dimensions of a New Identity,* Erikson once elaborates on the relationship between body symbolism and political rhetoric. In a digression originating in Erikson's fascination with Jefferson's abiding interest in the upright human body, he tells a fable:

> It was the time of the New Deal. Here was a great and wealthy country having undergone a traumatic economic depression which, as I can now see, must have seemed to paralyze that very self-made identity and put into question its eternal renewal. At that lowest period, a leader appeared who himself could not stand on his own feet because, alas, he was paralyzed from the waist down. But on the arm of a son or an aide, he appeared always erect; and his mood seemed to belie the catastrophe that had befallen him, and as his voice ringingly arose above any emotional depression, he was able to lift the spirit of the masses, and they marched—behind the man in the wheelchair. Happy days were here again.[11]

A man impressively taller than most of his contemporaries, Jefferson had described the natural bridge as "springing, as it were, up to heaven"[12] and referred to the British as being in America's bowels and therefore to be expelled.[13] Jefferson's imagery was a part of, and helped to create, some central American symbols. To stand erect is to be proud, strong, and American. What counts, Erikson notes, "is to be out front, and to be well equipped up front."[14] What is easily dispensable is the "shit" behind, from Indians to blacks to the Vietnamese at My Lai.

Bodily symbolism and its connection with political rhetoric is, in fact, a central theme in Erikson's theory of leadership. Take, for example, the way Erikson handles Gandhi's intense struggles with darkness, sexuality, and sin.

> One can see, then, why Gandhi, in all his preoccupation with sexuality and with dirt, with race and with poverty, gradually recognized the fact that civilized man can overcome his pride in his pseudospecies only by learning to differentiate rationally and compassionately between matters of unhygienic contamination and matters of mere symbolic uncleanness— a modern sense of discrimination which would no longer reject India's Untouchable castes upon whom all dirtiness had been ritually projected for centuries. But he also saw that "cleanliness," once it becomes a matter of pious compulsion, can be as dirty as its opposite; even an hypocritical moralism can be as dirty as sin.[15]

---

[10] Ibid., 107–108.

[11] Erikson, *Dimensions,* 98.

[12] Ibid., 87.

[13] Ibid., 89.

[14] Ibid., 90.

[15] Erikson, *Gandhi's Truth,* 196–197.

Erikson also notes carefully the way Gandhi's phallic maleness, his compulsive walking, and his virile near-nakedness were absorbed in his decisive wielding of political influence. And yet his aggressive maleness alternated with powerful images of maternal care. The spinning wheel was the central symbol of the *Ashram*. Gandhi cared for his followers as a woman tends to her brood. And in *Brahmacharya,* Gandhi perhaps disavowed his God-given organ of such singular potential but managed in the process to bring together a personal need and a national trend of Indian religiosity.[16]

The creative manipulation of bodily symbols need not serve healthy ends. Luther, for example, said: "I am like ripe shit, and the world is a gigantic ass-hole. They probably will let go of each other soon."[17] Erikson confronts this pathology directly.

> In its excess, Luther's obscenity expresses the needs of a manic-depressive nature which has to maintain a state of unrelenting paranoid repudiation of an appointed enemy on the outside in order to avoid victimizing and, as it were, eliminating itself.[18]

Luther, who raised human consciousness to new heights, also left an abiding sense of badness and sin in his theology. He "settled a personal account by providing a public accounting," as Erikson puts it.[19]

The centerpiece of Erikson's theory is that the leader articulates the latent issues of his age in his personal struggles. In probably his most famous paragraph, Erikson describes the connection between *public* and *private* in Luther:

> Millions of boys face these problems [struggles with the father] and solve them in some way or another—they live, as Captain Ahab says, with half of their heart and with only one of their lungs, and the world is the worse for it. Now and again, however, an individual is called upon (called by *whom,* only the theologians claim to know, and by *what,* only bad psychologists) to lift his individual patienthood to the level of a universal one and to try to solve for all what he could not solve for himself alone.[20]

The "collective patienthood" Erikson evokes here is the crisis of Western Christendom over man's relationship to God the Father, which found its direct political analogue in struggles with earthly fathers, princes, and popes. Luther did the dirty work of his age, Erikson concludes, and we have all benefited from an enhanced sense of self ever since.

It is at this critical juncture where psychology and history meet that Erikson's theory is most vulnerable. Notions of universal or collective patienthood are not exactly the kind of precise formulation of past group experience to which historians warm. *Young Man Luther* at least attempts to identify some specific correlations between the private man and the public issues at the beginning of the sixteenth century. After *Young Man Luther,* Erikson became steadily murkier, grander, more philosophical, and less historical. In *Gandhi's Truth,* it is never quite clear what

---

[16] Ibid., 402–403.

[17] Erikson, *Young Man Luther,* 206.

[18] Ibid., 246.

[19] Ibid., 250.

[20] Ibid., 67.

latent meanings in the group the Mahatma articulates. The "group" moves from the special needs of South African Indians to the unique and complex political strivings of Indians, to everyone everywhere. This last meaning is the most confusing:

> When I came to Ahmedabad, it had become clear to me (for I had just come from the disarmament conference of the American Academy of Arts and Sciences) that man as a species can no longer afford any more to cultivate illusions either about his own "nature" or about that of other species, or about those "pseudospecies" he calls enemies—not while inventing and manufacturing arsenals capable of global destruction and while relying for inner and outer peace solely on the superbrakes built into the superweaponry. And Gandhi seems to have been the only man who has visualized *and* demonstrated an overall alternative.[21]

Thomas Jefferson's idea that we need a revolution every 20 years (said, incidentally, offhand and informally in a letter) led to one of Erikson's more farfetched digressions:

> Twenty years is about the span of human development needed for the individual to acquire a sense of identity firm and informed enough to act: which requires enough experience to acknowledge the power of facts and the facts of power; enough practical idealism to attach infantile ideals to live persons and issues; and enough rebellious commitment to the future to leave behind some of the internalized debt of infantile guilt.[22]

Elsewhere in *Dimensions of a New Identity,* Erikson elaborates on Jefferson's ideal of the self-made man in terms of America's immigrant experience[23]; he explains Jefferson's love for the mulatto Sally Hemings as somehow fundamentally expressive of black and white in America; and he concludes with a vague idea about Jefferson and American adulthood.[24]

For all the limitations of his later work—when, it should be noted, he was clearly suffering from the Alzheimer's disease that ended up killing him—Erikson remains the towering figure in terms of style and method among all the work done on the psychology of leadership. One can reasonably question his life cycle theory or his ideas about adolescence, and many of his theories about the link between leaders and followers have not held up very well, but there is no one who wrote more eloquently or showed the way to use—and not abuse—historical sources in the psychological analysis of leaders.

II

After Erikson, a number of writers were drawn to examine leadership psychologically. One of the most noted and prolific is Bruce Mazlish, who through a number of works seeks to explore how psychoanalytic theory can be useful in deepening our understanding of history, especially in the biographies of leaders. Mazlish combines individual psychology with collective processes in what he calls "corresponding

---

[21] Erikson, *Gandhi's Truth,* 51.

[22] Ibid., 72–73.

[23] Ibid., 76–77.

[24] Ibid., 125.

processes," or the attempt to establish a correspondence between character traits and ideologies or doctrines.[25] He emphasizes the way doctrines reflect individual psychological characteristic. Since doctrines are widely shared, Mazlish argues that there develops a correspondence or coherence between individual psychological development and general historical progress. Ideas, in this schema, form the crucial link between individual and historical development. Mazlish argues that in corresponding processes personal, political, or economic developments cause and influence each other, which make for "powerful social change that we call history."[26] In *The Leader, the Led, and the Psyche: Essays in Psychohistory*, Mazlish takes the argument one step further by exploring how corresponding processes become part of a cultural dimension, contributing to the acceptance of the leader by the led. Mazlish argues that the appeal of the leaders for the led follows political identities the leaders shape that respond to the need of the followers through corresponding processes.[27]

In *Revolutionary Ascetic*, Mazlish takes a novel approach to leadership studies and presents a form of leader whose leadership combines spiritual self-denial and discipline with a form of profound libidinal love that the leader displaces into an abstraction like "the revolution" or "humanity." Revolutionary ascetic leaders need not be religiously motivated; what matters is that their personal motives are displaced into the political object. Mazlish introduces us to Lenin's profound sentimentality that for the author presents the autocrat as a "dictator with a difference."[28] Unlike Stalin, Lenin deeply cared about the revolution and the humanity of the Russian peasantry. To avoid reductionist criticism, Mazlish weaves psychological dynamics into the flow of economic, political, intellectual, and social history in his study of Cromwell, Robespierre, Mao, Lenin, and other revolutionary ascetics.[29]

That said, Mazlish—despite some of his own theorizing on method—is often simplistically reductionistic in the way he uses psychoanalytic theory. In his work on James and John Stuart Mill, as well as his work on Richard Nixon and Jimmy Carter, for example, Mazlish falls back on some rather tired analysis of Oedipal themes in his attempt to present a coherent picture of these historical figures.[30]

---

[25] Bruce Mazlish, *In Search of Nixon: A Psychohistorical Study* (New York: Basic Books, 1972); Bruce Mazlish, *James and John Stuart Mill: Father and Son in the Nineteenth Century* (New York: Basic Books, 1975); Bruce Mazlish, *Kissinger: The European Mind in American Policy* (New York: Basic Books, 1976).

[26] Bruce Mazlish, *James and John Stuart Mill: Father and Son in the Nineteenth Century* (New York: Basic Books, 1975), 8.

[27] Bruce Mazlish, *The Leader, the Led, and the Psyche: Essays in Psychohistory* (Hanover: University Press of New England, 1990).

[28] Bruce Mazlish, *Revolutionary Ascetics: Evolution of a Political Type* (New York: Basic Books, 1976).

[29] Ibid.

[30] Bruce Mazlish, *James and John Stuart Mill: Father and Son in the Nineteenth Century* (New York: Basic Books, 1975); Bruce Mazlish and Edwin Diamond, *Jimmy Carter: A Character Portrait* (New York: Simon & Schuster, 1980).

Mazlish also fails for the most part to bridge the gap between the individual leader and the richness of historical processes to which the leader relates and out of which he emerges. In this sense, Mazlish work, while always interesting, has more in common with the earliest of "pathographies" written by those close to Freud than with the more nuanced work of people like Erik Erikson, Robert Jay Lifton, or Heinz Kohut.

Betty Glad has proven to be a more subtle thinker in this field. Her two psychologically sensitive biographies of Jimmy Carter seek to avoid the reductionist argument by infusing the analysis with extensive biographical and political detail and avoiding undue psychobabble. Both in the first and second books on Carter, Glad examines Carter's character in relation to his political and social environment and highlights how the history of the presidency shaped around Carter's character.[31] In the second volume, Glad takes her analysis a step further by analyzing the character and personality of Carter's closest advisors, how they interacted with him and how they together shaped American foreign policy. She not only examines Carter but also Carter's relationship with Zbigniew Brzezinski, Cyrus Vance, and Edmund Muskie; their personalities; and how these relationships shaped the president's foreign policy fiasco during the Iran hostage crisis.[32]

One of the more frequent writers on the psychology of leadership in recent decades is Jerrold Post, a psychiatrist who works closely with the Central Intelligence Agency (CIA) on his studies. Post has been mostly concerned with charismatic narcissistic leaders. Using Kohut's language, Post argues that at the heart of the leadership situation is the relationship between the mirror hungry leaders and the ideal hungry followers.[33] Grandiose leaders embark on grand quests for confirmation of the special sense of self. Mirror hungry leaders fill the void, encapsulating a sense of insecurity and low self-esteem, with the admiration of followers. As a disguise, the narcissistic leader builds an elaborate superego ideal of absolute conviction and certainty—a crucial characteristic of charismatic leaders like Bill Clinton argues Post. Ideal hungry followers crave the absolutist convictions and the confidence displayed by the idealized leader with whom the followers can merge and feel worthwhile and complete. Jerrold Post concludes that together the narcissistic leader and the injured group become "lock and key," releasing energies and passions that can uplift or destroy a nation.[34]

Post has also made a number of contributions to the study of leadership with his colleague, Robert Robins, focusing on the significance of illness in understanding

---

[31] Batty Glad, *Jimmy Carter: In Search of the Great White House* (New York: Norton, 1980); Betty Glad, *An Outsider in the White House: Jimmy Carter, His Advisors, and the Making of American Foreign Policy* (New York: Carnell University Press, 2009).

[32] Betty Glad, *An Outsider in the White House: Jimmy Carter, His Advisors, and the Making of American Foreign Policy* (New York: Carnell University Press, 2009).

[33] Jerrold M. Post, "Narcissism and the Charismatic Leader-Follower Relationship," *Political Psychology*, 7 (1986): 675–688.

[34] Post, *Leaders and their followers in a dangerous world* (Ithaca, NY: Cornel University, 2004).

the shape of a leader's life.[35] Woodrow Wilson's debilitating stroke compromised his presidency and contributed to his failure to convince the Senate to ratify the League of Nations. Franklin Delano Roosevelt was so chronically ill at Yalta in 1945 that it may have affected his judgment as he redrew the map of Eastern Europe. A clinically paranoid Joseph Stalin deported over three million people to Siberia from 1941 to 1948, where almost half died of disease and starvation. The weird and unorthodox Dr. Theo Morell enabled Hitler's drug abuse, especially during the war as countless millions died.[36] And, finally, John F. Kennedy, who never recovered from his debilitating back pain as result of his wartime exploits, used codeine, Demerol, and methadone to control the pain; took Ritalin and barbiturates for sleep; tranquilizers for anxiety; and abused amphetamine to leverage the effects of Addison's disease.[37]

In all cases, behind closed doors every effort was made to conceal the illness and disability of the leader. The public never understood the degree of disability under which Roosevelt struggled from his polio, let alone the true state of his health at Yalta. It was years before the extent of Kennedy's reliance on drugs became known, as the mystique of his court was carefully choreographed. The insistence on full disclosure about a president's health, which is now common procedure in

---

[35] Jerrold M. Post, "The Season's of a Leader's Life: The Influence of the Life Cycle on Political Behavior," *Political Psychology* 2 (1980): 35–49. Post elaborates on "Early Life Transition, Mid-Life Transition, and Late Life Transitions." He identifies the first stage as the tumultuous struggles of adolescence, when important transformations shape political identifications in an effort to enhance psychological ego consolidation. Idealistic youth search for political and ideological vehicles to improve the world and better the condition of the downtrodden. When crisis shakes the national tent or failure devastates the hopes of an energetic generation, righteous rage becomes a manifest character disposition of a prospective young leader, shaped in that generation. Post mentions in this regard as relevant the example of Gamal Abdel Nasser, who during adolescence was deeply influenced by the political upheavals of Egypt. The righteous rage of his adolescence and the deep dissatisfaction with the political and social conditions of Egypt during his midlife crisis led Nasser to overthrow King Farouk and establish himself as the historical strong man of the Arab world. Post's second stage encapsulates turbulent midlife crises, where high levels of personal dissatisfaction lay at the roots of many political leaders to embark on revolutionary feats. During midlife crisis, many leaders find it difficult to reconcile their ambitions with their actual successes. As a result, they embrace revolution, argues the author. Equally important, Post's third stage highlights the imbalance between ambition and achievement, which has led many older leaders to commit great political blunders. Post exemplifies his argument by presenting the example of Mao's cultural revolution and the unresponsive, emotional, and senile Soviet leaders of the 1980s. The normal psychological reaction for the ageing include rigidity of thought, impairment of intellectual judgment, emotional overreaction, denial and disability, and a general tendency to exaggerate personality trait (earlier checked and balanced by political considerations). How significant a role did Alzheimer play for Regan during the Iran–Contra Affair? Post stresses the importance of understanding life circles that have serious implications for leader's decision-making abilities.

[36] David Irving, *The Secret Diaries of Hitler's Doctor* (New York: Macmillan, 1983).

[37] Jerrold M. Post and Robert S. Robins, *When Illness Strikes the Leader: The Dilemma of the Captive King* (New Haven, CT: Yale University Press, 1993). Note also Jerrold M. Post, *Leaders and Their Followers in a Dangerous World* (Ithaca, NY: Cornel University Press, 2004), 60–66.

American politics, only developed later. The most dramatic cover-up in American history around issues of the health of the leader, however, is that of Woodrow Wilson after his major stroke in 1919. Only three people had access to Wilson: his wife Edith, Dr. Grayson, and Wilson's aide, Joseph Tumulty. This peculiar and unofficial triumvirate assumed executive decision-making. After Wilson recovered enough to take back the reins of power, Ms. Wilson remarked, "You men make such a fuss. When Woody was ill, I had no difficulty running the country."[38]

Post and Robins also note another kind of circumstance around health that can have a dramatic effect on a leader–when he or she is terminally ill but refuses to let go of power. History can become subsumed to the needs of the dying leader. Mohammad-Rezā Shāh Pahlavi, for example, desired to modernize Iran by utilizing the country's resources to initiating his "white revolution." His plan had been for the white revolution to pick up pace gradually over 30–40 years, but then lymphocytic leukemia, a cancer that affects the white blood cells, struck Pahlavi. Sensing his end approaching, the Shah infused massive financial resources in the country's economy for speeding up the white revolution to insure his own symbolic immortality. Despite his original plans, the desperately ill Shah convinced himself that he could control the social dislocations caused by the rapidly rising expectations but found that the economy lacked a solid infrastructure able to absorb the rapid changes. The severe upheaval caused by the hasty implementation of many of his reforms proved conducive for creating a climate in which the ideas of a religious fanatic like Ayatollah Khomeini were able to flourish.[39]

Another figure who has written widely on aspects of the psychology of leadership is Stanley Renshon. He argues that for far too long psychological assessments of leadership have been myopic and reductionistic, attributing exclusive importance to psychological motivations while discounting political forces that restrict the leader's action. Renshon claims to utilize political context, role performance, and character-based personality traits to rectify this criticism. He emphasizes values, morals, and the overall ethical system as individual motivational principles, but also argues that for a leader it is necessary to have a balance between self and ideals. For Renshon, character integrity conceptually segregates the self from ideals and subjects the former to the service of the latter. Unrealistic levels of self-confidence and unhealthy levels of ambition, he argues, characterize grandiose and narcissistic personalities who can hijack the presidency. Such leaders relate to others with false and strategic empathy in order to sell their agenda rather than reach consensuses over policy. Renshon warns against psychological misfits who become presidential candidates possessing grandiose and narcissistic personalities.[40]

---

[38] Jerrold M. Post, *Leaders and Their Followers in a Dangerous World* (Ithaca, NY: Cornel University Press, 2004), 51.

[39] Ibid., 71.

[40] Stanley A. Renshon, *The Psychological Assessment of Performance of Presidential Candidates* (New York: New York University Press, 1996); Stanley A. Renshon, "Analyzing the Psychology and Performance of Presidential Candidates at a Distance: Bob Doll and the 1996 Presidential Campaign," *Journal of Leadership Studies* 3 (1996): 253–281. Note also Robert H. Swansbrough,

Such grand theorizing masks political bias, illustrating how perverted the uses of psychology in the study of leadership can be. In his book of the Clinton presidency, *High Hopes: The Clinton Presidency and the Politics of Ambition*, Renshon, an obvious conservative, argues that Clinton was unable to project a coherent political identity due to the fact that he was self-absorbed and was operating at a psychological level, out of touch with reality. Clinton's "grandiose self" is the key to his unconsolidated character integrity, according to Renshon. As a result, Clinton's wildly ambitious policy goals got him into serious political trouble on many fronts.[41] Clinton's weaknesses became the strengths of George W. Bush in Renshon's subsequent study, *In His Father's Shadow: The Transforming of George W. Bush*, published in 2005. In what reads now as almost amusing, if not certainly foolish, Renshon describes Bush as a "truly historical figure of the first rank" for his solid integrity and bedrock psychological core, which allows the president to keep a clear and narrow focus on his modest policy goals: tax relief, education reform, faith-based legislation, Medicare, social security, and national security (including two major wars). Renshon argues that the integrity of Bush's character allowed him to stand apart, follow his own values, and remain unbending in the face of diverging arguments—the true strength of a decisive president. Bush's integrity allowed him to become a transformative president who "turned away from domestic and international policy orthodoxies."[42]

"A Kohutian Analysis of President Bush's Personality and Style in the Persian Gulf Crisis," *Political Psychology* 15 (1994): 227–276. Swansbrough has argued that m*otivation* allows leaders to develop leadership styles conducive to their personality. Accordingly, leaders may challenge or respect constraints; they can be motivated primarily by policy goals or relationships building; and, they differ in the selection contextual information—some leaders open contextual information, while others utilize few loyal confidants and rely on their instincts, supported by self-confidence. George Herbert Walker Bush, *Swansbrough argues,* embodies the motivations of the achiever; he shaped a leadership style that challenged constraints but was built on relationships. Bush's information approach relied on rational calculations for decision-making and discussions with a smaller group of trusted advisors, particularly during the seminal time of the Persian Gulf crisis. Blema S. Steinberg, "Indira Gandhi: The Relationship between Personality Profile and Leadership Style," *Political Psychology* 26 (2005): 755–789. Steinberg, in her study of Indira Gandhi, seeks to explore the relationship between personality profiles and leadership style. She examines Gandhi's personality from the wide variety of open sources. On a parallel tangent, Steinberg explores Gandhi's leadership style during the time she was prime minister. The analysis reveals an excessively dynamic Gandhi, almost dysfunctional, with ambitious, reticent, contentious, and domineering personality traits. Gandhi's leadership style exhibited the ambitious and domineering traits, but also the reticent, retiring, and aggrieved—seemingly contradictory and incompatible traits in political leadership. Steinberg concludes by arguing that the model possesses predictive validity and attributes the perplexing behavior of Gandhi on her gender. Yet, the pieces of the puzzle clearly do not fit. The statistical models used to date for analysis of political leaders cannot be generalized. Steinberg herself recognizes that "for the most part, psychodynamic personality studies of political leaders have been insightful, but idiosyncratic and, thus, incapable of precise replication."

[41] Stanley A. Renshon, *High Hopes: The Clinton Presidency and Politics of Ambition* (New York: New York University Press, 1996).

[42] Stanley A. Renshon, *In His Father's Shadow: The Transforming of George W. Bush* (New York: Palgrave Macmillan, 2004); Stanley A. Renshon, "Presidential Address: George W. Bush's

Vamik Volkan, another writer who has written widely on the psychology of leadership, is more evenhanded and attempts to grasp some of the dynamics between a leader and a follower, as well as individual and group, by exploring ethnicity and nationality as crucial components of identity building for the study of leadership. Volkan says that, just as a person wears two layers of clothes, the undergarment and the outer layer, group members create individual identity and group identity. The undergarment fits the individual tightly according to his or her own body type and shape, while the overgarment, the ethnic garment, fits him or her loosely like a big canvas tent, encompassing the group's identity. Under such a tent, men and women, rich and poor, powerful and powerless, as far as nationality and ethnicity are concerned, are equal. They all equally take pride in the collective achievement and are equally shaken when events shake the tent. When darkness looms on the ethnic or national horizon, each individual collectively and tenaciously resolves to strengthen the tent again. Cultural rituals that distinguish between them and us emerge as an effort to restore the inner psychological balance—hence the need for enemies and allies.[43] From a Kleinian perspective, Volkan argues that splitting, projection, and externalization are the key concepts needed to understand the formation of ethnic and national high-level symbolism. The group's cultural amplifiers serve as positive suitable targets of externalization, while chosen enemies and their cultural identity serve as negative targets of externalization. Here the idea of enemies and allies serves as the foundation for identity.[44]

"Chosen traumas" and "chosen glories" become central to Volkan's thinking of leadership and international affairs.[45] In *Killing in the Name of Identity: A Study of Bloody Conflict*, Volkan argues that shared traumas and glories heighten group cohesion and promote a common identity. Volkan utilizes the word "trauma" to describe events that cause group members to feel victimized, injured, and humiliated by another group. Volkan links chosen traumas with the group's inability to mourn. Wars and narcissistic injuries cause a kind of mourning, comparable in some respects to individual mourning over the death of loved ones. If the mourning does not follow a normal course, these events become a chosen trauma and a political force in their own right. [46]

Time itself warps injured groups. In enduring unresolved political mourning, subsequent generations unconsciously repeat trauma in an effort to gain mastery over the humiliating original event, in the hope that by doing so they can gain control over their grief. Volkan adds:

Cowboy Politics: An Inquiry," *Political Psychology* 26 (2005): 585–614 presents essentially the same argument regarding Bush's character.

[43] Vamik D. Volkan, *The Need to Have Enemies and Allies* (New Jersey, NJ: Aronson, 1994), xxiii–xxv.

[44] Vamik D. Volkan, "The Need to Have Enemies and Allies: A developmental Approach," *Political Psychology* 6 (1985): 219–247.

[45] Vamik D. Volkan, *The Need to Have Enemies and Allies* (New Jersey, NJ: Aronson, 1994).

[46] Vamik D. Volkan, *Killing in the Name of Identity: A Study of Bloody Conflict* (Charlottesville, VA: Pitchstone Publishing, 2006).

> Once a trauma becomes a chosen trauma (a shared mental representation), the historical truth about it is not longer consequential; the central role that the event plays in the group's ethnic identity becomes more significant. Usually a chosen trauma in a group's history becomes condensed with similar traumas from the past.[47]

Slobodan Milosevic abuses the historical account of Prince Lazar's fall at the battle of Kosovo Polje in 1389, defending Serbia against the infidel Ottoman Turks. Milosevic projected on the mythical figure of Lazar many endured shared traumas to galvanize support for his ethnic cleansing policies. Milosevic's enflaming rhetoric caused the re-awakening of the perceived historical humiliation in Serbian population.[48] The leader of a group sharing a chosen trauma becomes the vehicle that re-traumatizes the group during times of stress.[49] "Even though the motor of war can be ignited by a variety of events, the emotional fuel is the chosen trauma," states Volkan.[50] At the same time, groups form rituals to preserve chosen glories, which shape the group's identity as much as chosen traumas. Attempts to re-create chosen glories or remedy chosen traumas lead groups to engage in purification, by purging foreign elements, in order to achieve a new cohesive identity and replace the injured sense of self—much like Milosevic's ethnic-cleansing wars.[51]

Crisis is crucial to Volkan thinking on leadership, since crisis will more dramatically reveal the leader's redemptive or destructive psychological qualities.[52] While viewing narcissism as pathological, Volkan distinguishes between malignant narcissistic leader and benign narcissistic leader. Yet they share common features. The charismatic narcissistic leaders, the author argues, personalizes issues of ethnicity and nationality, which crystallize for the group, at that particular moment, the difference between them and the enemy.[53] In *Blind Trust: Large Groups and Their Leaders in Times of Crisis and Terror*, Volkan argues that large groups function as individuals: When traumatized, they regress. Group regression may include any combination of symptoms, adaptation of group symbols, sensitization of borders, loss of individuality, dehumanization of the enemy, and unquestioned support for the leader, evident after September 11, 2001.[54] The relationship between narcissistic charismatic leaders and their followers, however, can become cathartic and redemptive. At times, narcissistic leaders produce positive and enduring changes that can

---

[47] Vamik D. Volkan, *The Need to Have Enemies and Allies* (New Jersey, NJ: Aronson, 1994), xxvi.

[48] Jerrold M. Post, *Leaders and Their Followers in a Dangerous World* (Ithaca, NY: Cornel University Press, 2004), 181–182

[49] Vamik D. Volkan, Gabriele Ast, and William Greer, Jr., *The Third Reich in the Unconscious: Transgenerational Transmission and Its Consequences* (New York: Brunner-Routledge, 2002).

[50] Vamik D. Volkan, *The Need to Have Enemies and Allies* (New Jersey, NJ: Aronson, 1994), xxxii.

[51] Vamik D. Volkan, *Bloodlines: From Ethnic Pride to Ethnic Terrorism* (New York: Basic Books, 1997).

[52] Vamik D. Volkan, "The Need to Have Enemies and Allies: A developmental Approach," *Political Psychology* 6 (1985): 219–247.

[53] Vamik D. Volkan, *The Need to Have Enemies and Allies* (New Jersey, NJ: Aronson, 1994).

[54] Vamik D. Volkan, *Blind Trust: Large Groups and Their Leaders in Times of Crisis and Terror* (Charlottesville, VA: Pitchstone Publishing, 2004).

uplift a nation. Volkan and Itzkowitz in *The Immortal Ataturk: A Psychobiography*, argues that at the core of Ataturk's motivation for saving and modernizing Turkey was his psychological urge to save his mother. This peculiar desire fueled Ataturk's narcissism and grandiose vision for a modern Turkey. [55]

Much of what bedevils the work of Volkan, Post, Renshon, and others is their tendency to isolate the leader from cultural, political, economic, and most of all historical context. Just as Hitler is a product of the 1930s and is hard to imagine in any other context, so Bill Clinton epitomizes the exuberance of the 1990s, and Slobodan Milosevic is the quintessential product of a disintegrating Yugoslavia and strident Serbian nationalism. These leaders, whatever their personalities, are shaped by events in profoundly significant ways. Too much psychologizing of the individual leader limits our understanding of the fit between leader and follower and how the group needs shape the contours of what may, or may not, be attempted by the leader. We are endlessly fascinated by stories about the lives of leaders, and psychological perspectives deepen our ability to understand their character, but we must beware the trivial, the banal, or the inane.

III

Robert Jay Lifton has written a series of books that offer a creative model for approaching leadership and followership that departs in significant ways from the paradigms that have dominated the field. Lifton conducted interviews and studies of four specific groups of people whose historical exposures have a bearing on important characteristics of the present era: Chinese and Westerners who underwent Chinese thought reform or, more colloquially, "brainwashing" in the early 1950s, Hiroshima survivors of the atomic bomb, antiwar Vietnam veterans, and surviving doctors who had been involved in the Nazi genocidal project.[56] Lifton's focus is always on themes, forms, and images that are in significant ways shared, rather than on the life of a single person as such. Lifton's approach required considerable innovation in the interview method.

In half a century of interviewing, Lifton has struggled with modifications of the psychiatric and psychoanalytic interview in order to approach and understand various kinds of people who have not sought therapeutic help but have been sought

---

[55] Vamik D. Volkan and Itzkowitz. *The Immortal Ataturk: A Psychobiography* (Chicago: Chicago University Press, 1984). Vamik D. Volkan, Norman Irkowitz, and Andrew W. Dod, *Richard Nixon: A Psychobiography* (New York: Columbia University Press, 1999), analyze both sides of Nixon's character, the dark and domineering aspects of Nixon and the peacemaker, to conclude that Nixon like Ataturk was e positive narcissist.

[56] Robert Jay Lifton, *Thought Reform and the Psychology of Totalism: A Study of "Brainwashing" in China* (New York: Norton, 1971); *History and Human Survival* (New York: Random House, 1970); *Death in Life: Survivors of Hiroshima* (Chapel Hill, NC: University of North Carolina Press, 1991 [1967]); *Home From the War: Vietnam Veterans: Neither Victims Nor Executioners* (New York: Simon and Schuster, 1973); and *The Nazi Doctors: Medical Killing and the Psychology of Genocide* (New York: Basic Books, 1986).

out by him. Lifton has developed a free interview style: It remains probing and encouraging the widest range of associations, and includes detailed life histories and explorations of dreams. But it focuses on the specific situation responsible for bringing the interviewee and interviewer together (most of the interviews have been individual ones) and takes the form of something close to an open dialogue emerging from that situation.

The relationship the two develop is neither one of doctor and patient nor one of ordinary friends, although at moments it can be seen to resemble either. Lifton has wrestled with what to call the subject in that relationship. "Research subject" seems unsatisfactory because it suggests that someone merely studied or investigated in a more or less passive way. "Patient" is entirely inappropriate, and "client" is not much better. "Historical actor" and "pivotal person" come closer, but they have their own ambiguities. Progress in this field may, in part, depend on such innovations in method. Once developed in the study of contemporary matters, such innovations could also be applied to the study of the past, although their usefulness lies mainly in relation to the search for and the interpretation of various kinds of records and documents.

Lifton's "shared themes approach" emphasizes shared exploration, mostly of the world of the person sought out but including a great deal of give-and-take and more than a little discussion of the author's own attitudes and interests. It requires a combination of human spontaneity and professional discipline. One's way of combining the two is always idiosyncratic and always less than ideal. Lifton moves outward from interviews with individual survivors to examine groups that they formed, leaders emerging from among them, and social currents that survivors create and are affected by. This approach requires close attention to historical context.

Through a detailed elaboration of the ethos of the survivor, Lifton unites individual psychological and historical currents. In his book on Hiroshima, for example, he compares survival of the atomic bomb to survival of other massive death immersions—Nazi persecutions, the plagues in the Middle Ages as revealed through records and natural disasters—and the deaths of close friends and family members. He then, in that and in subsequent studies, raises questions about the general importance of the survivor ethos of the present age and of the degree to which people have become historically prone to the survivor's retained death imprint, to his or her death guilt and his psychic numbing or desensitization to death-dominated images, and to his or her struggle for significance or what the author calls the survivor's "formulation." Those questions intrude into virtually all of Lifton's work, and they haunt the contemporary imagination.

In Lifton's one specifically biographical study of leadership, *Revolutionary Immortality*, Lifton discussed Mao Tse-tung's relationship to the Chinese cultural revolution in terms of Mao's many experiences of individual and revolutionary survival. Mao's use of the survivor state was related to his extraordinary accomplishments as a leader, and the general relevance of death symbolism was considered in the broadest historical perspective in relation to the Chinese cultural revolution. By connecting certain psychological characteristics of Mao's personal and revolutionary style with the predominant themes of the cultural revolution, Lifton attempted to combine the "great man" and "shared themes" approaches.

The central thesis of the book revolved around Mao's anticipation of his own impending death and his own and his followers' fear of the death of the revolution. What Lifton saw as the overwhelming threat that Mao faced was not so much death itself as the suggestion that his revolutionary works would not endure. Revolutionary immortality was, then, meant to be a shared sense of participating in permanent revolutionary ferment and of transcending individual death by living on indefinitely within continuing revolution, as expressed in Trotsky's principle of permanent revolution. That vision took on unprecedented intensity in the Chinese Communist experience. The quest for revolutionary immortality provided a general framework within which the political and economic struggles and antibureaucratic and antirevisionist assaults of the cultural revolution could be examined without being reduced to a particular psychological or psychopathological trait of any one person.

Also related to that quest was a pattern that reflected the excruciating Maoist struggles with technology. The author called that pattern "psychism," by which he meant an exaggerated reliance on psychic power as a means of controlling the external environment or an attempt to replace the requirements of technology with pure revolutionary will. Technology was desperately sought but feelings were cultivated. In that pattern of psychism, there was once more a coming together of Mao's personal revolutionary style, including what Chinese Communist commentators referred to as his revolutionary romanticism, and a number of larger currents surrounding the cultural revolution. The concept of psychism, like that of revolutionary immortality, was an attempt to say something about interface of leader, group, and history.

Revolutionary Immortality was not based on the kind of detailed interview approach described in relation to Lifton's Hiroshima work. Rather, it was a brief interpretive essay that drew heavily on documents and observations by others of the cultural revolution and on the writings of Mao. It included only a very limited number of interviews with participants and observers of the events described. As compared with the Hiroshima study, the Mao study was more tenuous and more vulnerable. In Lifton's study of the physicians in Nazi Germany, he returned to the use of interviews with "historical actors" to understand psychologically the meaning of important events in recent history and the contexts of meaning of Nazi leadership.

IV

An even more significant thinker on theoretical approaches to the psychology of leadership is Heinz Kohut (1913–1981), who is well known within psychoanalysis, and increasingly in the culture, for his innovative ideas about the self.[57] Many see him as the most creative thinker in psychoanalysis since Sigmund Freud. Kohut's significant contributions to the humanities, especially to history, and to politics

---

[57] Charles B. Strozier, *Heinz Kohut: The Making of a Psychoanalyst* (New York: Farrar, Straus & Giroux, 2001).

in general, are less well known and appreciated. Take, for example, his signal contribution from 1973 (published 3 years later), "Creativeness, Charisma, Group Psychology: Reflections on the Self-Analysis of Freud." [58]

In the paper, Kohut takes as his point of reference how difficult it is for analysts to think calmly about Freud, given their deep immersion in his works and even his inner world through the close study of *The Interpretation of Dreams,* which is so central to the curriculum of nearly all institutes. "The pull toward establishing a gross and uncontrolled identification with Freud is strong," he says, as is the equally intense and irrational debunking of the toppled father figure. For the most part, the powerful idealization of Freud for analysts "forestalls the development of certain exquisitely painful experiences of narcissistic imbalance in the analyst (such as pangs of jealousy and envy)" while for the movement as a whole it serves as a counterforce to the unfortunate tendency toward splinter groups. As Freud himself argued in 1921, psychoanalytic group cohesion is established in part and safeguarded by the imago of the leader, whom all members hold in common as their collective ego ideal, becoming in the process "that point to which all individuals look up, and to whose greatness they all submit in shared admiration and submission."

This relationship between Freud and psychoanalysts in general leads Kohut to talk at the outset of his paper about a "group self," by which he means (though he does not put it in these terms) the collective experience of we-ness that, following William James, can be understood as the analogue of self as that which "I" can conceive.[59] Kohut never concretely defined the group self—a deliberate avoidance, to be too concrete about defining "the self." Kohut uses the construct later in this same essay—in other papers he was writing in these years on leadership, rage, and related topics—and then most specifically in an interview not long before his death, in which he stressed again that the idea is that groups have a psychological cohesion and tendency toward fragmentation under duress similar to the way individual selves respond to trauma.[60] Kohut's ideas in this regard differ from what Volkan, Post, and others talk about in group "regression," which directly applies Freudian ideas about the individual to the group. Kohut is concerned with trauma and fragmentation, which can go in all kinds of unpredictable ways and certainly not in the reverse order of development (as Freud talks about with the individual).

---

[58] Heinz Kohut, "Creativeness, Charisma, and Group Psychology: Reflections on the Self Analysis of Freud," in *The Search for the Self: Selected Writings of Heinz Kohut, 1950–1978,* ed. Paul Ornstein (New York: International Universities Press, 1978), II, 801–802 and 837–838; Sigmund Freud, *Group Psychology and the Analysis of the Ego (1921), The Standard Edition of the Complete Psychological Works of Sigmund Freud,* trans. and ed. James Strachey, in collaboration with Anna Freud (London: The Hogarth Press, 1955).

[59] For a more detailed discussion of Kohut's use of "self" and its relation to William James, see Strozier *Heinz Kohut,* 194–198.

[60] Heinz Kohut, *Self Psychology and the Humanities: Reflections on a New Psychoanalytic Approach,* edited with an introduction by Charles B. Strozier (New York: Norton, 1986), 206–207.

In these opening comments about the group self in the charisma paper, Kohut makes two general points. One is that a firm group self-bound to a leader provides comfort and security to its members, fostering productivity in any number of valuable ways. He sees the work of the psychoanalytic community since Freud as based in such a relationship between the founding father and all those who have been laboring in the vineyard since the founding of psychoanalysis. The psychological basis of such a tie between leader and follower is based primarily on idealization and what Kohut derisively calls "submission." But it is his second point about creativity that moves the essay into a new understanding of the psychology of leadership. "Truly original thought," he says, "is energized predominantly from the grandiose self, while the work of the more tradition-bound scientific and artistic, i.e., productivity, is performed with idealizing cathexes."[61] This somewhat obscure passage, especially with its reference to the very old-fashioned idea of cathexes, can be unpacked to mean that at the heart of the relation between leader and follower lies the normalizing processes of idealization in the group self, but that truly original thought and action are grounded in the often erratic and potentially violent but enormously creative workings of grandiosity.

The concept of the group self is not a specific measurable sociological entity like class or race. Analogous to an individual self and its self-objects, a group self can only be grasped empathically from within the experience of "we-ness" in relation to the leader. That leader may be symbolized or internalized, but there is no "group self," as Kohut uses the term, outside of the group self-leader context. Kohut was keenly aware of the complexity of social, cultural, political, and historical processes but sought to introduce into such familiar ways of segmenting reality a psychological perspective. A good example of his appreciation for complexity is a passage from Kohut's essay, "On Leadership," written some 3 years before his charisma paper. He says:

> One of the difficulties of a psychoanalytic explanation of historical events (and other social phenomena) is the complexity of the interplay of various groups in producing social or historical action. The apparently passive tolerance in larger groups of the takeover of leadership and initiative by smaller groups may actually be more active than meets the eye. Thus, small pathological, or otherwise highly special and unusual, aberrant groups may be "passively" permitted to assume leadership in order to reach a goal which the majority may wish to disown yet also to reach. For example, people motivated by "normal" competitiveness and jealously may tolerate the merciless killing of the competitor by a paranoiac group which, after it has done its work, is itself condemned and removed from the social scene. These considerations not only are relevant with regard to the explanation of specific social phenomena, like the behavior of the German masses, the powerful Socialist Party, the Army, or the Church toward the Nazis before, during and *after* the Nazi regime in Germany, but also point the way to a promising direction of' remedial social action by psychology.[62]

Kohut then turns to examine the self-analysis of Freud in the late 1890s and early 1900s. What marked Freud's self-analysis as original was the systematic, scientific

---

[61] Kohut, "Creativeness," *Search* II: 801–802 and 837–838.

[62] Heinz Kohut, "On Leadership," *Self Psychology and the Humanities*, 53.

way he went about introspection that made his method generally available to others. His analysis, furthermore, was one that for the first time aimed at the "depth-psychological comprehension of the total personality" as opposed to the more narrow focus on symptom relief. But Freud was not entirely alone in his endeavors, as he only managed his analysis with the timely help of Wilhelm Fliess. Their remarkable relationship and the passion it engendered—the hundreds and hundreds of letters the two exchanged, and their "congresses" when they met and talked non-stop for days on end—is the stuff of many biographies.[63] But what interests Kohut is the texture of their relationship. He asks a simple question: What exactly did Fliess mean to Freud?

Wilhelm Fliess was clearly not the traditional analyst for a patient in the process of self-exploration. For one thing, he lived and worked in Berlin and thus far removed from Vienna. It is difficult to imagine treatment as we practice it today with someone outside of the room.[64] That separation between the two men is partly why Freud never came to understand transference—or the reactivation of past relationships in the present context of significant others—during all the years of his relationship with Fliess. Because he was not in a familiar healing relationship with his friend, Freud never experienced the feelings toward him that he would later understand are the heart of analysis. What mattered for Freud, Kohut argues, was a "transference of creativity" of his narcissistic, or self, needs. Freud came to require the imagined presence of Fliess as a crucial participant in his own inner struggles as he gained his great insights in human psychology in these years. It was, however, a scary process of discovery for Freud, filled with loneliness, doubt, and despair. During the years of discovery, Freud was in fact enfeebled and at the mercy of powerful forces that he could not fully control.

Much biographical evidence about Freud in this period of creative struggle supports Kohut's insight (though the air around Freud often reeks of hagiography).[65] Kohut also turns to biographical, literary, and artistic work on other geniuses during their creative struggles to extend his insights into Freud. Kohut was thus very interested in the way Picasso sought out Georges Braque during the discovery of cubism, especially the way he built up Braque in his mind as his alter ego (much like Freud greatly exaggerated the genius of Fliess during the years of their intense personal connection). At the height of Picasso and Braque's mutual exploration of the new art form, their paintings became virtually indistinguishable, as described by Mary Matthews Gedo (who was deeply influenced by and in dialogue with Kohut about Picasso in the early 1970s).[66] The reverse of this process of binding cohesion to

---

[63] Note especially *The Complete Letters of Sigmund Freud and Wilhelm Fliess, 1887–1904*, ed. Jeffrey Moussaieff Masson (Cambridge, MA: Harvard University Press, 1985).

[64] The exception today is the frequent use of phone sessions and now video chat, though such forms of therapeutic interaction best serve to complement direct contact, not supplant it.

[65] The standard biography of Freud is that of Peter Gay, *Freud: A Life for Our Times* (New York: Norton, 1988).

[66] Mary Matthews Gedo, *Picasso: Art as Autobiography* (Chicago: University of Chicago Press, 1982).

avert the potential fragmentation during intense periods of discovery is what Kohut calls "the disintegration of artistic sublimation." Nothing illustrates it better than Thomas Mann's *Death in Venice,* in which the writer Aschenbach unravels (and dies) in the steamy heat of plague-ridden Venice because of his love for the beautiful and unattainable boy Tadzio.[67]

All of this wide-ranging evidence gives us much understanding of the meanings of Freud's psychological state in his period of greatest creativity, as well as other geniuses in their periods of discovery. Kohut's interest clearly goes way beyond the specific case of Fliess and Freud, as his real concern is to figure out what self-functions the Fliesses of the world have for the Freuds of the world in periods of psychological enfeeblement. Kohut asks, as he moves deliberately from Freud's biography to psychohistorical analysis: "What are the characteristic features of the person who is especially suitable to become the admired omnipotent selfobject for the creative person during the period when he makes his decisive steps into new territory?" The answer is surprising. It seems the others in these relationships must possess "unshakable self-confidence" and express their opinions with an "absolute certainty" bordering on paranoia. What makes such people uniquely suited to play this role of omnipotent self-object is the ease with which they judge others and point out their moral flaws. Most of us have internal restraints on such exuberant self-expression. But no restraint exists for those charismatic or messianic figures who have identified with their own grandiosity or their idealized image of themselves. Without shame or hesitation, these figures "set themselves up as the guides and leaders and gods of those who are in need of guidance, of leadership, and of a target for their reverence."[68]

Charismatic and messianic figures have few feelings of guilt and seldom suffer any pangs of conscience for their behavior. They have fully identified themselves with their grandiose self. Most of us ordinary mortals seek ideals as "direction-settings symbols of perfection." We feel good about ourselves when we can approach such ideals and experience a fall in self-esteem when we fail, by too wide a margin, to meet those expectations. "The messianic leader figure, however, is done with the task of measuring himself against the ideals of his superego: his self and the idealized structure have become one." They are all or nothing. "There are no survival potentialities between the extremes of utter firmness and strength, on the one hand, and utter destruction (psychosis, suicide) on the other."[69]

One wants to know what differentiates the leader from narcissistically crippled people who in their self-absorption and misery usually lead narrow, isolated lives. Kohut addressed this question in his earlier essay, "On Leadership," in which he argues that the charismatic leader "develops a heightened sensitivity to the anonymous group and its motivations and is able to relate to it intensely." The leader, as

---

[67] Kohut, "Creativeness, Charisma," 820–823.

[68] Ibid., 825. The paranoid leader, it should be noted, is not the only possible leadership model for groups in states of enfeeblement. See, for example, the essay on Lincoln later in this book.

[69] Ibid., 826–827.

other narcissistically crippled people, perceives people as "types and clichés rather than as individuals," but compensates for this limitation by his "heightened grasp of the unconscious and preconscious tension states, of the fantasies, wishes, and fears of the group." This powerful resonance, however, has severe limits, for "the gifted leader can be effectively engaged only in the area in which the fantasies and wishes of the masses are like his own." He has no understanding of groups that do not precisely mirror the grandiose fantasies that he holds in common with the group. He finds contemptible the "motivations and attitudes which are not identical with his own," though his own self-loathing in time leads toward a "steadily increasing contempt for the masses who are enthralled with him."[70]

Charismatic and messianic leaders are unusually "sensitive to injustices" and quick to accuse others in very persuasive ways. That in turn evokes guilt and shame in their followers, who become submissive and allow themselves to be "treated tyrannically." Such behavior on the part of charismatic leaders appears to originate in a basic "stunting of their empathic capacity." They have little real understanding of other people's needs. In the childhoods of charismatic and messianic leaders, Kohut guesses, their initial experience of feeling bathed in mirroring and in the presence of idealized figures with which they can merge is followed by "abrupt and unpredictable frustrations." Their unique resolution of that trauma, perhaps drawing on some congenital abilities, is then to take over for themselves those self-object functions that should have been performed for them. The cost, however, is that they continue to live in a decidedly archaic world filled with rage at the torment they suffered in first knowing the security and comfort of empathy and then having it abruptly withdrawn. In response, they become "superempathic with themselves and their own needs" but furious with the world. They assert their perfection self-righteously and demand control over others to serve as vicarious regulators of their self-esteem. Their peculiar sensitivities put them in direct touch with the archaic needs of the group.[71]

Such are the Fliesses of the world—or the Hitlers, or Stalins, or bin Ladens, or any number of cult leaders who have imposed themselves on the religious landscape over the millennia.

Several historical examples might illustrate Kohut's theories of leadership. His favorite was that of Nazi Germany to which he returned in many different writings over the years, in seminars, and in frequent conversations.[72] His concern reflected the trauma of his youth and emigration. To understand Hitler and the Nazis from a self-psychological point of view, one must begin with the triumphal military victories of Prussia in 1866 against Austria and in 1870 against France that led to the consolidation of the new German Reich. A colossal new power dominating all of Central Europe and threatening peace to the east and in the imperial world suddenly

---

[70]Kohut, *Humanities* 56–57.

[71]Kohut, *Creativeness* 830–832.

[72]Besides the paper, "Creativeness," under discussions, note Kohut, "On Leadership," *Humanities* 64ff and 204–205; and "On Empathy," *Search* 4: 525–535.

sprang up, demanding its rightful "place in the sun." The grandiose ambitions of Otto von Bismarck mirrored those of millions of Germans who relished their new status in the world. New political structures privileged the military elite as militarism in general came to characterize the Reich in its assertive and increasingly coercive diplomacy. Victory over all of Europe and domination in the world matching that of Rome seemed easily within its reach as Germany and the European powers drifted thoughtlessly toward war in 1914. That war then developed in contradictory ways for the Germans. In the east, they won great victories and took over vast western lands of the Russian empire in the Treaty of Brest-Litovsk in 1917, negotiated by Lenin in a desperate attempt to bring peace so he could make his Communist revolution. In the west, however, where the war really mattered, Germany eventually suffered a terrible and humiliating defeat. With their lines about to break and a full-scale invasion of Germany in the offing, Marshal Paul von Hindenburg purposely sent a Jewish representative of Germany, a diplomat and Social Democrat named Matthias Erzberger, to sign the armistice in the forest of Compiegne, some 40 miles northeast of Paris. It was a fateful move that became a key element in the subsequent German myth of a "stab in the back" by Jews. That surrender and subsequent disgrace of the Treaty of Versailles that imposed huge sanctions on a ravaged Germany made no sense to a people who had been fed propaganda of great victories.

The free-wheeling social and cultural character of the Weimar Republic over the next decade belied the malevolent forces in the margins of the group self that pulled Germany ever deeper into despair, fed in time by economic collapse, loss of security, and widespread unemployment. A self-proclaimed Messiah appeared on the horizon with the absolute certainty about the future that only paranoia grants. His book, *Mein Kampf*, tells it all. Germans have suffered and been humiliated by the perfidy of the Jews, even though as Aryans they own history. There will be redemption, and that Germany must expand into the barren areas of the east as it realizes its historical mission. The logic is that Jews will die, although that idea is not in *Mein Kampf* one can say reasonably that the Holocaust is the logical extension of Hitler's ideas.

The inspiring and even idealistic message of Hitler that Aryans must triumph in history because of their racial superiority proved wildly appealing to Germans, even to those who were more onlookers than activists. It was, however, a world-view built on hatred that bound the most primitive instincts of the group self to a frantic embrace of their new charismatic leader. The psychological instability of the alliance forced ever-expanding forms of revenge on the despised, military victories to undo the humiliation of Versailles, and soon the Holocaust that was the only thing that ultimately could bring about total redemption.

Another example (in less detail) would be the rise of Osama bin Laden in the Middle East and the murderous jihad he has unleashed on the world. For several centuries, indeed ever since the Crusades, the power and prestige of the Moslem world has been in decline, culminating in its dismemberment after World War I. In the twentieth century, Moslem land has been raped for oil, its sacred sites desecrated, and seemingly endless examples of humiliation inflicted on Moslems. The fatwas of bin Laden, especially the crucial ones of 1996 and 1998, trot out this history of abuse by the "Crusaders and Zionists" in flowery language that seems to celebrate their victimization in rhetoric that evokes *Mein Kampf*. Most of all it is the humiliation of Moslems that haunts bin Laden. He offers himself up to the Moslem group self as the messianic leader who will redeem history by wiping out Israel, kick the Americans out of Saudi Arabia, and purify Islam in the face of its corrupt and secular leaders. The rage of bin Laden drips off the page as he rises heroically and with utter certainty to relate his message of Moslem triumph in history. Violence is intrinsic to the process. The fatwa of 1998 proclaimed a universal war against the Crusaders and Zionists that set in motion the attack on the Cole, the bombings of the embassies in East Africa, and, of course, the dreadful attacks on September 11, 2001.[73]

Kohut also recognizes there are some very important historical situations in which charismatic leadership can heal the enfeebled group self and play a positive role. His favorite example along these lines is that of Winston Churchill in World War II. Churchill's mystique, he felt, "emanated... predominantly from the grandiose self," that is, he was a leader with the psychological potential to abandon traditional values and be at risk of threatening, rather than preserving, the democracy he served. In a paper written in 1966, "Forms and Transformations of Narcissism," Kohut argued that Churchill at some archaic level of self-experience probably believed he could fly. For one thing, in his life he "repeated again and again, in an ever enlarging arena, the feat of extricating himself from a situation from which there seemed to be no escape by ordinary means." Kohut was particularly struck by a story Churchill tells about his childhood in his autobiography. Young Winston was on vacation and playing a game of chase with a cousin and a younger brother. He came to a ravine and saw a fir tree down below. Winston spread his arms to catch the wind. It was 3 days before he regained consciousness and 3 months before he crawled out of bed.[74]

Churchill had been repeatedly rebuffed in the 1920s and 1930s in his attempts to assume leadership of the Conservative party and become Prime Minister, despite, or perhaps because of, his charisma and many talents. But when England was threatened as never before, when the Luftwaffe was bombing London and threatening an invasion that could mean the end of Western civilization, when the British felt endangered, helpless, and afraid, he was the natural person to assume leadership and direct the war effort. His calm certainty of victory resonated with the British people (and others, one might add) at deep levels that helped secure defeat of the Nazis. He loved to mock Hitler, who said he was going to wring the English chicken's neck. Churchill said: "Some chicken, some neck." When the war was over, however, and the times called for rebuilding, for the making of a new and just society along social welfare lines, for adjusting to the loss of the empire, and for getting reacquainted

---

[73] The fatwas (and much else) are available online and in Osama bin Laden, *Messages to the World: The Statements of Osama bin Laden*, ed. Bruce Lawrence (New York: Verso, 2005). The best general account of the rise of bin Laden are Lawrence Wright, *The Looming Tower: Al-Qaeda and the Road to 9/11* (New York: Knopf, 2006), and Steven Coll, *The Bin Ladens: An Arabian Family in the American Century* (New York: Penguin Books, 2008).

[74] Kohut, "Forms and Transformations of Narcissism," *Search* 1:443–444.

with the task of democratic compromise and bickering, Churchill was cast aside like an old towel.[75]

Heinz Kohut's ideas about the psychology of leadership make a unique contribution to the field and definitely extend and deepen Freud's discussion in 1921, not to mention most other scholarly contributions. Kohut helps us appreciate the psychological bond between leaders and followers. He identifies, among other things, that there is a psychology of leadership that only makes sense in the context of a psychology of followership without which charismatic or messianic leaders would never arise. His is not a fully developed theory. That was not his point. Much work is needed to fill in the huge conceptual gaps that remain before one could talk meaningfully about a nuanced psychological theory of leadership. But he certainly points the way toward such a theory, while cautioning to beware the charismatic leader.

---

[75] Kohut, "Charisma," *Search* II: 827–828. The story of the chicken's neck is from my interview with Kohut in *Humanities* 248.

Part II
Studies

Chapter 4
Lincoln and the Crisis of the 1850s: Thoughts on the Group Self

Charles B. Strozier

In 1858, Lincoln was a political figure little known outside of Illinois. For 4 years, he had vigorously opposed the prospect of slavery's extension into the territories, which was made politically feasible with Stephen A. Douglas's doctrine of popular sovereignty that was introduced in the Kansas-Nebraska Act (1854). Lincoln believed strongly by 1858 that Stephen Douglas was the principal spokesman for a disastrous set of policies dealing with issues that the country faced. The country's founders, in Lincoln's view, had reluctantly accepted slavery as a Southern institution. They recognized its existence and even validated its perpetuation with the three-fifths compromise. Such constitutional protection had justified federal laws governing the return of fugitive slaves for over half a century. It was thus illegal and unconstitutional to talk of abolition and the mobilization of a national effort to end the South's peculiar institution. Lincoln hated the realities of tracking down fugitive slaves but reluctantly accepted the practice. He told Joshua Speed in 1855:

> I also acknowledge *your* rights and *my* obligations, under the Constitution, in regard to your slaves. I confess I hate to see the poor creatures hunted down, and caught, and carried back to their stripes, and unrewarded toils; but I bite my lip and keep quiet.[1]

Nevertheless, Lincoln believed that the constitutional recognition of slavery in the South by no means meant that the founders approved of an institution that excluded a whole race from the benefits of the principles outlined in the Declaration of Independence. The only way the founders had to secure passage of the Constitution was to allow slavery to exist. But just as God defines ethical perfection, Lincoln continued, so the Constitution sets up a standard for legal action. "If we cannot give freedom to every creature," Lincoln argued in the summer of 1858, "let us do nothing that will impose slavery upon any other creature."[2] Slavery, Lincoln stated again and again in the 1850s, was morally wrong, a "monstrous injustice," as he

C.B. Strozier (✉)
John Jay College, Center on Terrorism, New York, NY 10019, USA
e-mail: charlesbstrozier@yahoo.com

[1] Roy P. Basler, ed., *The Collected Works of Abraham Lincoln*, 8 volumes (New Brunswick, NJ: Rutgers University Press, 1953), II, 320.
[2] Ibid., 501.

C.B. Strozier et al. (eds.), *The Leader*, 2nd ed., DOI 10.1007/978-1-4419-8387-9_4,
© Springer Science+Business Media, LLC 2011

called it in 1854.[3] "I have always hated slavery I think as much as any abolitionist," he proclaimed in 1858.[4] Furthermore, this powerfully negative judgment of slavery, he argued, lay behind most of the founders' thinking when they accepted the three-fifths compromise. It took 100 years of agitation, Lincoln once noted, to abolish the slave trade in Great Britain.[5] Men like Thomas Jefferson and George Washington had been tied to slavery economically but were politically and morally opposed to it. Life as they knew it in the South seemed inconceivable without slaves, but all had hoped for a better day when slaves could be freed and returned to Africa, and the ideals of life, liberty, and the pursuit of happiness genuinely engaged. Lincoln recognized the inconsistencies in this position but accepted the muddle as all too human. His great hero was Henry Clay, who could eloquently criticize those who would blow out the moral lights around everyone while sipping a mint julep served by a black house slave.

Thus, the heart of Lincoln's opposition to slavery was moral and constitutional. The people of the South, he said, had an "immediate and palpable and immensely great pecuniary interest" in their institution, but for those in the North "it is merely an abstract question of moral right, with only *slight* and *remote* pecuniary interest added."[6] However, the abstract issue for Lincoln was not as far removed from political reality as the term might suggest. "When the white man governs himself that is self-government; but when he governs himself, and also governs *another* man, that is *more* than self-government—that is despotism."[7] The moral issue was abstract only in that the Declaration of Independence defined a standard of equality that did not explicitly include the Negroes. The founding documents defined republican institutions and established the criteria for assessing the ethics of political action in modern society. The documents, however, were complex, varied, contradictory, and human. Lincoln argued vehemently after 1854 in favor of the abolitionists to the extent that they opposed the extension of slavery while he also argued for the return of fugitive slaves. "Stand with anybody that stands RIGHT," he thundered. "Stand with him while he is right and PART with him when he goes wrong. Stand WITH the abolitionist in restoring the Missouri Compromise; and stand against him when he attempts to repeal the fugitive slave law."[8]

Lincoln also had strong economic views on the poisonous effect of slavery on white workers. "As I would not be a slave," he wrote, "so I would not be a master. This expresses my idea of democracy."[9] In general, Lincoln was a decided economic optimist. When he wrote about inventions or technological progress, he became almost boyish in his buoyant, hopeful, and assertive enthusiasm. "All creation is a

---

[3] Ibid., 255.

[4] Ibid., 492.

[5] Ibid., 482.

[6] Ibid., 349–352.

[7] Ibid., 266.

[8] Ibid., 273.

[9] Benjamin Quarles, *Lincoln and the Negro* (New York: Oxford University Press, 1962), 35.

mine," he began his first lecture on discoveries and inventions, "and every man a miner." Lincoln went on to stress the uniqueness of humans, who may work like animals, but, unlike them, improve on their workmanship.[10] Lincoln's view of technology was clearly optimistic; it was almost somewhat naive. He seemed to accept unquestionably that technological progress carried with it moral improvement. And that is the link to slavery. The slave was kept apart from the just rewards for his or her labor. That degraded the slave and his or her master and perverted democratic institutions. Our republican form of government as defined by the Constitution required free labor, which in turn brought opportunity, progress, and hope. Slavery dashed all to the ground.[11]

Yet the evil of slavery went along, in Lincoln's thought, with a mournful sense of racial inequality between white and black.[12] For there is no denying that at this point in his life, Lincoln in the 1850s was convinced that blacks were inferior and did not deserve social or political equality with whites. He made that point often, though most vociferously at Charleston in 1858: "I am not, nor ever have been in favor of bringing about in any way the social and political equality of the white and black races." Lincoln would not make voters or jurors of blacks, nor qualify them to hold office, nor allow them to intermarry with whites. He believed that the physical differences of the races would always keep them from living together on equal terms and that whites would always be superior. Just because he did not want a Negro woman to be his slave did not mean he wanted her for a wife; he could just leave her alone.[13]

---

[10] *Collected Works*, II, 437–442.

[11] Gabor Boritt, *Lincoln and the Economics of the American Dream* (Memphis, TN: Memphis State University Press, 1978); Eric Foner, *Free Soil, Free Labor, Free Men: The Ideology of the Republican Party before the Civil War* (New York: Oxford University Press, 1970), 45; Quarles, *Lincoln and the Negro*, 30–38.

[12] The issue of Lincoln and race has been hotly debated since Lerone Bennett, "Was Abe Lincoln a White Supremacist?" *Ebony* 23 (1968): 35–38, 40, 42. Herbert Mitgang replied to Bennett quickly and self-assuredly, "Was Lincoln Just a Honkie?" *New York Times Magazine* (February 11, 1968), 34–35, 100–107. In fact, quite a lot of scholarship preceded Bennett's 1968 article. See, for example, Edward Magdol, "Owen Lovejoy's Role in the Campaign of 1858," *Journal of the Illinois Historical Society* 59 (1959): 403–416; Quarles, *Lincoln and the Negro* (1962); and Arvarh E. Strickland, "The Illinois Background of Lincoln's Attitude toward Slavery and the Negro," *Journal of the Illinois State Historical Society* 55 (1963): 474–494. See also Leon Litwack, *North of Slavery: The Negro in the Free States, 1790–1860* (Chicago: University of Chicago Press, 1961); and Martin Duberman, ed., *The Antislavery Vanguard: New Essays on the Abolitionists* (Princeton, NJ: Princeton University Press, 1965). Since 1968 a number of important works have appeared on this issue. The best general study is Foner, *Free Soil;* a careful analysis is George W. Frederickson, "A Man but Not a Brother: Abraham Lincoln and Racial Equality," *The Journal of Southern History* 41 (1975). Compare Stephen B. Oates, *Lincoln's Journey to Emancipation: Our Fiery Trial* (Amherst, MA: University of Massachusetts Press, 1979). The historiographical story is nicely summarized in Arthur Zilversmit's presentation of the topic of Lincoln and race, February 12, 1980, Abraham Lincoln Colloquium, State Historical Library, Springfield, IL, that will appear in the forthcoming *Papers* of the Abraham Lincoln Association, vol. II.

[13] *Collected Works*, III, 145–146; see also II, 405–498.

These are not pleasant statements. As the historian Kenneth M. Stampp has put it, Lincoln's speech at Charleston represents Lincoln's "fullest and most explicit declaration of belief in white supremacy."[14] Charleston, however, was not an isolated event in Lincoln's struggle with the issue of racial equality. Clearly, before an audience that leaned South in sentiment, Lincoln was rather more explicit in stating his white supremacist views. It has been frequently noted that Lincoln altered his emphasis on these matters, depending on which part of Illinois he found himself in; indeed, during the debates, Stephen Douglas himself charged Lincoln with inconsistency on exactly this issue. But it would be naive to ignore the essential racism that informed Lincoln's thought wherever he spoke. In Peoria in 1854, he frankly acknowledged that his own feelings would not allow him to entertain the notion of political and social equality between the races. And, he added as a shrewd politician, "If mine would, we well know that those of the great mass of white people will not."[15] Even in Chicago, Lincoln stressed the numerous categories of inequality between white and black in the same breath that he claimed minimal rights of life, liberty, and the pursuit of happiness for Negroes in America.[16] The Declaration of Independence, Lincoln noted in Springfield in 1857, never intended to assert that all men are equal in all respects. Such a notion is patently absurd, in any event. The Declaration simply defined basic rights and clarified a "standard maxim for free society" that, although never attained, could be admired, striven for, and perhaps, in time, approximated.[17]

The fact that Lincoln held back from the notion of full equality for blacks does not necessarily cast doubt on the sincerity of his insistence that they be granted minimal rights under the Constitution. For example, when Lincoln argued that the Declaration of Independence defined a standard maxim for free society, he was nudging his fellow citizens toward giving rights to blacks that they did not then possess. In the 1850s, such an assertion had overtones of abolitionism, which was the label that would most harm Lincoln politically (and the one that Stephen Douglas was most eager to pin on him). Lincoln made tortuous, indeed specious, distinctions after 1854, but he recognized the humanity of blacks. They were people, albeit inferior in some odd and almost incomprehensible way. Our sensibilities tend to emphasize the prejudices that remained in the man we generally admire as a paragon of American virtue. But in the 1850s, white supremacy was taken for granted; what was remarkable was that Lincoln had the courage to brand slavery *wrong*, oppose its extension into the territories on moral and political grounds, and risk association with abolitionism. As Frederick Douglass pointed out, Lincoln was always devoted entirely to the welfare of whites. He was willing to postpone, deny, or sacrifice the rights of blacks. He came to the presidency as opposed only to the spread of slavery.

---

[14] Kenneth Stampp, *The Imperiled Union: Essays on the Background of the Civil War* (New York: Oxford University Press, 1980), 128.
[15] *Collected Works*, II, 256.
[16] Ibid., 520.
[17] Ibid., 405–406.

His patriotic dreams embraced only whites. He supported the Fugitive Slave Law and would have eagerly suppressed any uprising. Whites were his natural children; blacks were his only by adoption. Yet, Douglass concluded, "measuring him by the sentiment of his country. . . he was swift, zealous, radical and determined."[18]

It was not easy for Lincoln to resolve his genuine and growing hatred of slavery with his white supremacist views. Furthermore, to abolish slavery was not only unconstitutional but also impractical, for what would happen to the slaves? They would become unequal members of a society in which they could never fully participate: "If all earthly power were given me," said Lincoln in 1854, "I should not know what to do, as to the existing institution. My first impulse would be to free all slaves, and send them to Liberia—to their own native land."[19] Lincoln saw acutely that colonization of blacks would be expensive, dangerous, and time-consuming, but he also felt it might be the only viable solution. There seemed to be only two alternatives: Free the slaves and keep them in America as "underlings" or make them fully equal. Both alternatives seemed to him impossible from a white perspective.[20] And so he toyed for years with colonization schemes, as absurd and offensive in retrospect as they seemed sensible and humane at the time. In 1852 he eulogized Clay's efforts since 1816 to return blacks to Africa:

> May it indeed be realized. . . If as the friends of colonization hope, the present and coming generations of our countrymen shall by any means, succeed in freeing our land from the dangerous presence of slavery; and, at the same time, in restoring a captive people to their long-lost father-land, with bright prospects for the future; and this too, so gradually that neither races nor individuals shall have suffered by the change, it will indeed be a glorious consummation.[21]

Lincoln himself was an active member of Springfield's Colonization Society, to which he spoke on January 4, 1855.[22] When Lincoln talked of the "ultimate extinction" of slavery in the "house divided" speech, he may have had colonization in the back of his mind.[23]

The confusions, contradictions, and specific distinctions built into Lincoln's thought about the interrelated issues of slavery and racial equality in the 1850s reflected the fact that his primary concern lay elsewhere—with the preservation of

---

[18] Frederick Douglass, "Oration in Memory of Abraham Lincoln, Delivered at the Unveiling of the Freedmen's Monument in Memory of Abraham Lincoln in Lincoln Park, Washington, DC, April 14, 1876," in *The Life and Writings of Frederick Douglass*, ed. Eric Foner, 8 volumes (New York: International Publishers, 1955), 4, 312. Compare Christopher Breiseth, "Lincoln and Frederick Douglass: Another Debate," *Journal of the Illinois State Historical Society* 68 (1975): 9–26.

[19] *Collected Works,* II, 255.

[20] Ibid., 255–256.

[21] Ibid., 132.

[22] Ibid., 298299; Earl Schenck Miers, ed., *Lincoln Day by Day: A Chronology*, 1809–1865, 3 volumes (Washington, DC: Lincoln Sesquicentennial Commission, 1960), II, 114.

[23] Frederickson, "A Man but Not a Brother," 50, makes this point, repeating, without credit, Harry V. Jaffa, *Crisis of the House Divided: An Interpretation of the Lincoln-Douglas Debates* (Seattle, WA: University of Washington Press, 1959), 61.

the union. For the political issue in the slavery question was not abolition but extension, and on that question Lincoln saw the country hurtling toward civil war. The Constitution was vague in what it intended to happen regarding slavery in newly acquired territories. A sensibly worked-out compromise in 1820 had seemed to settle the matter forever. However, the huge acquisitions from Mexico after 1848 and renewed tensions between North and South on a variety of other fronts fatefully reopened the whole issue of slavery's spread. After much agony and near war, a second compromise was tried in 1850. It seemed secure at first but quickly fell apart under pressure from the man most responsible for putting it together—Stephen Douglas. Douglas was an opportunist, inordinately ambitious, and very interested in the railroads. As chairman of the Senate Committee on the Territories, he wanted to push through a bill in 1854 that would quickly organize Kansas and Nebraska. Effective state government would then make possible the construction of a transcontinental railroad. In one blow, Douglas hoped to solve the most vexing political issue of the day and, of course, assume leadership of the country for his labors.

The key, he felt, lay in allowing the states to decide for themselves whether they would be free or slave. To justify this sidestepping of the issue of slavery, Douglas invoked the concept of popular sovereignty. For Douglas, popular sovereignty was a convenient and perfectly legitimate evasion of the moral passions that inflamed the debate over slavery. He personally did not care whether slavery was voted up or down. Let the people decide. For Lincoln, however, popular sovereignty was a grossly inappropriate concept for dealing with the question of slavery in the territories. The founders, he felt, never intended to allow slavery to extend beyond its original location in the states of the South. If left alone, slavery would in time wither away. But slavery must not be given a new lease on life in the territories. Thus, the democratic principle of local self-government in the territories had to give way to the larger concern for legitimate government and the principles of the Declaration of Independence.

II

On June 16, 1858, in the sultry heat of the legislative chamber, Abraham Lincoln spoke to the assembled members of the State Republican Convention. That afternoon the convention had nominated him as its candidate for the US Senate. Lincoln spoke to accept the nomination and to outline his sense of current issues and future agendas.

The speech began with a rhetorical flourish—constituting some 7% of its total—that has immortalized the speech in our political history:

> If we could first know *where* we are, and *whither* we are tending, we could then better judge *what* to do, and *how* to do it.

> We are now far into the *fifth* year, since a policy was initiated, with the *avowed* object, and *confident* promise, of putting an end to slavery agitation.

> Under the operation of that policy, that agitation has not only, *not ceased,* but has constantly *augmented.*

In *my* opinion, it *will* not cease, until a *crisis* shall have been reached, and passed.

"A house divided against itself cannot stand."

I believe this government cannot endure, permanently half *slave* and half *free*.

I do not expect the Union to be *dissolved*—I do not expect the house to *fall*—but I *do* expect it will cease to be divided.

It will become *all* one thing, or *all* the other.

Either the *opponents* of slavery will arrest the further spread of it, and place it where the public mind shall rest in the belief that it is in the course of ultimate extinction; or its *advocates* will push it forward, till it shall become alike lawful in *all* the States, old as well as *new*— *North* as well as *South*.[24]

There were, however, two distinct parts to the "house divided" speech. The familiar opening flourish built psychologically on Lincoln's own experiences, feelings, and needs. His rhetorical domestication of politics nicely expressed his own deepest concerns and could be grasped clearly by a country dangerously close to civil war. But the heart of the speech—and what most of it dealt with—outlined a remarkable Southern conspiracy to nationalize slavery. Lincoln developed his theory in the context of a brief history of recent events, which, if examined dispassionately, he argued, showed clear "evidence of design" and "concert of action." Lincoln felt the conspiracy was hatched early, for the "first point gained" was the Kansas-Nebraska Bill of 1854, which had opened up the territories to slavery on the spurious grounds of popular sovereignty. Then, in 1856, came the election of President Buchanan, a weak but decidedly pro-Southern Democrat. Thus was the second point gained. The third and final point came immediately following Buchanan's inauguration when the Supreme Court announced its decision on the Dred Scott case. In this decision, the "machinery" of the conspiracy reached full operating condition. It declared that no black slave or his descendant could ever become a citizen; that neither Congress nor a territorial legislature could exclude slavery from any territory; and that it was up to the separate slave states to deal with whether a slave was made free by passing into free states. In theory, at least, this part of the decision virtually endorsed Southern kidnapping of free Northern blacks.

"Several things will now appear less dark and mysterious," Lincoln commented, "than they did when they were transpiring." And he continued:

We can not absolutely know that all these exact adaptations are the result of preconcert. But when we see a lot of framed timbers, different portions of which we know have been gotten out at different times and places and by different workmen—Stephen [Douglas], Franklin [Pearce], Roger [Taney] and James [Buchanan] for instance—and when we see these timbers joined together, and see they exactly make the frame of a house or a mill, all the tenons and mortices exactly fitting, and all the lengths and proportions of the different pieces exactly adapted to their respective places, and not a piece too many or too few—not omitting even scaffolding—or, if a single piece be lacking, we can see the place in the frame exactly fitted and prepared to yet bring such piece in—in such a case, we find it impossible to not believe that Stephen and Franklin and Roger and James all understood one another

---

[24] *Collected Works*, II, 461–462.

from the beginning, and all worked upon a common plan or draft drawn up before the first lick was struck.

Lincoln's interpretation of events dramatically shifted the attention from Kansas and the other territories to Illinois and the free states of the North. We may go to sleep pleasantly in the belief that Missouri will be voted free, Lincoln argued, but "we shall awake to the reality, instead, that the Supreme Court has made Illinois a slave state." And as if that were not enough, Lincoln further argued that the country could also look forward to the reopening of the slave trade with Africa. If it is a sacred right of white men to own slaves, then how can it be less a sacred right to buy them where they can be bought cheapest? That clearly was Africa rather than Virginia.

The conspiracy argument of the speech clarifies significantly the force of the opening flourish. The house, in Lincoln's view, will not endure divided. Either slavery will be nationalized and our free institutions will crumble, or the North will arrest the spread of slavery and put it on a course of ultimate extinction. Many observers immediately saw in this stark vision a call for war to end slavery. To see the inevitable so clearly appeared to hurry it along. Thus Charles Lanphier, editor of Springfield's *Register* (a Democratic paper), lambasted Lincoln for his bellicosity.[25]

Lincoln, however, neither retreated from his conspiracy theory nor relinquished it easily. He was irritated that Douglas chose largely to ignore the charge.[26] Lincoln returned to conspiracy throughout the debates with Douglas in the late summer and fall of 1858.[27] As late as September 16, 1859, Lincoln told an audience in Columbus, Ohio, that the Republican party must stand firm against the conspiracy to revive the African slave trade, pass a congressional slave code, and push through an extension of Dred Scott that would explicitly make slavery legal throughout the United States. These developments are not immediately upon us, Lincoln noted. But beware:

They are not quite ready yet. The authors of these measures know that we are too strong for them; but they will be upon us in due time, and we will be grappling with them hand to hand, if they are not now headed off.[28]

And as late as June 12, 1863, he wrote: "The insurgents had been preparing for [the war] more than thirty years, while the Government had taken no steps to resist them."[29]

It is dramatically obvious in retrospect how wrong Lincoln was in his conspiracy theory.[30] For as he formulated it, the conspiracy went well beyond the schemes

---

[25] Illinois State *Register,* June 19, 1858, 2.

[26] *Collected Works,* II, 20–22.

[27] For example, ibid., III, 20.

[28] Ibid., 404.

[29] Ibid., IV, 263.

[30] Almost all commentators on Lincoln and on the 1850s agree with the observation. Don E. Fehrenbacher, *Prelude to Greatness: Lincoln in the 1850s* (Stanford, CA: Stanford University Press, 1962), 80, noted that there is "no evidence of any organized movement in 1858 to push slavery into the free states, or of any disposition among members of the Supreme Court to attempt such folly." For a complete discussion of the Dred Scott case, see Fehrenbacher, *The Dred Scott*

of Southern fanatics. The leaders, in Lincoln's view, were the preeminent political figures of the day: president of the United States, James Buchanan; chief justice of the Supreme Court, Roger B. Taney; and, of course, Stephen Douglas. Because Douglas was generally acknowledged as the most important Democratic senator, Lincoln's sense of the conspirators' base of operations included all three branches of government: executive, judicial, and legislative. There appears to have been some collusion between Buchanan and Taney over the Dred Scott case, but beyond that, it is most unlikely that an elaborate conspiracy among Douglas, Buchanan, and Taney could have hatched in 1854, developed in 1856, and matured in 1857. For one thing, Buchanan and Douglas hated each other. Douglas had expected to receive a prized position in the Buchanan administration but was instead unaccountably snubbed and isolated entirely from any position of influence. Douglas then opposed Buchanan on the Lecompton Constitution, and Buchanan retaliated by trying to remove Douglas's patronage base in Illinois. This political battle preoccupied the state in the months before Lincoln delivered his house divided speech. There is also only meager evidence of radical Southerners calling for a revival of the slave trade. It is hard to imagine the leaders of the three branches of government actually planning such an act. Nor was a national slave code envisioned by serious politicians. There had been enough trouble with the Fugitive Slave Law, which was a part of the Compromise of 1850. Lincoln had not only lost perspective but he had also misinterpreted the drift of politics.

Lincoln's ideas about politics in the late 1850s border on a paranoid interpretation of events. Why he responded to what was happening in the country with such

---

Case: Its Significance in American Law and Politics (New York: Oxford University Press, 1978). James G. Randall, *Lincoln the President: Springfield to Gettysburg*, 2 volumes (Gloucester, MA: Eyre and Spottiswoode, 1945), 1, 108, termed Lincoln's conspiracy theory "quite fanciful and nonexistent." Allen Nevins, *The Emergence of Lincoln*, 2 volumes (New York: Scribner's, 1950), I, 362, called Lincoln's theory a "partisan analysis" which "in the eyes of posterity, was pitched on a disappointingly low plane." And in the view of David Donald, *Liberty and Union* (Lexington, MA: D. C. Heath, 1978), 71, "These utterances in the house divided speech reveal more about the state of Lincoln's mind and the receptivity of the Northern audiences that cheered his speeches than they do about historical reality." There has been one major dissenter to this interpretation, Harry Jaffa, *Crisis of the House Divided: An Interpretation of the Lincoln-Douglas Debates* (Seattle: University of Washington Press, 1959), 81, 277–278. Jaffa, however, marshals evidence regarding only the Dred Scott decision. Lincoln's theory went well beyond that. Jaffa's interpretation has been echoed by George W. Frederickson, "A Man but Not a Brother: Abraham Lincoln and Racial Equality," *The Journal of Southern History* 41 (1975): 45, "It is important to recognize that the years after 1854 not only saw an effort to extend and nationalize slavery but also provided the occasion for a torrent of racist propaganda." In support of this assertion, Frederickson footnotes his own *Black Image in the White Mind: The Debate on Afro-American Character and Destiny, 1817–1914* (New York: Harper Torchbooks, 1971), 44–164; and Eugene H. Berwanger, *The Frontier against Slavery* (Urbana: University of Illinois Press, 1967), 123–137. These sources, however, support only Frederickson's notion that there was a "torrent of racist propaganda." His idea that there was an effort to nationalize slavery remains unproven. Oddly enough, Richard Hofstadter, *The Paranoid Style in American Politics and Other Essays* (New York: Knopf, 1966), passes over Lincoln and the 1850s.

miscalculated fervor is perplexing. It is quite possible he was simply seizing the public's mood and giving it voice. Certainly, he was a reasonable man. There is little in his early development that even hints at an individual proclivity toward paranoia. He was then—and later—noted for his generosity toward his enemies, his warmth and understanding, his empathy, and his humor—all traits decidedly missing in paranoid leaders. It is rather that he sensed the crisis and made it his own, in large part as a reflection of his empathy, rather than despite it. He articulated its latent meanings as few others could. He gave it shape, if not direction. The fact is that paranoia pervaded people's minds as the political crisis that would soon lead to war spread in the 1850s. Lincoln responded empathetically to their deepest fears. "He knew the American people better than they knew themselves," said Frederick Douglass.[31]

Paranoia was rampant throughout the land. Lincoln's opponent in the Senate race, Stephen Douglas, returned Lincoln's charges with his own, rather more deviously conceived, exaggeration of the implications of Lincoln's program for the country. During the debates, Douglas exhorted his listeners to vote for Lincoln,

> If you desire negro citizenship, if you desire to allow them to come into the State and settle with the white man, if *you* desire them to vote on an equality with yourselves, and to make them eligible to office, to serve on juries, and to adjudge your rights, then support Mr. Lincoln and the Black Republican party, who are in favor of the citizenship of the negro.[32]

Lincoln repeatedly tried to answer Douglas by pointing out that he was neither an amalgamationist (in favor of bringing the races fully together) nor an abolitionist; that just because he wanted to grant a Negro woman her legitimate rights did not mean he wanted to marry her; and that his moral opposition to slavery in no way represented an abolitionist desire to forcibly free the slaves.[33] It is hard to believe Douglas was not aware of these distinctions, but then it is equally difficult to understand the meanings of Lincoln's conspiracy theory, which put Douglas at the center of a malevolent plot to nationalize slavery.

Politics in America breeds competition, suspicion, and overstatement. Individuals of roughly comparable ability and party-backing struggle against each other for elected office. At stake are their own fortunes and those of their parties as well as those of the literally thousands of hangers-on who expect to benefit from victory. In America, the political system as it evolved in the Jacksonian era put unusual stress on the competitive personal aspects of vying for elective office. A long tradition of virulence legitimated the most outrageous charges and countercharges. In the fiercely contested election of 1828, for example, Andrew Jackson was called the son of a prostitute and a Negro, a usurper, a gambler, a cockfighter, a brawler, a drunkard, an illiterate, and a person unfit for high office. His wife, furthermore, was called an adulteress. John Quincy Adams, it seems, was a panderer, who had bought the presidency, was opposed to American institutions, and had grossly misspent public funds during his administration. Even Henry Clay was not spared. He

---

[31] Frederick Douglass, Oration in Memory of Abraham Lincoln 4, 318.

[32] *Collected Works*, III, 9.

[33] Ibid., 16, 29, 145–146, 221–222, 248–249, 299–300.

was described as a traitor who had instigated the assassination of William Morgan to prevent the exposure of freemasonry. If 1828 is an extreme example, it is not an unrepresentative one. At all levels of government, this attacking, competitive style prevailed. And the people loved it. Speeches, parades, kegs of whiskey—all helped stir partisan feeling. People endured two-hour-long speeches as the norm and then read a fiercely loyal summary and analysis of the speeches in their violently partisan paper of choice the next day. It was the kind of environment that encouraged political battles and forced extreme positions on otherwise mild men. Something in American politics of the time pushed opponents to their limits.

Until the 1850s, however, the dominant theme in this process was the coarseness of the attack, which seemed to be prompted less by paranoia than by the burning desire to win. For example, as head of the New York Regency, Martin Van Buren was a decidedly unlovely figure in the 1820s and 1830s, but he was not paranoid. Something new appeared on the scene in the 1850s. The dark shadow of paranoia that has always lurked on the fringes of American politics and culture came to block out the sun entirely. Suspiciousness reached extreme proportions. A basically conservative man such as Lincoln shuddered in terror at an imagined conspiracy to nationalize slavery. A less attractive but impressively shrewd politician such as Douglas became increasingly brittle and vulnerable. He might or might not have believed all that he attributed to Lincoln in 1858, but he certainly felt legitimately hounded by President Buchanan in their fight over control of the Democratic party after 1857.[34] Douglas also came under mounting pressure from the Southern wing of the party, which wanted no compromise on anything relating to slavery. Furthermore, what Lincoln and Douglas experienced and felt was repeated in a host of leaders throughout the country. A man such as William Seward, who had resisted compromise in 1850, came to see the inevitability of open conflict to resolve the issue of slavery. Seward, interestingly enough, felt almost as strongly against nativism—the powerful movement that affirmed old ideals of the nation and vigorously opposed the recent immigration from Europe. It has been suggested that Seward lost out to Lincoln in the Republican Convention of 1860 because he (Seward) had offended nativists over the years.[35]

The case of the abolitionists is a fascinating example of the changes in politics and culture from the 1830s to the 1850s. Abolitionists had long reacted with moral outrage and a mounting sense of frustration to the continued existence of slavery. In the 1830s, when the movement began, a strong religious fervor encouraged abolitionists to commit themselves to a variety of reform movements (especially temperance) and remain peaceful, even pacifistic, in their means. As Lawrence Friedman has persuasively argued, however, the degree of genuine pacifism that

---

[34] See Christopher Breiseth, "Lincoln, Douglas and Springfield," *The Public and Private Lincoln: Contemporary Perspectives,* ed. Cullom Davis *et al.* (Carbondale, IL: Southern Illinois University Press, 1979), 101–120.

[35] David M. Potter, *The Impending Crisis, 1848–1861,* ed. Don E. Fehrenbacher (New York: Harper & Row, 1976), 246. See also Kenneth M. Stampp, *An Imperiled Union: Essays on the Background of the Civil War* (New York: Oxford University Press, 1980), 156–157.

infused the abolitionists of the 1830s is open to some question.[36] The basic issue the abolitionists failed to grapple with was whether violence was acceptable if used defensively. All agreed the goal was political reform through moral persuasion. The problem, however, was that few considered how to react to violence if directed at themselves. They soon discovered that this question of whether defensively employed violence was consonant with their moral and religious beliefs was the central dilemma they faced. Thus Elijah Lovejoy, an abolitionist editor in Alton, Illinois, saw two printing presses destroyed. On the day of arrival of his third press, he and a group of followers were huddled inside the warehouse with guns to ward off attackers. Lovejoy himself, though he never fired a gun, died with a bullet through his heart in the melee that followed.

The reaction to Lovejoy's death provides an interesting litmus test of how genuinely pacifistic the abolitionist movement was in the 1830s. Most abolitionists never really questioned the propriety of Lovejoy's willingness to counter violence with violence. The issue for them was the brutality of the scene, the evils of slavery, and the devastating power of the mob. Only Sarah Grimké and a handful of other abolitionists strongly objected to Lovejoy's decision to defend himself. Lovejoy, Grimké felt, had seriously compromised the moral integrity of the reform movement by his willingness to defend the press with his guns.

In the 1830s, this debate was remote from the political mainstream. However, the easy accommodation to defensive use of violence was to have fateful consequences for the abolitionists. When they lost their firm commitment to pacifism, in a sense they lost their moral innocence. Pacificism was clearly desirable, but the overriding concern was the end of slavery. And that goal became increasingly elusive for the abolitionists. They watched with growing alarm as the political power of the white-led South, based in slavery, seemed to grow stronger over the years. Moral reform had backfired. Southern power was spreading everywhere, and its bellicosity was growing shriller every day. The abolitionists felt a mounting sense of suspicion, disorientation, frustration, and anger from 1848 on, which resulted in a loss of cohesion within their movement, that rapidly affected the means they felt were appropriate and necessary to end slavery. Tactics were reconsidered. The old moral pacifism gave way to an accommodation to violence as the only way to end the curse of slavery. John Brown's attack on some pro-slavery settlers in 1856 thus helped reshape attitudes and prepare the ground for his attempted raid on Harper's Ferry in 1859. The articulate black leader, Frederick Douglass, had been informed by Brown of the raid on Harper's Ferry (though Douglass warned him against the plan), and abolitionist William Lloyd Garrison applauded Brown's courage and commitment.

The interesting thing about the example of the abolitionists is that it illustrates how extreme suspiciousness can effectively undermine firmly held beliefs and even passionately valued moral codes. It is said that when the firing on Fort Sumter—the start of the war—was announced in the Senate, a woman cheered lustily from the

---

[36]Lawrence J. Friedman, "Antebellum American Abolitionism and the Problem of Violent Means," *The Psychohistory Review* 9 (1980): 26–32.

balcony; she was an abolitionist and for her only war could mean the end of slavery.[37] For the spiritual children of Lyman Beecher, the start of war was a long way from their 1830s program of moral reform through committed pacifism. Mounting frustration had fed abolitionists' fears of Southern power, making them increasingly combative and eventually violent. The more the abolitionists felt out of control (especially after 1848), the more they were filled with rage.

Freud first noted how psychological symptoms often spread. Thus obsessions that begin in a relatively circumscribed form usually become a way of thinking. The Rat Man, for example, first feared that the rat punishment described by the sadistic Captain Nowak would be imposed on his father and the Rat Man's friend, Gisela. But the devastating fears he experienced in connection with rats spread to all facets of his life, and his obsessive rituals to ward off danger had to increase proportionately. In the transference, Freud arrested the spread and focused the fears, anxieties, and conflicts on himself.[38] The same spreading phenomenon is true for phobias and can be true for hysterics (e.g., Anna O.).[39] The point is that the underlying conflict, once expressed in a specific form of symptomatology, will invent new variations on the same theme if for some reason the conflict itself is exacerbated. This notion of spreading symptomatology has relevance for an attempt to grasp the underlying issues of the 1850s in what Kohut called the group self. We must, however, make something of a translation from classical psychoanalysis, for it is not the relationship between conflict and symptom that concerns us but the meaning of the fragmentation of experience of the group self. As individual members of small, defined groups—abolitionists, Irish immigrants in Boston, Southern white aristocrats—experience intense feelings of suspiciousness, competitiveness, rage, and envy, the effects of a larger group-fragmentation anxiety become evident, spreading fear and hatred in the group self.

The suspiciousness of the 1850s in America was indeed widespread. The transformation of the abolitionist movement in the process of its accommodation to violence refracted the image of Southern white bellicosity and increasing preparedness for war. Southerners also felt they were under attack. They saw abolitionists crusading against the essence of their way of life, spurring slave revolts and poisoning minds everywhere.

"The antebellum South," Kenneth M. Stampp has recently noted, "was a land troubled by a nagging dread of slave insurrections; indeed, it is impossible to understand the psychology of white Southerners, or the events of the sectional conflict, without taking this fact into account."[40]

---

[37] Bruce Catton, *This Hallowed Ground* (New York: Simon & Schuster, 1955), 23.

[38] Sigmund Freud, *The Standard Edition of the Complete Psychological Works of Sigmund Freud,* ed. James Strachey (London: Hogarth, 1962), X, 153–230.

[39] Ibid., II, 21–47.

[40] Stampp, *An Imperiled Union,* 242–243.

George Fitzhugh, a conservative Southern ideologue who sarcastically described the abolitionists as devoted to the "uncouth, dirty, naked little cannibals of Africa,"[41] also expressed the projective fantasies behind the paranoia: "Whilst they dare invoke anarchy in Europe, they dare not inaugurate New York Free Love, and Oneida Incest, and Mormon Polygamy. The moral, religious and social heresies of the North are more monstrous than those of Europe."[42] Furthermore, the white Southern sense of abolitionism was psychologically and politically expansive: It included anyone who was not actively on the side of the South. Lincoln, for example, was perceived as part of the abolitionist conspiracy to destroy the South; he would contain slavery to kill it and work determinedly to keep slaves out of the territories. Many Southerners saw the election of Lincoln in 1860 as an act of aggression deliberately perpetrated against themselves. Within a month and a half after the election, South Carolina seceded; and before Lincoln left Springfield for Washington on February 11, 1861, the seven states of the Deep South had seceded. After 1858, the South even turned on Stephen Douglas, who attempted to stand between North and South and find some compromise ground that would focus attention on unity, growth, and the railroads and away from slavery, secession, and war. In the debates with Lincoln, it became clear that Douglas was not an unquestioning supporter of the South. The South regarded Douglas's reservations as treason to their cause and, without Southern support, Douglas's 1860 presidential hopes were doomed.

In this toxic political climate, even Lincoln grew increasingly and somewhat rigidly certain of his views. At first, his position was tempered and moderate. In 1854, in a speech in Peoria, Lincoln went to some length to express his understanding of the South's position: "Before proceeding," he interjected after an assault on slavery and its extension,

> let me say I think I have no prejudice against the Southern people. They are just what we would be in their situation. If slavery did not now exist amongst them they would not introduce it. If it did now exist amongst us, we should not instantly give it up.[43]

By 1857, Lincoln had stopped trying to empathize with the South and instead focused his attention on what the founders really intended in the Declaration of Independence as a way of supporting his own position. "They meant to set up a standard maxim for free society," he said in Springfield in response to the Dred Scott decision,

> which should be familiar to all and revered by all; constantly looked to, constantly labored for, and even though never perfectly attained, constantly approximated, and thereby constantly spreading and deepening its influence, and augmenting the happiness and value of life to all people of all colors everywhere.[44]

---

[41] George Fitzhugh, *Cannibals All!! or Slaves without Masters,* ed. C. Vann Woodward (Cambridge, MA: The Belknap Press of Harvard University Press, 1852), 252.

[42] Ibid., 11.

[43] *Collected Works,* II, 73.

[44] Ibid., 91.

The generosity of Lincoln's outlook, however, gave way to the assertive sense of noble and moral rightness in the "house divided" speech (the opening flourish) that was psychologically the counterpart of the deep-seated fears of a conspiracy to nationalize slavery (the bulk of the speech). Events had pushed Lincoln to assume an increasingly shrill tone in asserting his own moral and political rectitude.

The evolution of Lincoln's articulate, pained, and sensitive thoughts on slavery from empathic opposition to a belief in conspiracy that was closely tied to his own sense of moral correctness suggests the broader significance of these issues for the group self. Indeed, it was characteristic in the 1850s to assert loudly how right one was and how wrong everyone else was. It was this holier-than-thou quality that so alienated the society from the abolitionists. Their self-protective response to this alienation was to withdraw even further, which in turn heightened both their sense of superiority and of being under siege.[45] The vocal Southern whites similarly grew progressively assertive and grandiose in their claims for the superiority of Southern life. George Fitzhugh, for example, became a passionate defender of slavery after 1854 and an equally vigorous critic of free society and Northern ideas of personal liberty.[46]

The sectional, class, and racial conflicts that increasingly devastated mid-nineteenth-century America developed over a long time. The American colonies were, of course, separate entities, but they were culturally homogeneous and constitutionally united in their common relationship to England. After the Revolution, each state surrendered a measure of its sovereignty to the newly formed federal government. States' interests, nevertheless, as well as local or even parochial interests, remained the most significant center of initiative. For the next few decades, sectional rivalry continued as an important theme. The noisy struggle over tariffs, for example, pitted the North and West against the South; banking issues tended to forge a West–South alliance against the North; and issues of internal development tended to isolate the South, which benefited relatively little from such projects. Such divisions were clearly important and kept the new country politically, socially, economically, and culturally heterogeneous.

The basis for a cohesive group self, however, was being forged. A firm idealization of the Constitution and the Declaration of Independence fed on idealizing cultural needs after the Revolution. Parson Weems's *Life of Washington* (1802), for instance, created George Washington as a mythic hero, admired for his role in shaping the war and our political institutions but revered primarily for his personal, moral virtues; it was Weems who invented the story of the cherry tree. Collectively affirmed idealizations, in turn, supported a strong sense of agreement on such things as the extension of the suffrage, the value of internal development, and the importance of such Republican virtues as openness, honesty, integrity, health, abundance,

[45]Lawrence J. Friedman, "Garrisonism, Abolitionism, and the Boston Clique: A Psychosocial Inquiry," *The Psychohistory Review* 7 (1978): 6–19.

[46]Fitzhugh, *Cannibals All!!;* see also Fitzhugh, *Sociology for the South or the Failure of Free Institutions* (New York: Burt Franklin, 1854).

and strength. After the Revolution, almost all agreed, furthermore, that the Indians should be forced off their lands, blacks kept on the plantations in a condition of slavery, and the class status quo left unchanged. In the period after 1825, the imposing figure of Andrew Jackson heavily influenced the gradual erosion of state sovereignty and the emergence of a federal government that was relatively effective and increasingly powerful. In 1828, for example, the so-called tariff of abominations infuriated South Carolina, which feared that high tariffs would ruin its declining economic state. John Calhoun then formulated the first fully developed theory of the right of secession. The South Carolina Legislature responded by voting to secede if the tariff was not repealed. Jackson, himself a Southerner, would not tolerate such divisive sectionalism. In 1832 he mobilized troops for a movement into South Carolina while he also pushed the Force Act through Congress. The issue was compromised and left many raw feelings, but a crucial point had been demonstrated. The new American self was not to be easily undone by internal strife.

The Jacksonians generally succeeded in sidestepping the issue of race. Neither major party opposed slavery per se, which meant that both Democrats and Whigs agreed to preserve intact a system that kept some three million blacks in bondage. The Constitution recognized the legitimacy of slavery, and the South increasingly built its economy around the institution; the racism of Northern whites and the abundance of land muted any latent discontent with existing political and social arrangements. To someone like Lincoln, it was not surprising that Southerners could believe slavery was wrong and still own slaves. Because the economic and social system of the South was built on slavery, anyone who lived there would necessarily participate in the prevailing patterns of behavior. The crucial point for Lincoln was whether one recognized the essential wrongness of slavery and hoped it would die a natural death; one's correct attitude about the future of slavery need not inform present actions. There were, to be sure, Northern dissenters from this easy accommodation to the existence of slavery, but the voice of opposition was generally still and went unheeded politically.

The tensions and splits in the group self were, however, fundamental, and the course of events after 1848 increasingly eroded the assumptions of the Jacksonians. The major challenge came from the acquisition of vast new tracts of land after the Mexican War. No one knew what laws should govern settlement of these lands. The South felt it had the right to extend slavery wherever and whenever it desired, whereas Northern and Western opinion grasped with a new understanding the significance of slavery spreading indiscriminately into the territories. The debate over the war itself focused the issues. The national parties that had so effectively buried sectional discord for some 25 years soon gave way to ideological alliances that had little to do with traditional Whig or Democratic positions. The Compromise of 1850 papered over these basic changes in the political climate, but their full meaning struck home after the passage of the Kansas-Nebraska Act in 1854. The Whig party quickly dissolved and the Democrats divided into warring factions. Disgruntled Northerners—old Whigs, Democrats, nativists, and Free-Soilers—coalesced around the Republican party, which in 1856 nominated John Charles Fremont in an intensely ideological campaign.

The rapidity of these changes astounded contemporaries and continues to amaze historians. In a matter of a few years, a largely stable, cohesive society disintegrated into separate and warring factions. The developments of the 1850s naturally had antecedents. Southern white culture had long since acquired distinctive characteristics that made it extremely sensitive to slights and eager to defend its rights.[47] On the other side, the abolitionists were insistent about the righteousness of their cause, and many were willing to forgo their earlier pacifism in order to achieve their goal. But it was politics and society in a new key in the 1850s. A terrible sense of urgency infected all aspects of public life. The confused party situation between 1854 and 1856, for example, created high levels of anxiety for everyone and prodded even the ordinary citizen to sort through political priorities; for the reflective, the period often became the turning point of their adult lives. Lincoln before 1854 was a comfortable Whig, who opposed Jackson and Jacksonian leaders, favored strong banks and internal developments, and idealized Henry Clay. He seldom thought much about slavery, though he clearly felt it was wrong. Suddenly, after 1854, the rules changed, and Lincoln became a different person.

Sectional rivalry now disintegrated into rhetorical, and, at times, bloody regional warfare. Congressman Preston Brooks of South Carolina beat Senator Charles Sumner senseless on the Senate floor on May 22, 1856, over derogatory remarks the latter had made about his relative, Senator Andrew P. Butler. John Brown's "Holy Crusade" on slavery took shape as paramilitary action that avowedly aimed at revenge and fomenting social revolution in the South. Brown's great disappointment in the raid on Harper's Ferry was that the blacks in the area never rose up to fight in response to his call; what he failed to realize was that they had never heard it in the first place. The passion of rhetoric escalated on all sides, from George Fitzhugh and Jefferson Davis to Charles Sumner, William Lloyd Garrison, and John Brown. Even traditional political rivalries acquired a shrillness that suggested underlying themes of larger significance.

As the crisis intensified in the 1850s, there were a variety of compensatory responses to the imminent collapse; there was a fervent spirit of revivalism sweeping the land.[48] Periods of religious enthusiasm were not new in American history, but the oddly conservative character of the "New Light" movement in the 1740s gave way, after 1820, to a more expressive religiosity that featured the weeklong revivals of Charles Grandison Finney. In Illinois in the 1840s, Peter Cartwright, a noted preacher, was able to move large crowds to hysteria and religious ecstasy, though he proved less able in his political efforts to defeat Lincoln for Congress in 1846. After 1852, at least in Illinois, something of an unconscious dread of the underlying meaning of the revivals became intertwined with the process of building the nascent field of psychiatry. Thus the records of the first mental institution in the state, Jacksonville

---

[47] Steven M. Stowe, "The 'Touchiness' of the Gentleman Planter: The Sense of Esteem and Continuity in the Antebellum South," *The Psychohistory Review* 8 (1979): 6–15.

[48] Fehrenbacher, *Prelude to Greatness*, 14.

State Hospital, list for 8% of admissions between 1852 and 1860 the following closely interrelated set of causes for illness: religious enthusiasm, excessive reading of the Bible, church difficulty, spiritualism, Millerism (adherence to William Miller's Second Adventist Church), and "Spiritual Rappings." These records suggest a confusion of cause and effect, of symptom for real illness. Nevertheless, the categories of diagnosing mental illness in the state's first institution for the insane reveal a deeply ingrained fear of intense religiosity as potentially pathological.[49]

The fragmenting self struggled desperately to heal its widening split and to restore cohesion. If the spreading revivalism was one such attempt, another, of broader cultural and social significance, was the cult of domesticity that came to define the idealized style of family life in the 1850s. Changes in values leading to this cult became apparent after 1820 but greatly intensified in the 1850s. For women, the cult sharply defined ideal virtues—piety, purity, passivity, and domesticity—and their loathsome opposites. The home itself became a haven or refuge from the outside male jungle of work and politics. Children were the exclusive responsibility of women in their accepted role as mothers. Sexuality per se was severely repressed, but a warm sentimentality suffused all the essential relationships, especially that of mother and child.

Themes in family history, even their indirect expression in popular literature, seldom appear or disappear in as short a period as a decade. However, one book and its warm reception suggest a unique intensification of the cult of domesticity in the 1850s. Harriet Beecher Stowe's *Uncle Tom's Cabin* appeared in serial form in 1851 and was published in book form the following year. Its characters are etched in our consciousness by now: Eliza and George, Tom, St. Clare, Little Eva, Miss Ophelia, and Simon Legree. The dramatic appeal of the story aroused millions to the evils of slavery in the wake of the reopened debate after 1848. But it is worth noting that the central themes of *Uncle Tom's Cabin* deal with family and domestic issues. The "message" and central point of the book is that blacks are fully human, indeed at times more upright, Christian, responsible, and worthy than their dissolute white masters, and the proof of that central point is that blacks, like whites, have families and family ties. Eliza and George, for example, are models of fidelity, integrity, and mutual respect in an age haunted by these issues. Eliza is the ideal mother. Her escape from the Shelby plantation with young Harry to avoid being sold is achieved at a great cost. The plantation is the only home she has ever known, and her escape means leaving her "loved and revered" husband. "But," Stowe notes, "stronger than all was maternal love, wrought into a paroxysm of frenzy by the near approach of a fearful danger."[50]

Finally, the complex relationship between fragmentation anxiety—the fear of disintegration—and compensatory maneuvers to heal splits in the group self is perhaps nowhere better illustrated than in the course of nativism in the 1850s. On the one hand, nativist feelings of hatred for Catholics, Irish, and Germans—or, more

---

[49] Admissions records of the Jacksonville State Hospital, 1852–1860, Illinois State Archives.

[50] Harriet Beecher Stowe, *Uncle Tom's Cabin* (New York: Collier Books, 1966 [1852]), 104.

simply, anyone or anything foreign—came to dominate politics in many parts of the country. Building on the tradition of antimasonry from the early 1830s, the tensions between native-born Protestant whites and Catholic foreigners reached major proportions in the early 1850s. The nativist movement had by then already generated its own literature (e.g., *The Awful Disclosures of Maria Monk*) and would soon establish its own party, the Know-Nothings. It was a party of hate, as Lincoln saw more clearly than most of his contemporaries.[51]

The importance of nativism cannot be overemphasized. It blended curiously with Free-Soil, antislavery sentiment, for nativists hated the aristocratic white South as much as they did Catholic foreigners. As historian David Potter has put it, both nativism and antislavery

> reflected psychologically a highly dramatized fear of a powerful force which sought by conspiratorial means to subvert the values of the republic: in one case this was the slavocracy, with its "lords of the lash," in the other, the Church of Rome with its crafty priests and subtle Jesuits.[52]

In social terms as well, nativist feeling seemed to govern essential human relationships and define normative behavior. In the Jacksonville asylum's records, for example, at least 40% of the patients between 1852 and 1860 were foreign-born, and that figure could be much higher.[53] These patients were, on the whole, young female domestic servants, recently arrived, lonely and different. "Homesickness" is not infrequently cited as the "supposed cause" of illness in the admitting records.

And yet nativist sentiment built as it destroyed and affirmed essential values as it intolerantly castigated foreigners. It was a curious kind of populism, typically American, terribly important, and often profoundly misunderstood. Thus in many areas, nativism carried the spirit of reform, whether it was against slavery or for temperance. Furthermore, a powerful nationalism informed all nativist programs and politics. The fact that the Know-Nothing Convention in June, 1855, disintegrated into sectional rivalry is less surprising (or interesting) than is the "Union Degree," exalting nationalism, that the group had instituted in its ritual. As many as one million, five hundred thousand members of the Know-Nothing party took the Union Degree and pledged themselves against sectional forces from either North or South.[54]

---

[51] Even Mary Lincoln despised the Irish and leaned toward the Know-Nothings. See Justin C. Turner and Linda Levitt Turner, eds., *Mary Todd Lincoln: Her Life and Letters* (New York, Knopf, 1972), 46. Compare Lincoln's own views, *Collected Works*, II, 323.

[52] Potter, *The Impending Crisis*, 252

[53] Approximately 40% of the patients clearly indicated to the staff of the hospital when admitted that they had been born abroad. However, for those whose place of origin is listed as an eastern state—a sizable number—many could well have been born abroad but lived in the East long enough to establish residency before moving to Illinois. I suspect, for example, that many Irish immigrants named Massachusetts or New York as their place of origin.

[54] Potter, *The Impending Crisis*, 254. Note David Bryon Davis, *The Slave Power Conspiracy and the Paranoid Style* (Baton Rouge: Louisiana State University Press, 1969).

The most important and dangerous by-product of a fragmenting self is rage. Rage can express itself in almost infinitely variable ways, turning on the self one moment, on a loved figure the next. Freud all but missed the significance of rage, both because of the kind of patients he saw and because of his larger theoretical interests in aggression and the death instinct. Kohut' s work, however, helps us appreciate the central position of rage in human existence and its relationship to the dissolving self.[55] The loss of cohesion in the self generates rage in its wake. The rage can express itself in a kind of affect storm (e.g., a child's temper tantrum) or it can become quite elaborately organized, defining an angry, hostile, and vulnerable style that attempts to ward off further fragmentation. For the group there are fascinating analogues to these characteristics of rage in the individual: the fury of war, for example, elaborately structures systems of hate, fear, and suspicion that can become built into social institutions in the same way a narcissistic patient so often organizes himself or herself around rage.

As the crisis of the 1850s matured, rage pervaded American life. War increasingly seemed inevitable. There is no easily discernible turning point in this process, which is not surprising since it is inherently irrational. Thus the Compromise of 1850 appeared to settle the interrelated issues of slavery and the territorial expansion of the country but actually foreshadowed the dramatic realignments of the political parties 4 years later. A number of events in 1856 revealed the mounting rage in the group self breaking through—the caning of Charles Sumner, for example—but then all was quiet again, and there was even a degree of consolidation during the early part of Buchanan's administration.

John Brown's own rage escalated with that of the group self as the raid on Harper's Ferry in 1859 sent tremors of real war through the country. And finally, the blustering and strutting of the secession crisis, from Lincoln's election to his inauguration, fed the deepest levels of rage as the self split into two parts. Its dissolution over a decade unraveled the fragile idealizations of the past—those collective strands of value that bound the self—and prompted an eruptive, peremptory grandiosity. The rage that this process generated in the end could only be absorbed by war itself.

---

[55] Heinz Kohut, "Thoughts on Narcissism and Narcissistic Rage," in *The Search for the Self: Selected Writings of Heinz Kohut 1950–2978,* ed. Paul H. Orenstein, 2 volumes (New York: International Universities Press, 1978), 2, 615–658. See also Charles B. Strozier, "Heinz Kohut and the Historical Imagination," *Advances in Self Psychology,* ed. Arnold Goldberg (New York: International Universities Press, 1980), 397–406.

Chapter 5
Mirror Image of the Nation: An Investigation of Kaiser Wilhelm II's Leadership of the Germans

Thomas A. Kohut

> *This Kaiser, about whom you are in an uproar, is your mirror image!*
> —Friedrich Naumann's admonition to the German people in January 1909.[1]

> *Never before had a symbolic individual been so completely reflected in an epoch, an epoch in an individual.*
> —Walter Rathenau on Wilhelm II in 1919.[2]

In recent years, Kaiser Wilhelm II has been the subject of renewed historical interest. For decades, however, historians have ignored the Kaiser while focusing considerable attention on the period of German history that bears his name. The striking, if lamentable, reality that not one full-scale scholarly biography of Wilhelm II has yet been published[3] testifies to the fact that until now historians have chosen to investigate Wilhelmine Germany while minimizing the significance of Wilhelm II. At the same time, a spate of popular biographies of the Kaiser have been written by more or less amateur historians.[4] The general public, it seems, remains curious

---

T.A. Kohut (✉)
Sue and Edgar Wachenheim III Professor of History, Williams College, Williamstown, MA, USA
e-mail: thomas.a.kohut@williams.edu

[1]Friedrich Naumann, "Hilfe," January 1909 in *Das deutsche Kaiserreich,* ed. Gerhard Ritter (Göttingen: Vandenhoeck and Ruprecht, 1975), 318.

[2]Walter Rathenau, "Der Kaiser," in *Walter Rathenau: Schriften und Reden,* ed. H. W. Richter (Frankfurt: S. Fischer Verlag, 1964), 247.

[3]Fortunately this situation has been remedied as Lamar Cecil and John C.G. Röhl have published just such biographies: Lamar Cecil, *Wilhelm II,* 2 vols. (Chapel Hill: University of North Carolina Press; 1989–1996); Jhon C. G. Röhl, *Wilhelm II,* 3 vols. (Munich: C.H. Beck Verlag; 1993–2008). The work that comes closest to a scholarly biography of Wilhelm II is Michael Balfour's *The Kaiser and His Times* (New York: Norton, 1972) which, however, is based exclusively upon published sources.

[4]These include J. Daniel Chamier, *Fabulous Monster* (London: E. Arnold, 1934); Virginia Cowles, *The Kaiser* (New York: Harper & Row, 1963); H. Kurtz, *The Second Reich: Kaiser Wilhelm II and His Germany* (London: MacDonald, 1970); Tyler Whittle, *The Last Kaiser. A Biography of Wilhelm II, German Emperor and King of Prussia* (New York: Times Books, 1977); Alan Palmer, *The Kaiser: Warlord of the Second Reich* (London: Weidenfeld and Nicolson, 1978).

C.B. Strozier et al. (eds.), *The Leader,* 2nd ed., DOI 10.1007/978-1-4419-8387-9_5,
© Springer Science+Business Media, LLC 2011

about the Kaiser. This combination of popular interest and scholarly neglect corresponds to the mixture of adulation and irritation with which Wilhelm was viewed by his contemporaries. He seemed at once a fascinating, mythical figure of heroic proportions and an inconsequential and pathetic posturer. It is the thesis of this study that both the images of the Kaiser reflect the reality of Wilhelm II's leadership of the Germans, a leadership that was dynamic and compelling, yet weak and ineffectual.

This paradoxical view is based upon the distinction between the two principal leadership functions of the German kaiserdom. Wilhelm was expected to combine what his best friend and political confidant, Philipp Eulenburg, described as "the two images of the governing statesman and the sleeping Hero-Kaiser."[5] On the one hand, Wilhelm II was to be a political leader: a framer and implementer of specific policies. He was to function as a traditional politician, basing his actions on an assessment of what would be to his own advantage and to that of the nation. In this context "political leadership" is defined primarily in terms of rational self-interest. On the other hand, Wilhelm II was to be the spiritual reincarnation of Friedrich Barbarossa, symbolically awakened from his deep sleep in the Kyffhauser grotto to restore, in the words of one contemporary speaking of Wilhelm II, "the German glory which he took with him into the depths of the mountain."[6] He was, in other words, to be a symbolic leader, an emotional and spiritual personification of the German nation. He was to function as the charismatic representative of the German people, giving exalted expression to deeply felt popular ideals and aspirations. In this context, "symbolic leadership" is defined primarily in terms of public image.

Wilhelm II, on the basis of this distinction, was a successful symbolic leader and an unsuccessful politician. This chapter seeks to demonstrate that the nature of Wilhelm's personality and, in particular, his narcissistic psychopathology made him uniquely able to function as a symbol of late-nineteenth and early-twentieth-century Germany. The contradictory and disjointed state of the Kaiser's psyche enabled him to reflect his regionally, socially, politically, and intellectually divided nation; and his efforts to promote psychological cohesion for himself also suited in large measure the needs of many of his countrymen. However, Wilhelm's inner disharmony and disorganization, and his inability to define psychologically a homogeneous personal self-interest made him ineffective as a political leader and prevented him from being able to pursue policies reliably and consistently. This study, then, is a psychohistorical investigation of Wilhelm II's leadership of the Germans. Its purpose is not to "diagnose" the Kaiser psychoanalytically as narcissistically disturbed but rather to make sense of the significant, yet seemingly insubstantial, impact of this

---

[5] Philipp Eulenburg to Friedrich von Holstein, December 2, 1894. Johannes Haller, *Aus dem Leben des Fürsten Philipp zu Eulenburg-Hertefeld* (Berlin: Gebrüder Paetel, 1924), 171.

[6] F. J. Scherer, *Die Kaiseridee des deutschen Volkes im Liedern seiner Dichter seit dem Jahre 1806,* trans. Terence Cole (Arnsberg: Verlag, 1896), 5–6. Both this and the preceding quotation are in Elisabeth Fehrenbach, "Images of Kaiserdom: German Attitudes to Kaiser Wilhelm II," in *Kaiser Wilhelm II: New Interpretations,* ed. John C. G. Röhl and Nicolaus Sombart (Cambridge: Cambridge University Press, 1982), 269–285.

perplexing figure, to shed light on his relationship with his subjects, to assess his place in modern German history.

Wilhelm II's Personality in the Light of Psychoanalytic Self-Psychology

Within the limits of the present investigation, it is not possible, of course, to present a detailed description of the etiology and symptomatology of narcissistic psychopathology as understood by contemporary psychoanalysis. Suffice it to say that the view of narcissistic disorders adopted in this article is based upon a recent advance in psychoanalytic theory, the psychology of the self, which focuses on human narcissistic needs.[7] From this perspective such disorders are understood to be the result of a defect or weakness in the essential structure of the personality. Narcissistic pathology is, in other words, "self-pathology": disorganization, disharmony, or debility of the self. The defective or weakened self generally has its origins in the faulty interaction between child and caretakers who were unable to provide needed psychological sustenance in early life. On the one hand, the caretakers may not have been able to provide the child with the opportunity to merge with an adult's sense of calmness and strength that would enable him or her ultimately to internalize a sense of security and stability. On the other hand, they may not have been able to respond to the child with affirming pride that would enable him or her ultimately to internalize a sense of inner self-confidence and self-esteem.

As a result of these developmental deficiencies, the narcissistically disturbed adult experiences a sense of inner imbalance and a fear of psychological fragmentation. External display of pseudo-excitement or frenzied activity can ward off feelings of inner apathy and deadness. Anxious grandiosity may cover a frightening sense of inferiority and depression. The internal fragility of the personality makes such individuals extremely sensitive to the way in which others respond to them, and their behavior is characterized by precipitous and intense reactions. Seemingly minor slights and rejections are experienced as profoundly threatening and often produce outbursts of rage, vengeful brooding, or an outwardly haughty withdrawal that covers the deeply felt sense of humiliation. Lacking basic internal security, harmony, and self-esteem, narcissistically disturbed individuals are exquisitely dependent on others for psychological survival. They seek to obtain from their environment that which is missing inside themselves. Others are primarily of interest not as separately experienced individuals but insofar as they can help to maintain, enhance, or restore psychic equilibrium. Like the child whose self-esteem and psychological balance are maintained through his or her feeling that one is a

---

[7] For further information about self-psychology see, among others: Heinz Kohut, *The Analysis of the Self* (London: The Hogarth Press, 1971); Heinz Kohut, *The Restoration of the Self* (Chicago, IL: University of Chicago Press, 2009); Heinz Kohut, *How Does Analysis Cure?* (Chicago, IL: University of Chicago Press, 1984); Paul Ornstein, ed., *The Search for the Self: Selected Writings of Heinz Kohut*, 4 volumes (New York: International Universities Press, 1978); Arnold Goldberg, ed., *Advances in Self Psychology* (London: Karnac Books, 2011).

part of his or her parents and that they are a part of him or her, the narcissistically disturbed adult experiences himself or herself as part of others and others as
part of himself or herself. The hollowness at the center of the personality creates
an addiction-like craving for relationships with people he or she can admire and
depend upon, in whom he or she can find strength and security. Or, to counter-
act feelings of worthlessness, he or she may need to exhibit oneself and boastfully
evoke attention in the hope that the confirming and admiring response of others will
nourish his or her famished self. Without the continuous sustenance of such "selfobject" relationships—relationships with others (objects) that are experienced as part
of the self—the narcissistically disturbed individual experiences a frightening loss
of psychological continuity and cohesion.

Much of Kaiser Wilhelm II's personality behavior can readily be understood
within the framework of this theoretical approach to narcissistic psychopathology.[8]
It becomes possible to explain both his mythic external grandeur and his inner insub-
stantiality, his charismatic appeal and his ostentatious ineffectuality, in basic human
terms. Those among Wilhelm's contemporaries who knew him best recognized the
lack of integration at the core of his personality. Bernhard von Bülow, for example,
Wilhelm's chancellor and friend for many years, was "often concerned about his
psychic balance."[9] "Wilhelm's character was full of contradictions," Bülow wrote
in his memoirs.

> Prince Guido von Henckel-Donnersmark [sic] liked to say that the Kaiser reminded him of
> a dicebox in which the dice rattled against each other. His personality was not cohesive,
> self-contained, or harmonious; its various aspects did not interfuse as do even stubborn
> substances and elements during the process of amalgamation.[10]

Even perceptive casual acquaintances, though dazzled by the Kaiser's position and
demeanor, could sometimes discern the incoherence of Wilhelm's self. After a lunch
with Wilhelm in the summer of 1891, Viscount John Morley noted in his dairy:

> I was immensely interested in watching a man with such a part to play in Europe. . ... Energy,
> rapidity, restlessness in every movement from his short quick inclinations of the head to the
> planting of the foot. But I should be disposed to doubt whether it is all sound, steady and
> the result of a—what Herbert Spencer would call—rightly coordinated organization.[11]

The rattle of Wilhelm's inner dicebox resounds throughout this study. By way
of introduction to the Kaiser's personality, however, it is appropriate to comment briefly at this point on some of the manifestations of his self-pathology. As

---

[8] Those wishing to learn more about Wilhelm's personality and development should see: John C.G.
Röhl, "The Emperor's New Clothes: A Character Sketch of Kaiser Wilhelm II," 23–62; Thomas
A. Kohut, "Kaiser Wilhelm II and His Parents: An Inquiry into the Psychological Roots of German
Policy towards England before the First World War," 63–90; and Lamar Cecil, "History as Family
Chronicle: Kaiser Wilhelm II and the Dynastic Roots of the Anglo-German Antagonism," 91–120;
all in Röhl and Sombart, *Kaiser Wilhelm II.*

[9] Bernhard Füirst von Bülow, *Denkwürdigkeiten,* I (Berlin: Ullstein Verlag, 1930), 56–61.

[10] Ibid., 461.

[11] Diary entry, July 9, 1891. Viscount John Morley, *Recollections,* I (London: MacMillan,
1917), 272.

beautifully evoked by the image of tumbling dice, Wilhelm's politically trouble-some capriciousness and unpredictability can be traced to a lack of consolidation at the core of his personality. This central weakness was covered by a display of brittle self-certainty. The Kaiser did not possess the inner strength to admit that he did not know something. He felt compelled to express opinions on almost every subject, and he would commit himself to a position or policy with little or no infor-mation about it. He seemed unable to listen to the advice of his ministers, frequently interrupting and monopolizing the conversation. Politically, the Kaiser's display of self-certainty took the form of the frequent assertion of his absolute sovereignty by divine right. He declared in a speech in Königsberg in 1910, for example: "I see myself as an instrument of the Lord. I go my way without regard for the views or opinions of the day."[12] On the surface, Wilhelm's statement seems a powerful and self-confident assertion of virtually unlimited political authority. One gets the sense, however, that its primary psychological purpose for Wilhelm was to borrow from God that strength he missed within himself. Wilhelm's invocation of the deity in this context was ultimately an attempt to shield himself from his critics and to bolster his precarious sense of personal autonomy.

In general, Wilhelm's display of self-certainty can be understood as an attempt to protect his fragile self from outside attack. His extreme vulnerability was such that when he felt himself insufficiently appreciated, let alone condemned, he reacted with explosive rage or icy resentment, and his reign was marked by an unprece-dented number of trials for lese majesty. The Kaiser also felt threatened by his own compelling need to depend emotionally upon his environment to supply him with direction and purpose. It was a fact often remarked upon by the Kaiser's advisors that he had the politically alarming tendency to adopt the opinions and goals of the person with whom he had last spoken. His assertion of personal and political absolutism was thus an attempt to convince others *and himself* of his psychological independence. In the final analysis, Wilhelm's declarations of absolute sovereignty were a defensive facade behind which he hungered for the approval and guidance of others. On close inspection, this facade proved to be painfully transparent, and those like Philipp Eulenburg who knew the Kaiser best recognized that though Wilhelm pretended to hold other people in contempt, "he actually feared their judgement of him—without ever being able to admit that this was so." He was at heart motivated by what his friend described as "a feminine tendency to wish to please."[13] It would in fact be difficult to imagine a leader more keenly sensitive to the attitudes and responses of others or more profoundly influenced by "the views or opinions of the day" than Kaiser Wilhelm II.

Unable to internalize a sense of basic self-esteem and security through the steady interaction with empathic caretakers in early life,[14] the Kaiser relied upon "selfobjects" to direct his ambitions and determine his ideals. The very lack of

---

[12]Speech of August 25, 1910. Karl Wippermann, ed., *Deutscher Geschichtskalender* (Leipzig: W. Grunow, 1885–1934), vol. for 1910 (II), 9.

[13]Philipp Eulenburg, "Kaiser Wilhelm II," Bundesarchiv Koblenz, Eulenburg Papers, vol. 80.

[14]For a discussion of the origin of these developmental deficits, see T. Kohut, "Kaiser Wilhelm II and His Parents."

self-consolidation that resulted in Wilhelm's dependence on external emotional support, however, also gave him an extraordinary impressionability and personal pliancy that enabled him to adapt himself to his environment in ways designed to elicit the affirming and supportive responses he required. The Kaiser, in other words, was a consummate actor able to play those parts that would bring him needed psychological sustenance. Contemporaries recognized the assumed quality of Wilhelm's personality. Eulenburg liked to call him "Wilhelm Proteus" after the legendary Greek prophet who could assume any shape he chose. And when asked how she and the Kaiser had gotten along, the great French actress Sarah Bernhardt replied: "Why admirably, for are we not both, he and I, fellow troupers."[15] Of course all leaders at times attempt to hide their private personalities behind a public mask. In Wilhelm II's case, however, one gets the sense that his behavior was little more than a continuous theatrical performance and that the Kaiser was an actor without a character of his own. In his need to complete himself through interaction with his surroundings, Wilhelm actually became the parts he played. The remarkably convincing impression created by Wilhelm's dramatis personae on the casual observer can thus be traced to the integrity and intensity of the Kaiser's performances, to the fact that he could only feel harmonious when he experienced himself as being affirmed and appreciated by those around him.

Similarly, Wilhelm's craving for external reassurance was at the source of his anxious and seemingly unrestrained grandiosity. The Kaiser's driven display of himself most often took the form of flamboyant speech-making and traveling that was so frequent that Wilhelm became known as the *Reisekaiser,* or the "traveling emperor." In his private life, the Kaiser's civilian and military entourage provided Wilhelm with the same sense of affirmation that he derived from his state visits, gala receptions, orations, and parades. It is no accident that from his accession in 1888 until his death in exile in Holland in 1941, Wilhelm consistently surrounded himself with a narrow and relatively homogeneous group of self-consciously "charming" and "clever" aristocratic gentlemen. Not only did this inner circle share a similar social, political, intellectual, cultural, and even emotional outlook, they also seemed to recognize that their principal purpose for the Kaiser was to provide him with psychological support. Like the excitement of constant exposure to new people and places, the colorful and witty stories of these raconteurs kept the Kaiser entertained. Like the cheers of the crowds, the enthusiasm of the entourage for the Kaiser and their exaggerated deference to him bolstered Wilhelm's fragile sense of self-esteem. Philipp Eulenburg, a personality typical of those around the Kaiser, appreciated Wilhelm's vital need for external confirmation. He advised his friend Bülow in June 1897, as the latter was on his way to assume the post of state secretary in the foreign office, on how best to handle the Kaiser:

> Wilhelm II takes everything personally. Only personal arguments make an impression on him. He wants to instruct others but does not take to being instructed himself. He cannot

---

[15] Valentine Chirol, *50 Years in a Changing World* (New York: Harcourt, Brace, 1928), 276.

tolerate anything that is boring. Slow, stiff, or overly serious people get on his nerves and have no success with him. Wilhelm II wants to shine and do everything himself and make all decisions. . . . He loves acclaim, is ambitious, and jealous. In order to get him to accept an idea, one must present it as if it had come from him. You must make everything easy for him. . . . Never forget that now and again His Majesty needs praise. He is one of those characters who without occasional recognition from the lips of significant people becomes depressed. You will have access to all your wishes so long as you do not neglect to express recognition of His Majesty when he has earned it. He is grateful for it like a good, clever child.[16]

Not only did Wilhelm depend upon those around him to assure himself of his own importance, he also depended upon his entourage to supply him with the direction and purpose he lacked within himself. Indeed, several recent studies, as well as the voluminous published correspondence of Philipp Eulenburg, reveal the extent of the entourage's impact upon the Kaiser. Through Wilhelm, this narrow elite was able to exert a subtle yet pervasive political influence on the conduct of Wilhelmine government.[17]

As a result of these features of the Kaiser's personality, many of his contemporaries concluded that Wilhelm II was mentally "abnormal," meaning by this designation that the Kaiser's puzzling behavior was the product of some hereditary or physiological disorder. Bülow, however, did not regard Wilhelm to be abnormal in this sense of the term. The Kaiser, he believed, simply suffered from extreme hubris, a hubris that covered his profound insecurity:

> For Wilhelm II his hubris expresses itself in an addictive self-aggrandizement, that not only arouses antipathy, but is also politically dangerous. It is largely the product of his wish to hide the inner uncertainty, even anxiousness, that the Kaiser more frequently experiences than the world realizes. Fundamentally, he is not a brave but a fearful personality.[18]

As Bülow and Eulenburg recognized, the key to the Kaiser personally and politically was to understand his central weakness. This weakness would have deleterious political consequences for Germany. But paradoxically, in attempting to compensate for and overcome his psychic deficit, Wilhelm developed some exceptional symbolic leadership capacities. Put another way, the Kaiser's lack of a secure sense of psychological cohesion and continuity—that is, his narcissistic psychopathology— is at the heart of his historical significance.

---

[16]Bülow, *Denkwürdigkeiten*, I, 5.

[17]See John C. G. Röhl, ed., *Philipp Eulenburgs politische Korrespondenz,* 3 volumes (Boppard-am-Rhein: Harald Boldt Verlag, 1976–1981); Röhl, "Introduction," 1–22; Wilhelm Deist, "Kaiser Wilhelm II in the Context of His Military and Naval Entourage," 169–192; Isabel V. Hull, "Kaiser Wilhelm II and the 'Liebenberg Circle, ' " 193–220; all in Röhl and Sombart, *Kaiser Wilhelm II.* See especially Isabel V. Hull, *The Entourage of Kaiser Wilhelm II, 1888–1918* (Cambridge: Cambridge University Press, 1982).

[18]Bülow, *Denkwürdigkeiten,* I, 140.

The Kaiser, the Press, and German Public Opinion

"In politics no one does anything for another," Otto von Bismarck wrote in 1857, "unless he also finds it in his own interest to do so."[19] With this statement, perhaps the greatest political leader of the nineteenth century summed up what one biographer of the great statesman has described as his "fundamental rule of all political behavior." For Bismarck, the pursuit of rational self-interest was natural to the conduct of individuals, groups, and states; indeed, it was a part of God's divine order. As a result, the statesman was morally compelled to define the interest of state and to dedicate himself to its fulfillment.[20] Bismarck believed that "the only sound basis" for the conduct of the nation-state was "its egoism and not romanticism."[21] Personal feelings, the wishes of powerful elites or political parties, popular opinion were all to be subordinated to the realization of the state's self-interest. They were to be manipulated in the service of the rational conduct of foreign policy; they were never to be allowed to shape it. It seemed almost inevitable to Bismarck that the state would follow a foreign political course based upon its self-interest. In November 1887, for example, Bismarck assured Lord Salisbury (who was worried that the accession of the then Prince Wilhelm to the imperial throne would lead to an anti-English shift in German foreign policy) that no individual, be he Kaiser or Chancellor, could steer the ship of state off its predetermined course. You need not be concerned, Bismarck wrote the British prime minister, that Wilhelm will pursue an anti-English policy. "Neither this nor the opposite would be possible in Germany." Whoever is Kaiser "will and can only be influenced by the interests of the German Empire. The path that must be taken in order to uphold these interests is so urgently prescribed that it is impossible to depart from it."[22]

Unfortunately, Bismarck's prediction about the future of Anglo-German relations was mistaken, and his optimistically rational conception of the nature of political behavior proved to be out of tune with the mass politics of the twentieth century. With the accession of Wilhelm II in 1888, *Realpolitik* in Germany gave way to the politics of symbolism. When Bismarck retired in anger to Friedrichsruh in 1890—dismissed by a headstrong Kaiser who wished to steer the ship of state himself—Germany's course was no longer self-evident either domestically or internationally. What was certain was that both the youthfully impetuous Kaiser and his youthfully impetuous nation wanted the speed increased, the ship's screws turned faster. Germany had entered the Wilhelmine era.

---

[19] Herman von Petersdorff *et al.*, eds., *Bismarck: Die gesammelten Werke,* 15 volumes (Berlin: O. Stollberg, 1923–1933), II, 231; XIV, 473. Quoted in Otto Pflanze, *Bismarck and the Development of Germany: The Period of Unification, 1815–1871* (Princeton, NJ: Princeton University Press, 1963), 84.

[20] Otto Pflanze, *Bismarck,* 84–85.

[21] Petersdorff, *Bismarck: Werke,* XIV, 160–161. In Pflanze, *Bismarck,* 79.

[22] Letter from Bismarck to Salisbury of November 22, 1887. Bernhard Schwertfeger, ed., *Die Diplomatischen Akten des Auswärtigen Amtes, 1871–1914,* 5 volumes with 2 additional volumes (Berlin: Deutsche Verlagsgesellschaft für Politik und Geschichte, 1923–1925), I, 288–291.

This transformation of German political life is dramatically represented in the shift in style of leadership from Bismarck to Wilhelm II, from the Chancellor's efforts to realize the rational interests of state to the Kaiser's attention to public opinion and his popular image. Indeed many of Wilhelm's advisors, products as they were of the nineteenth- century perspective on political life, could not understand the Kaiser's preoccupation with his relationship with his subjects, particularly as it was reflected in and influenced by the press. "Complaints from everyone that His Majesty dodges political reports," Friedrich von Holstein, a longtime privy councilor in the foreign office, wrote shortly after Wilhelm's accession. "At the same time he reads thirty to forty newspaper clippings one after the other and makes marginal comments on them. A curious personality."[23]

Wilhelm's tendency, noted by his disgruntled advisors, to concentrate on newspapers as well as on political reports was a reflection of the Kaiser's frequent sense that public opinion played a crucial role in determining political behavior. In 1895, during the Armenian crisis, the British military attaché in Berlin complained to Wilhelm that an article in the Russian paper *Grashdanin* was symptomatic of a fundamental Russian antipathy toward England that was preventing rapprochement between the two countries. The Kaiser's telling response was that the *Grashdanin*

> like the Press in Russia generally has no appreciable influence on account of its limited circulation; certainly nothing like the influence of the Press in other countries, particularly in England. It is precisely this Press and British public opinion dominated by it that we have to thank for the whole sorry scandal of the Armenian question.[24]

Wilhelm II did not attribute the bloody Near Eastern crisis to the actions of the Turks and Armenians or to the policies of the European world powers actively seeking to defend and promote their national self-interest in the foundering Ottoman Empire. He did not even blame the British Government directly for attempting to hasten and exploit the process of Turkish collapse—as did many in the German Foreign Office. Instead, the Kaiser blamed the English press because of its influence on public opinion. By the same token, he discounted the political significance of the Russian press. Because of its limited circulation, *Grashdanin* had no real impact on the great mass of the Russian people. The fact that newspapers were read by those who directed the policies of the Russian Government seemed irrelevant to the Kaiser. For him, in this instance at least, it was mass public opinion and the press (insofar as it influenced mass public opinion) that determined the nation's course and defined the nature of its leadership.

It became one of Wilhelm's principal occupations to follow the press because of the importance of public opinion to him and because of the enormous power of the

---

[23]Letter to Hugo von Radolin of November 28, 1889. Norman Rich and M.H. Fisher, eds., *The Holstein Papers*, 4 volumes (Cambridge: Cambridge University Press, 1955–63), III, 323.

[24]Letter from Wilhelm II to State Secretary in the Foreign Office Marschall von Bieberstein of October 25, 1895. Johannes Lepsius *et al.*, eds., *Die grosse Politik der europäischen Kabinette*, 40 volumes (Berlin: Deutsche Verlagsgesellschaft für Politik und Geschichte, 1922 ff.), XI, 8–11. This source will subsequently be abbreviated *GPEK*.

press in its position as a medium between ruler and subject, simultaneously influencing and reflecting public opinion. He ascribed such major political developments as the growth of Anglo-French diplomatic and even military cooperation by early 1906 to the fact that the German press had "scolded" the two countries "together."[25] With its *influence* on popular opinion in France and England, the German press, Wilhelm believed, had produced decisive political action—one quite to Germany's disadvantage. As a *reflection* of public opinion, however, the press indicated future political action. In 1896, for example, Wilhelm anticipated that the English would soon decide to seize Germany's colonies because "the newspaper expectorations from England which announce the steady increase in anti-German feeling demonstrate that the antipathy is more deep-seated than has hitherto been believed."[26] In a way that his advisors did not, Wilhelm recognized that public opinion had become a crucial political factor in late-nineteenth- or early-twentieth-century Europe. Although he could proclaim and at times believe that he was completely above "the views and opinions of the day," his conduct as German emperor was often based upon the attitude that he expressed in December 1896 to the British ambassador in Berlin that despite his personal desire to promote Anglo-German understanding, he was simply "not able to act in opposition to the interests and wishes of the German people."[27]

Both the Kaiser's recognition that he must be a "modern monarch," sensitive and responsive to the needs of his subjects, and his belief in the political importance of public opinion and the press as a mediator between the ruler and his subjects were a direct result of Wilhelm's narcissistic psychopathology. His preoccupation with the "interests and wishes of the German people"—often to the neglect of the interests of the German state—was a direct result of the enormous significance that public opinion (via the press) had for Wilhelm personally. Because it affected him so powerfully, he appears to have naturally assumed that public opinion had a commensurate impact on political life in general. In the theoretical language of psychoanalysis, public opinion via the press can be said to have served as a "self-object" for the Kaiser: as an aspect of his external world that provided the direction and support that he could not find within himself.

Lacking a clear sense of consistent inner purpose, Wilhelm relied on public opinion—as he relied on other, often discordant, self-objects—to shape his attitudes and organize his activities. In general, the Kaiser seemed unable to develop a position on his own. Like iron filings that only assume a recognizable pattern in the presence of a magnetic field, Wilhelm formed opinions in reaction to the opinions of others. At times, the Kaiser simply adopted the views of those around him as his own. But even on those not infrequent occasions when he adopted a view diametrically opposed to that of the person with whom he was talking, Wilhelm needed

---

[25] Wilhelm II's marginalia to report from Monts in Rome to Chancellor Bülow of March 3, 1906; Ibid., XXI (1), 246–248.

[26] Telegram from Wilhelm II to Chancellor Hohenlohe-Schillingsfürst of October 25, 1896; Ibid., XIII, 3–4.

[27] Telegram from Wilhelm II to Chancellor Hohenlohe-Schillingsfürst of December 2, 1896; Ibid., XIII, 9–10.

the structured position of another to which he could impulsively react in defining his own point of view. It is significant in this context that so many of the Kaiser's telegrams and letters are essentially accounts of his conversations with others; his position only formulated in his descriptions of his replies. The same impulsive reactivity characterizes the principal way in which Wilhelm developed his opinions and articulated them to his advisors: namely, through extensive marginal comments on newspaper, diplomatic, and governmental reports. These marginalia reveal the degree to which Wilhelm was influenced by public opinion as it was reflected in the press. Not only can one see that the Kaiser actually read many newspapers, but it becomes clear that many of his personal opinions and political judgments were formed in direct response to press reports of popular feeling. In a psychological sense, public opinion can be described as having participated in the process of determining the Kaiser's point of view. Moreover, by following the manner in which the press reacted to his actions, Wilhelm was able to gauge the popular impact of his behavior. He lacked the internal capacity to evaluate the appropriateness of his actions, and he needed to rely upon the responses of his environment to regulate his impulsive activities. Like the timely intervention of his aides who were able to prevent the Kaiser from embarking on a potentially disastrous political course, the negative responses of the general public expressed through the papers could lead Wilhelm suddenly to change a position to which moments before he had seemed unalterably committed.

But while public opinion helped to shape Wilhelm's ideas and direct his actions, for him its principal function, like that of his entourage, was to offer external affirmation. Despite the fact that Wilhelm II was an emperor, raised from earliest childhood to be a public figure *par excellence,* he still experienced intense gratification at being the focus of popular attention. Bülow remarks in his memoirs on how quickly the cheers of the crowds would bring Wilhelm to a state of unbridled excitement: "In the course of my time in office I seldom went anywhere with the Kaiser when he did not declare after his ceremonial entrance that it had been the most lovely reception of his life."[28] The exquisite pleasure that Wilhelm experienced on such occasions had a direct influence on his actions; when he felt himself appreciated by British public opinion and supported by the British press, for example, Wilhelm sought to pursue a warmly pro-English policy.[29]

Both Wilhelm II's belief in the enormous influence of public opinion on political life and its powerful impact on himself personally placed the Kaiser in a problematical position. The political and personal dilemma that confronted Wilhelm in his relationship to public opinion found expression in a letter to Czar Nicholas II in May 1909. Wilhelm wrote that he felt "blamed" for the tension in Europe following Austria's annexation of Bosnia–Herzegovina in October of the preceding year. "Especially the Press in general," he complained, "has behaved in the basest way against me." Despite their inaccuracy, Wilhelm believed that the newspaper attacks

---

[28] Bülow, *Denkwürdigkeiten,* I, 164–165.
[29] See, for example, after the death of his grandmother, Queen Victoria, in early 1901.

against him should be taken seriously since "the fact must be taken note of that the papers mostly create public opinion." He concluded:

> As sovereigns who are responsible to God for the welfare of the Nations entrusted to our care it is our duty therefore to closely study the genesis and development of "public opinion" before we allow it to influence our actions. Should we find that it takes its origin from the tarnished and gutterlike sources of the above named infamous press our duty will and must oblige us to energetically correct it and resist it.
>
> Personally I am totally indifferent to newspaper gossip, but I cannot refrain from a certain feeling of anxiety, that if not corrected at once, the foul and filthy lies which are freely circulated about my policies and country, will tend to create bitterness between our two people by virtue of their constant and uncontradicted repetition. Public opinion wants clear information and leading.[30]

In the first place, the Kaiser's letter to the Czar gives expression to the dilemma inherent in Wilhelm's position as an "absolute" monarch in an age of growing mass political participation. As an autocrat, he was above newspaper criticism and yet obviously susceptible to it. He was theoretically accountable only to God and yet recognized that his leadership rested ultimately on his standing with his subjects. Wilhelm was confronted with the task of reconciling the facade of absolute self-certainty that seemed so necessary to his personal and political functioning with his appreciation of the powerful impact that press and public opinion had both on him and on modern political life. He had to reconcile his need to appear "totally indifferent to newspaper gossip" with his driven need to devote so much energy to the reading of newspapers.

The contradiction in Wilhelm's political position was probably inevitable given the changing realities of monarchical rule in turn-of-the-century Europe. The dilemma that confronted Wilhelm also had to be faced in one way or another by all the European hereditary sovereigns of his era. But though the Kaiser's political predicament was by no means unique, he was faced psychologically with a profoundly personal dilemma that arose directly out of Wilhelm's emotional dependence on the feelings and opinions of his subjects.

In the course of this study, considerable attention has been devoted to the three basic self-object functions that public opinion served for Wilhelm II, and the reader may well have experienced a sense of discomfort at the emphasis placed on these self-object needs of the Kaiser. After all, everyone needs the responses of others throughout one's life to help establish goals and set priorities and to assess the appropriateness of one's behavior. Everyone needs the affirming responses of others throughout one's life to feel truly alive and truly worthwhile. What makes Wilhelm unique was not that he needed self-objects to sustain him, but that he needed them so much. Wilhelm's dilemma, in other words, was that to a significant degree he was at the mercy of popular responses to him. Just as he could feel exhilarated by the adulation of the masses, as he could feel uplifted upon entering a city by the cheers of the crowds, as he could feel gratified by favorable newspaper reaction to

---

[30]Letter in English of May 9, 1909. Isaac Don Levine, ed., *Letters from the Kaiser to the Czar* (New York: Frederick A. Stokes, 1920), 230–234.

one of his speeches, he could feel correspondingly devastated when he felt himself unappreciated, undermined, or criticized by his subjects.

There is evidence to suggest that public condemnation contributed directly to a series of "nervous breakdowns" that Wilhelm suffered during the course of his reign.[31] The most famous of these occurred in the aftermath of the publication of the Kaiser's notorious interview with the English newspaper the *Daily Telegraph* in late October 1908, when Wilhelm's indiscrete remarks produced national indignation and the demand of the Reichstag that restraints be placed on the Kaiser's conduct.[32] One of Wilhelm's first such breakdowns occurred after he was roundly criticized for an inflammatory speech to the Brandenburg Provincial Diet on February 26, 1897. Bülow recalled that

> the Kaiser was so disappointed by the failure of his speech, which could not be kept from him, that... he suffered a nervous collapse.... He had anticipated that his "forthright" speech would be a huge success.[33]

It is not enough to say that Wilhelm simply felt criticized. On this occasion, and to a degree on all occasions when he felt out of tune with his countrymen, the intensity of his reaction indicates that Wilhelm experienced his subjects' response to his speech as a denigration of something that he had proudly created and displayed and as a devastating subversion where he had expected—indeed counted on—popular acclaim to support him emotionally. It is difficult to know with certainty how these breakdowns would be characterized in the terminology of contemporary psychiatry or what their precise precipitants may have been. They were doubtless the produce of various intersecting factors. Nonetheless, these incapacitating episodes of intense anxiety and depression do demonstrate that the supporting and sustaining responses of the Germans were essential to the Kaiser's personal and political functioning.

Although the extent of Wilhelm's dependence on public opinion placed him in a precarious psychological position, the nature of public opinion itself tended to increase Wilhelm's emotional vulnerability. The popular mood was a particularly problematical self-object for the Kaiser to have adopted. In the first place, public opinion was, and remains, difficult to define and evaluate. Wilhelm could rarely get a direct sense of what the Germans were thinking and feeling. It was mainly through the medium of the press, in its capacity as a reflection of public opinion, that the Kaiser could experience his vitally important relationship with his countrymen. This relationship was subject to countless distortions. No matter how many articles the Kaiser read, he never was actually exposed to public opinion in the press. He was only exposed to newspaper opinions and reportage.

---

[31] This was the term used by both Wilhelm and his aides to characterize these periods of intense anxiety and depression.

[32] Telegram from von Jenisch to Bülow of November 14, 1908. Bundesarchiv Koblenz, Bülow Papers, vol. 33. Also: Bülow, *Denkwürdigkeiten*, II, 377 and 386.

[33] Ibid., I, 50.

Not only did Wilhelm feel compelled to base himself on an inevitably distorted press image of public opinion; public opinion was also based upon an inevitably distorted press image of the Kaiser. "It is remarkable," Zedlitz-Trützschler, Wilhelm's court marshal for many years, noted in his diary in 1904,

> how sensitive the Kaiser is to the press. In and of themselves harmless inaccuracies and untruths about his life can greatly upset him when they are reported to him or when he comes across them in his own reading.[34]

Wilhelm's distress at the publication of misinformation about himself can be attributed to his concern that the Germans would develop misconceptions about him that could lead to a skewing of the popular responses on which he so depended. These problems of conception were compounded by the fact that the divisions in Wilhelmine Germany meant that at any given moment there existed many different—often incompatible—public opinions. Wilhelm, with his internal inconsistencies, had come to rely upon a self-object that itself profoundly lacked consensus. Furthermore, the frequent dramatic shifts of the German popular mood during the course of Wilhelm's reign added to the inconsistency of the support that it provided the Kaiser. Unable to function for any length of time without the support of his subjects, Wilhelm's leadership bears the mark of these features of German public opinion. The confusion of the Kaiser's aims, his inability to pursue policies steadfastly and consistently, his frequent precipitous changes in course are in part to be attributed to the ill-defined, inevitably distorted, contradictory character of public opinion as it was reflected in the press. Finally, it should be pointed out that the directions in which Wilhelm was propelled via his reliance on German public opinion were very different from those in which he was propelled by the other self-objects, like his entourage or his relatives, on which he also depended. The inconsistency of the Kaiser's political views and conduct was thus increased by the inconsistency of the environment on which he relied to help him organize and direct his activities.

But if Wilhelm's dependence on public opinion contributed to the ineffectiveness of his political leadership, in his efforts to deal with the political and personal dilemma that arose out of his dependence he demonstrated an interest and skill in swaying public opinion unprecedented for a leader of his era, let alone for a hereditary monarch. Wilhelm sought to overcome his sense of helplessness in his relationship with his subjects by attempting to control the feelings and opinions of the Germans primarily through the medium of the press, now in its capacity as an influence on public opinion. As he stated so emphatically in his letter to the Czar: "Public opinion wants clear information and leading." If Kaiser and country were in fundamental agreement, Wilhelm was not confronted with the paradox of being an absolute monarch whose leadership depended upon popular support since it was only when he and his subjects were out of step that the Kaiser realized that it was they and not he who set the pace. In fact, by using the press to

---

[34]Diary entry of November 21, 1904. Graf Robert von Zedlitz-Trützschler, *Zwölf Jahre am deutschen Kaiserhof* (Berlin: Deutsche Verlagsanstalt, 1924), 97.

encourage the German public to adapt itself to his policies and priorities, Wilhelm diminished his dependence on his countrymen and increased his political authority. Psychologically, too, by exerting his control over public opinion, Wilhelm was acting to insure the sustaining and supportive responses of his subjects, thereby reducing his sense of emotional helplessness and vulnerability. By establishing a measure of control over the feelings and opinions of the Germans, the Kaiser increased his control over himself and over his political and psychological destiny. As a direct result of his narcissistic psychopathology, Wilhelm came to develop a style of symbolic leadership that was more contemporary than traditional, more propagandistic than dynastic; it was a style of leadership suited to modern mass society.[35]

In its crudest form, Wilhelm's "leading" of public opinion involved the effort to prevent the publication of newspaper or journal articles that he deemed misleading, inappropriate, inaccurate, or malicious before they could corrupt the popular image of Wilhelm or of his policies. He constantly put pressure on his aides to suppress critical articles and prosecute "hostile" editors and was constantly irritated that there were limits on the government's authority to censor the German press.[36] Where it was not possible to prevent critical or erroneous articles from appearing, the Kaiser sought "energetically to correct" any possible popular misconceptions by publishing government denials or bulletins, and by using press leaks, friendly persuasion, or pressure to get his point of view expressed in those papers sympathetic to the government. At a particularly sensitive period in Anglo-German relations, for example, the Kaiser, annoyed at the publication of several articles in Germany critical of the English royal family, ordered that with the upcoming visit of the Prince of Wales "our Press must in the last 8 days before his arrival print only amicable articles about his trip."[37] Not only was the prince to be spared embarrassment at the hands of the German press, but the German people were to be encouraged to share Wilhelm's enthusiasm for the visit. In general, during those periods when the Kaiser felt favorably disposed toward the English, he sought to foster a similar sense of mutual goodwill on the part of the German and English people. When friendly articles toward Germany were printed in the English newspapers, Wilhelm ordered that they be translated and reprinted with approving commentary in the German press,[38] and he had officials of the government, academicians, and sympathetic journalists write essays for the papers, expressing the myriad economic, cultural, diplomatic, and military advantages for Germany of close friendship with England. He encouraged organizations, such as the Hamburg Chamber of Commerce, which

---

[35] Nicolaus Sombart, "Der letzte Kaiser war so, wie die Deutschen waren," *Frankfurter Allgemeine Zeitung,* January 27, 1979.

[36] Letter from Hohenlohe-Schillingsfürst to Holstein of May 28, 1896. Politisches Archiv Bonn, Holstein Papers, vol. 54.

[37] Wilhelm II's marginalia to telegram from Metternich in London to the Foreign Office of January 14, 1902. PA Bonn, England 81, Nr. lb secr., vol. 1.

[38] As, for example, Wilhelm II's marginalia to report from Metternich in London to Bülow of December 27, 1904. PA Bonn, England 78, vol. 23a.

had vested interests in improved relations between the two countries, to hold rallies and meetings to promote Anglo-German friendship.

The effort to engender popular support for a policy or position of the Kaiser by influencing the press and organizing public demonstrations found its clearest and most effective expression in the systematic propaganda campaign directed by Wilhelm and Admiral Tirpitz to create widespread German enthusiasm for the development of the navy. After the defeat of the government's naval bill in the Reichstag in March 1897, Wilhelm—although hurt and angry and thinking of insti-gating of a coup d'etat—took decisive action to transform German public opinion and thereby end the discrepancy between his own desire for naval increases and his subjects' apparently manifest indifference to naval development. To a report that increasing numbers of middle-class Germans were beginning to recognize that German commerce could not flourish without a powerful navy, Wilhelm ordered: "This mood must be methodically exploited and strengthened by the Press. At the same time the people must be oriented and incited against the Reichstag."[39] Approximately 3 months later, on June 18, 1897, Wilhelm appointed Tirpitz state secretary in the Naval Office. Wilhelm's order, however, had expressed the prin-ciple that would animate one of the first effective propaganda campaigns in the history of modern politics. Together, the Kaiser and Tirpitz through concentrated mass political action were able to achieve what more traditional political lob-bying had failed to accomplish. The government, in conjunction with powerful industrial and commercial circles, skillfully manipulated the press, abetted various popular naval and colonial leagues, and generally spent vast amounts of financial and political capital to produce a groundswell of popular support for the develop-ment of the German navy. Within a year, the Reichstag had passed a naval law setting forth the long-range expansion and modernization of the navy. What the Kaiser had described as "the struggle for the fleet" had been won with astonishing ease.[40]

If Tirpitz and the Kaiser shared an appreciation of the political importance of public opinion, there was a difference in the approach the two men took in attempt-ing to influence it. For Tirpitz, the propaganda campaign on behalf of the navy was a way to increase the naval budget, enlarge the navy, and, perhaps in the surge of patri-otic fervor for naval development, to distract the Germans from growing domestic tension. Although Wilhelm also yearned for the creation of a glorious German fleet, his attempt to influence public opinion was less calculated and more emotional. At heart, he was motivated by the need to make his subjects feel what he himself experienced. They were to share, affirm, and reflect his enthusiasm for the navy. By "leading" public opinion to support the government's naval building program, the Kaiser sought to create an identity of political and psychological outlook between himself and the Germans.

---

[39] Wilhelm II's marginalia to report from Monts in Munich to Hohenlohe-Schillingsfürst of March 23, 1897. PA Bonn, Deutschland 138, vol. 10.

[40] Letter from Wilhelm II to Eulenburg of August 20, 1897. Bülow, *Denkwürdigkeiten,* I, 137–139.

That Wilhelm's attempt to influence his subjects through the press was ultimately a subtle yet significant form of emotional communication with them is revealed by his order in early February 1896 that an article in the English newspaper *The Speaker* be translated and published in the German press. The article was a critical account of the successful British campaign against the Ashanti in West Africa. It concluded with the statement: "The most powerful nation in the world had crushed a naked African savage, and had celebrated its victory by treating him, his family, and his envoys considerably worse than it would have ventured to treat a party of pickpockets"—to which Wilhelm had noted in English in the margin "as it treats everybody."[41] At first glance, it seems incomprehensible that the Kaiser would want this article, on a subject apparently irrelevant to German concerns, circulated throughout the country. Wilhelm's reaction to the article and his desire that it be reprinted becomes understandable, however, in the context of the events following the Kruger telegram. On January 3rd, a month before the Kaiser's order regarding *The Speaker,* Wilhelm had sent a telegram to President Paul Kruger of the South African Republic, congratulating him on the Boer defeat of a band of British irregulars led by Leander Starr Jameson. The publication of the Kaiser's telegram produced a storm of anti-German feeling in England. Wilhelm was personally criticized by his English relatives and condemned in the British press. There were calls for an alliance between England and her traditional enemies, France and Russia, against Germany. Wilhelm was completely unprepared for the British reaction. He felt hurt and angry, and he even feared that because Germany did not possess a powerful navy, the English might be planning a surprise attack.[42] Wilhelm felt vulnerable and, as his marginalia to *The Speaker* indicates, treated with contempt by "the most powerful nation in the world"—a phrase in the article that Wilhelm had underlined. At such a time it was especially important for the Kaiser to have the support of his countrymen. By exposing his subjects to *The Speaker's* article on the Ashanti campaign, he hoped that their reaction would mirror his. If the Germans could share his experience of being treated with disdain, they might also conclude that a mighty navy could bring England to accept and respect Germany as another world power.

As described earlier, the very lack of inner consolidation that made Wilhelm so dependent on the support of his environment also gave him the psychological flexibility to assume the roles that would bring him the responses he needed. In his interaction with his subjects, the Kaiser was able to take on those characteristics that he sensed were expected of him. Only 3 years into Wilhelm's reign, the Portuguese diplomat, Eça de Queiroz, wrote of him:

---

[41] Wilhelm II's marginalia to *The Speaker of* January 25, 1896. PA Bonn, England 81, Nr. 2, vol. 12.

[42] Letter from Wilhelm II to Hohenlohe-Schillingsfürst of January 7, 1896, in Bundesmilitärarchiv Freiburg, RM 2, vol. 1558. Letter from August Eulenburg to Hohenlohe-Schillingsfürst of January 15, 1896, in Karl Alexander von Müller, ed., *Furst Chlodwig zu Hohenlohe-Schillingsfürst: Denkwürdigkeiten der Reichskanzlerzeit* (Berlin: Deutsche Verlagsanstalt, 1931), 158–159. Order of January 16, 1896, in ibid., 152.

> In this sovereign what a variety of incarnations of Royalty! One day he is a Soldier-King, rigid, stiff in helmet and cuirass,... regarding the drill-sergeant as the fundamental unity of the nation... Suddenly he strips off the uniform and dons the work-man's overall; he is the Reform-King attending only to questions of capital and wages, ... determined to go down in history embracing the proletariat as a brother whom he has set free.
>
> Then all unaware he becomes the King by Divine Right, driving over the frontiers all who do not devotedly believe in him.
>
> [Then he becomes the] Courtier-King, worldly, pompous, thinking only of the brilliancy and sumptuosity of etiquette... The world smiles and presto! he becomes the Modern King... treating the past as bigoted, ... determined to construct by the aid of Parliamentarism the largest amount of material and industrial civilization, regarding the factory as the supreme temple, dreaming of Germany as worked entirely by electricity.[43]

On a more individual level, Wilhelm's versatile theatricality, coupled with his broadly based general education and his innate intellectual capacity to grasp and retain vast amounts of information, enabled the Kaiser to establish an immediate personal contact with his subjects. Wilhelm variously presented himself as composer, painter, art historian, anthropologist, archeologist, historian, theologian, engineer, military strategist, sea captain, ship's architect, and businessman; the list of his interests and activities goes on and on. The Kaiser, it would seem, had the capacity to be all things to all people. Whether in personal conversation or in "the variety of his incarnations of Royalty," Wilhelm was able to engage his subjects individually. From worker to aristocrat, most Germans at one time or another felt personally connected to their Kaiser. Like his travels throughout Germany, which gave his countrymen the opportunity to see him face-to-face, the diversity of his interests and his many royal roles narrowed the gap between ruler and subject. Through a sense of shared interests and aspirations, a special emotional bond linking Wilhelm to the Germans contributed to the success of his leadership.

Reflecting the fact, however, that his adaptability was a manifestation of inner instability, Wilhelm could not maintain or integrate his incarnations of royalty; his knowledge lacked depth; his interests proved ephemeral. Although his versatility was impressive to the general public, those who had extended contact with the Kaiser knew him to be a dilettante. As his longtime chief of the naval cabinet, Admiral von Müller, noted in his diary:

> No thoughtful observer from this period can be in any doubt that the Kaiser understood much, very much very superficially, that he was very self-absorbed and believed that he could make judgments about things which he actually neither could nor needed to make judgments about.[44]

Lord Esher recorded in his diary on September 27, 1908, that the British statesman, Sir Edward Grey, after many years' experience in dealing with the Kaiser, had become convinced that Wilhelm's diversity was a sign not of strength but of emotional weakness. Grey, Esher wrote,

---

[43] Henry Wickham Steed, *Through Thirty Years,* I (New York: Doubleday, Page and Co., 1924), 21. Originally printed in *The Times.*

[44] Walter Görlitz, ed., *Der Kaiser: Aufzeichnungen des Chefs des Marinekabinette Admiral Georg Alexander von Müller uber die Ära Wilhelms II* (Göttingen: Musterschmidt Verlag, 1965), 34.

is not an admirer of the German Emperor. He thinks him not quite sane, and very superficial. This has always been my view. That he is picturesque and has a certain gift for language is true, but he is not a consistent or persistent thinker.[45]

As with so many other features of the Kaiser's personality, the diversity that enhanced his symbolic leadership contributed to the ineffectiveness of his political leadership by working to dissipate his energies, divide his attention, and encourage his inconsistency.

In considering the Kaiser's leadership, attention has been focused on the communication between Wilhelm and the Germans. Wilhelm, it has been argued, was not an effective political leader, a leader able to set an independent course and, through the power of his ideas and the influence of his political activity, to bring the nation into step behind him. Rather, what is significant about the Kaiser, and indeed marks his place in history, was his ability to sense vague, inchoate popular emotions, to experience them intensely himself, and to reflect them back to his subjects in a comprehensible and exalted form. In a way, one could describe the Kaiser's effective leadership as more a "followership" of sorts. There was, however, a significant transformation of popular feeling, an articulation and glorification of popular feeling, that makes "leadership" the appropriate characterization. In mirroring the nation, the Kaiser presented the Germans with a defined and enlarged image of themselves. The essence of this process of leadership, then, consisted of Wilhelm's capacity to experience and express popular feelings. Because it was primarily through symbols that the Kaiser communicated emotions in a concrete and broadly recognizable form, the term "symbolic leadership" has been chosen to define this process.

As was the case with Wilhelm's appreciation of the increasing significance of public opinion and press, his appreciation of the impact of symbols on popular feeling was a consequence of the impact that symbols had on him personally. In fact it would appear that for the Kaiser, symbols were not symbols at all. To him they were real—tangible and enduring expressions of feeling that could fulfill his need for constant reassurance. On a personal level, the many honors and titles he bestowed on others and that were bestowed on him were not mere formalities to the Kaiser. They were statements of direct appreciation and recognition. Politically, the state visits and the obligatory decorations and tributes exchanged between heads of state were not mere representations of the underlying state of relations between countries—relations ultimately determined by rational self-interest. For Wilhelm, they seemed at times in and of themselves determinants of the state of relations between countries.

As was the case with his preoccupation with public opinion and the press, Wilhelm's advisors could not understand the vast importance he attributed to what seemed to them to be insignificant symbolic gestures. Bülow, for example, criticized the Kaiser for his tendency "to regard banal civilities and empty phrases as

---

[45] Maurice V. Brett, ed., *Journals and Letters of Reginald, Viscount Esher,* II (London: I. Nicolson and Watson, 1934–1938), 344.

material successes of political consequence."[46] Wilhelm reacted with intense pleasure to such formal honors as being named Admiral of the Fleet in both the Russian
and the British navies. To him, these were not honorary titles, but actual commis-
sions carrying great political and military significance. After Queen Victoria had
made the Kaiser an admiral in her navy in 1889, he told Bismarck that "he now
had the opportunity and right to intervene directly in the construction, organization,
and administration of the English Fleet."[47] And intervene the Kaiser did—to the
dismay of his advisors and to the indignation of the British.[48] Wilhelm's interven-
tions, although designed to reduce tension, usually had the opposite effect, like that
produced by his letter to the First Lord of the British Admiralty, Lord Tweedmouth,
in February 1908. At the critical moment during the heated Anglo-German naval
rivalry, when the British Admiralty was about to submit its estimates on the rate
of German naval development to Parliament as part of its consideration of the
naval budget, the Kaiser, in a private letter, sought to assure Lord Tweedmouth that
Germany intended no challenge to British naval supremacy. He complained that
the admiralty's estimates about the German navy as they had been reported in the
papers were erroneous, and he justified his direct involvement in this sensitive matter by virtue of the fact that his letter was written "by one who is proud to wear the
British Naval Uniform of an Admiral of the Fleet, which was conferred on him by
the late great Queen of blessed memory."[49] As rumors of the existence of Wilhelm's
letter began to sweep England, the British press reacted with anger and suspicion.
The Times editorialized:

> if there was any doubt before about the meaning of the German naval expansion, none can
> remain after an attempt of this kind to influence the minister responsible for our navy in a
> direction favorable to German interests, an attempt, in other words, to make *it* more easy
> for German preparations to overtake our own.

The article concluded:

> If the complimentary title of Admiral of the Fleet is held to warrant a foreign Potentate in
> interfering in our domestic affairs by secret appeals to the head of a department on which
> the national safety depends, the abolition of dynastic compliments of this kind is an urgent
> necessity.[50]

When the German ambassador in London, Count Metternich, reported the British
outrage at the letter to Berlin and expressed his concern that it would increase the
mistrust and tension between the two countries, the Kaiser reacted with disbelief. "I
do not share Metternich's fears," he wrote in the margin of the ambassador's telegram. "The English have not yet become so totally crazy." *The Times'* editorial he

---

[46] Bülow, *Denkwürdigkeiten,* I, 526.

[47] Ibid., 93–95.

[48] Throughout his reign, the Kaiser sent suggestions to the British Admiralty, Lord Salisbury, and
others in England on ways to improve the Royal Navy.

[49] Letter of February 16, 1908. *GPEK,* XXIV, 34.

[50] *The Times,* March 6, 1908.

could only attribute to the machinations of his uncle, Edward VII, "who is worried that the letter makes such a calming impression."[51]

Even when played out on a political stage, Wilhelm's independent actions contained emotional messages expressed in grand symbolic form. His messianically tinged journey to the Holy Land in late 1898, his romantically brutal "Hun" speech to the German troops embarking for China during the Boxer Rebellion in 1900, his dramatic alliance with the Czar signed at Björkö in 1905 are all examples of the kind of theatrical epics enacted by the Kaiser which, although serving ostensibly rational political purposes, conveyed an emotional message of mythic grandeur. The political significance of these actions was usually limited to the negative reaction that they produced as the Kaiser's ostentatious demonstrations of German cultural, diplomatic, or military authority were viewed with alarm and annoyance in foreign capitals. Psychologically, these essentially symbolic actions can be understood on several levels. In the first place, they can be regarded as having served a defensive purpose for Wilhelm. The heroic journeys, the bellicose statements, and the bold political initiatives were from this perspective attempts to mask Wilhelm's chronic insecurity. This, at least, was Bülow's interpretation. "The Kaiser," he wrote in his memoirs, "through loud speeches and strong words sought to deceive others and himself about his inner uncertainty and anxiousness."[52] Secondly, it can be argued that Wilhelm simply lacked the unity of purpose necessary to formulate and consistently carry out clear-cut policies. He did not possess the inner strength to tolerate the tension and uncertainty that accompany the steady and cautious realization of distant political objectives. The Kaiser could only produce sudden bursts of dramatic action designed to effect immediate political change. Finally, it seems likely that on the deepest level these symbolic gestures were yet another manifestation of Wilhelm's driven need for external recognition and appreciation. The dramatic political displays were designed to attract attention and to elicit admiration; they were meant to be awe inspiring. When these actions were not understood or well received, Wilhelm reacted with surprise, anxiety, and depression. After the Björkö Treaty was effectively scuttled by both the Russian and German governments (each recognizing that the treaty was simply not compatible with either Russian or German national self-interest), Wilhelm appeared on the verge of a nervous breakdown. Instead of the acclaim he had expected, he felt humiliated by the treaty's repudiation.[53]

"Fundamentally, the populace *wished* to see itself represented in a proud and magnificent fashion," Thomas Mann wrote in 1905 of the relationship between ruler and subjects in his allegorical critique of Wilhelmine Germany, *Königliche Hoheit*.[54] Indeed, it seems clear that in the grandeur of the Kaiser's symbolic leadership a widespread yearning for a sense of national greatness found effective

---

[51] Wilhelm II's marginalia to telegram from Metternich in London to the Foreign Office of March 6, 1908. *GPEK,* XXIV, 39–40.

[52] Bülow, *Denkwürdigkeiten,* I, 570.

[53] Ibid., II, 149.

[54] Thomas Mann, *Gesammelte Werke,* II (Oldenburg: S. Fischer Verlag, 1960), 43.

expression. Determining popular attitudes, feelings, and opinions about events, ideas, or individuals is one of the historian's most important tasks. Unfortunately it is a task invariably undertaken with some trepidation, scholarly misgivings, and insecurity. Because of the vital historical importance of this task, however, the historian is obliged to make statements about the popular mood, even with the knowledge that these will be necessarily speculative and tentative and subject to the criticism of colleagues. It is, needless to say, impossible, given present historical methods and the available evidence, to determine scientifically just what the Germans' response to Wilhelm II might have been. Lacking quantitative measures of the popular mood, surveys, or opinion polls, the historian is forced to rely upon qualitative evidence, upon the comments of perceptive contemporary observers, to get a sense of what the Germans thought and felt about their Kaiser.

Clearly, it is impossible to draw general conclusions about the Germans' attitudes, feelings, and opinions about Wilhelm without being subject to a host of legitimate historical criticisms. Specifically, with some notable exceptions, the views of the Kaiser's contemporaries quoted in this article reflect the views of the Prussian establishment, the literati, and the German bourgeoisie. Socialists and other political radicals, Jews, and some South Germans had a very different view of Wilhelm II than, say, Thomas Mann or Friedrich Meinecke.[55] Nonetheless, despite the fact that every historical generalization is inevitably a distorted, indeed inaccurate, oversimplified, and limited characterization of the past, such generalizations can also contain a measure of historical truth. As long as these distortions, inaccuracies, oversimplifications, and limitations are acknowledged, there is a place in historical scholarship for the general statement. In the first place, there is ample qualitative evidence (some of which will be cited in the following pages), evidence drawn from both the Kaiser's supporters and detractors, to suggest that for much of his reign Wilhelm II enjoyed significant popularity among large sections of the German population. Furthermore, those observers cited in this article wrote not only as representatives of a specific party, class, or region of the country, but also as Germans. Thus, although opinions about Wilhelm II during the course of his reign differed widely in different parts of Germany and in different segments of German society, there was, one senses but cannot of course prove, an underlying feeling in Germany, experienced by most Germans at one time or another—often against their better judgment—a feeling of proud identification with the heroic image of the German Kaiser. No matter how much they may have detested him as a political leader or disliked him as a man, as the personal symbol of the German nation, Wilhelm II could evoke widespread and intense popular enthusiasm.

Despite the limited political benefit of Wilhelm's symbolic actions and despite their having exposed him to the risk of shattering disappointment, there is ample qualitative evidence to suggest that the Kaiser's emotional message of pride and magnificence was fundamentally in tune with the wishes of many of his countrymen. The sumptuous banquets, the memorable state visits, the impressive parades,

---

[55] I am indebted to Lamar Cecil for emphasizing to me the importance of this issue.

the imposing military maneuvers, the decorations, and uniforms, all conveyed the simple message of national power and glory the Germans readily understood and appreciated. The spectacular journeys, the fiery speeches, and the dramatic diplomatic initiatives all proclaimed to the applause of the enthusiastic nation the importance of Germany's place in the world. Although ill advised politically, an emotional gesture like the Kruger telegram was extraordinarily popular in Germany. Even a seasoned diplomat like the Prussian minister in Munich, Count Anton von Monts, despite his criticism of nearly everything else about the Kaiser's reign, could write to Bülow 1 month later: "The only thing that is going well is our foreign policy. The Kruger telegram has my complete approval. If only one doesn't back down."[56] Wilhelm's sense of triumphant satisfaction at the English defeat by the Boers was shared by Monts and many other Germans. Feeling themselves treated with insufficient respect by the British and envious of Britain's mighty empire, the Kaiser and his subjects appear to have identified on some level with the tiny Boer Republic's act of heroic defiance. Wilhelm's telegram to President Kruger gave dramatic expression to this identification with the Boers. It was a symbolic act of emotional defiance of the British paralleling the Boer's military defeat of Jameson's raiders.

If the Germans were a self-object for the Kaiser, it seems evident by the same token that the Kaiser was a self-object for the Germans. In an age of nationalism, Wilhelm became a personification of the German nation; he was experienced by his subjects as their representative, as an embodiment of their ideals and aspirations. As Ludwig Thoma, a leading South German liberal and cofounder of the journal *März*, recognized, Wilhelm's glorification of himself served to affirm the glory of his countrymen. Thoma wrote, in 1908:

> It was precisely the remarkable penchant for the operatic that brought our loyal citizenry to see in Wilhelm lithe embodiment of its ideal. What epic emotions were unleashed by the monarch's every pleasure cruise. What lyricisms have been written and spoken when he did nothing more than participate in a parade. There was no room for sobriety and nothing could occur in silence. Even the simplest thing took place in a Bengal light. The imagination of the bourgeoisie was inspired and aroused daily by the personality of the Kaiser. In every popular court of judgment on him, Wilhelm never found himself opposed, even in those places where he actively searched for opposition.[57]

Through his personality and symbolic actions, the Kaiser held a mirror up to the Germans in which an image of themselves was reflected larger than life. It was for the most part an image they very much wanted to see.

There is one further aspect of Wilhelm's personality which must be considered in the context of the Kaiser's leadership of the Germans: namely, his tendency, described by Eulenburg in 1903 in a letter to Bülow, "to regard and evaluate *all* things and *all* people solely from a personal point of view." Because of his dependence on the responses of his environment, Wilhelm experienced as a personal reaction to himself what to an outside observer might seem an event utterly unrelated

---

[56]Letter of February 24, 1896. Bülow, *Denkwürdigkeiten*, I, 34–36.

[57]Quoted in Friedrich Hartau, *Wilhelm II: In Selbstzeugnissen und Bilddokumenten* (Reinbek: Rowohlt Taschenbuch Verlag, 1978), 144.

to the Kaiser. In the words of Eulenburg's letter to Bülow: "Objectivity is lost completely, and subjectivity rides on a biting and stamping charger." When, Eulenburg continued, news of the failure of the German South Pole expedition arrived, Wilhelm became enraged. "With his tendency to take everything personally, the poor man experiences this expedition as an *insult.*"[58]

The Kaiser's rearing subjectivity led him to take a personal view of political life, and, specifically, to understand politics largely in terms of personalities. In part because of their personal authority, in part because of their impact on public opinion, Wilhelm believed other leaders, and especially other sovereigns, to be politically decisive. The symbolism inherent in the Czar's visit to France in 1901, for example, seemed to Wilhelm to pose a much greater menace to Germany than did the formal alliance concluded between France and Russia some 7 years before, and he demanded that more forts be built along the Rhine, that more garrisons be sent to Posen and West Prussia, and that the size of the navy be increased.[59]

Consistent with this personalized view of politics, Wilhelm regarded countries as if they were living, breathing, and, above all, emotional individuals. To the Kaiser, countries did not pursue policies determined by their rational self-interest; instead, they were "insulting," "proud," "cowardly," "adoring," and so on. From this perspective, policies were organized expressions of feeling, and it was the role of the leader to pursue a course compatible not with the national interest but with the national character. In conducting foreign policy, the statesman was confronted with the difficult task of reconciling the feelings of his own people with the feelings of foreign peoples. In a discussion with Joseph Chamberlain in late November 1899, the Kaiser described the national character of the Germans and advised the British colonial minister on how best to deal with them. As Bülow reported the contents of this conversation to Holstein:

> His Majesty added that it would be to the advantage of the English to treat the sensitive, obstinate and rather sentimental Germans with caution, not to make them impatient, but to show them goodwill in little things. The German is "touchy." The more this fact is borne in mind on the English side, the more useful it will be for the relationship between the two countries.[60]

It is striking and significant that the Kaiser's description of his countrymen was also a description of himself. Indeed, there was a subtle blurring in Wilhelm's mind of the distinction between himself and the Germans. Thus, he experienced blows to German national pride as a blow to his own self-esteem. Upon learning that two German missionaries had been murdered in China in 1897, the Kaiser demanded reprisals "that, with total severity and if necessary with the most brutal disregard

---

[58]Letter from Eulenburg to Bülow of July 26, 1903. "Nordlandreise II: Psyche." Bundesarchiv Koblenz, Eulenburg Papers, vol. 74.

[59]Telegram from Wilhelm II to Bülow of August 20, 1901. *GPEK*, XVIII (1), 14–16. For a clear exposition of Wilhelm's understanding of politics in terms of personalities see Lamar Cecil, "History as Family Chronicle."

[60]Letter from Bülow to Holstein from Windsor of November 24, 1899. Bundesarchiv Koblenz, Bülow Papers, vol. 91.

for the Chinese people, would finally demonstrate that the German Emperor will not allow himself to be trifled with and that it is ill advised to have him as an enemy."[61] By the same token, Wilhelm experienced insults to himself as insults to the nation as a whole. He reacted to the possible cancellation of the Prince of Wales's visit to Germany in 1902—which, according to Bülow, he would regard "as a slight directed against Him personally"—by threatening "to recall the German ambassador in London."[62]

Ultimately, of course, it was the powerful current of nationalism—of the individual's definition of himself or herself on the basis of the nation to which he or she belongs—that accounted for the Kaiser's having become, as a symbol of the nation, the focus of popular ambitions and ideals. Nevertheless, Wilhelm II, through his personality and behavior, increased substantially the extent to which he became the personal representative of the Germans. By presenting his subjects with an intensely personalized view of political life, a view that focused popular attention on individual and collective personalities, Wilhelm focused popular attention directly and by implication on his own personality. In his lack of psychological distinction between himself and his subjects, the Kaiser encouraged the Germans to regard him as the personification of their nation. Once again the message was simple, direct, and compelling: Politics was essentially an expression of feelings. Again, it was a message his subjects readily understood and accepted. It is easier to consider politics in terms of the influence of an important individual and to consider the relations between states as if they had human personalities than it is to think of politics as the rational competition for subtle economic, diplomatic, or military advantage between value-neutral nation-states. The universal language of emotion is easier to comprehend than is the low-key, complex, and intellectual language of self-interest. Wilhelm II's effective communication of the language of emotion to his subjects can in part be attributed to the fact that it was his native tongue.

Wilhelm's personalization of politics, however, contributed directly to the reactive character of German foreign policy during his reign. Much of Wilhelm's "policy" can in fact be understood as a series of reactions to what he regarded as blows to his own and to his nation's fragile honor. The typical response to such an "insult" was an expression of vengeful anger followed by an effort to restore the self-esteem of Kaiser and the country through some bold and dramatic action. When, for example, Wilhelm learned that his envoy in China, Kiemens von Ketteler, had been killed during the Boxer Rebellion in June 1900, he demanded a joint European action against the Chinese. He insisted, however, that German troops play the leading role. "The German representative," he telegraphed the state secretary in the Foreign Office, "will be avenged by my troops. Peking must be razed."[63] The news that the situation in China was being brought under control without any glorious

---

[61] Telegram from Wilhelm II to the Foreign Office of November 6, 1897. *GPEK*, XIV (1), 67.

[62] Telegram from Bülow to Metternich in London of January 21, 1902. PA Bonn, England 81, Nr. 1b, secr., vol. 1.

[63] Telegram from Wilhelm II to Bülow of July 19, 1900. *GPEK*, XVI, 14.

German victories, indeed even before the German commander of the European forces had arrived on the scene, "completely upset His Majesty," according to Eulenburg. "He spoke in the strongest possible terms about Russia and England, who had 'betrayed' him, not even sparing his advisers," and finally demanded that Eulenburg "send a telegram to the Foreign Office ordering the immediate conclusion of a defensive and offensive alliance with Japan, a country which until that time he had held in the utmost contempt." It was only with difficulty that Eulenburg was able to persuade the Kaiser to drop the idea.[64] It seemed to Wilhelm that Germany had lost the opportunity to redeem its honor and restore its strength in the eyes of the world. Feeling exposed and threatened, he reacted with the impulsive desire to find a new ally to support and strengthen his country and himself.

Reflecting the personality of the Kaiser, German foreign policy throughout his reign was characterized by general passivity, punctuated by sudden, frantic bursts of activity. There was no long-range purpose or clear program. Foreign governments were never certain where the Kaiser stood or what he would be likely to do in the future. As a result, they came to mistrust and to fear him. Similarly, in internal affairs, the conduct of government was characterized by a series of crises, scandals, and sudden shifts in direction. This pattern of unpredictability, of successive upheavals on both the foreign and domestic fronts, can be attributed in part to Wilhelm's impulsive, anxious, dramatic reactivity. The Kaiser did not possess the inner consolidation necessary to define a cohesive self-interest either for himself or for his nation. Lacking inner direction and purpose, Wilhelm's course was determined by the buffeting seas around him. His old nemesis, Sir Edward Grey, proved to be prophetic when he wrote at the time of the *Daily Telegraph* affair:

> The German Emperor is ageing me; he is like a battleship with steam up and screws going, but with no rudder, and he will run into something one day and cause a catastrophe.[65]

Wilhelm II's Symbolic Leadership of the Germans

In considering Wilhelmine Germany, it is easy to overlook the fact that although the concept of "Germany" was old, Germany itself was not. By the time of Wilhelm's accession in June 1888, the German nation had been in existence a mere 17 years. Without the benefit of a longstanding tradition of national cohesion, the country that Wilhelm led was still attempting to answer such basic questions as: What is Germany? How is it to be governed? Where does Germany fit in with the rest of the world? Not only did Germans have to come to terms with these existential issues relatively suddenly, but they were also confronted with the economic, social, political, and psychological dislocations and divisions brought on by the

---

[64] Bülow quoting Eulenburg in *Denkwürdigkeiten,* I, 456.

[65] Dudley Sommers, *Haldane of Cloan: His Life and Times, 1856–1928* (London: G. Allen and Unwin, 1960), 203.

rapid industrialization that transformed Germany after 1871. As a result of these sudden and sweeping developments, Germans found themselves in profound disagreement over the nature of state and society. Tradition, rather than promoting consensus, tended in fact to promote disunity. Germany was an uncertain aggregate, containing numerous historical tensions that constantly threatened its cohesion. These included: tension between the forces of centralism and those of particularism (Germany was made up of 25 heterogeneous states); the heritage of the Prussian–Austrian dualism; tension between Prussian state militarism and the more liberal political tradition in the southern and western parts of the country; tension between authoritarian government and middle-class constitutional aspirations; tension among diverse economic interests; tension between the agrarian East and the industrial West; tension between Protestantism and Catholicism; tension between the German majority and Polish, Danish, French, and Alsatian minorities; and sharp divisions and antagonisms among various social classes and castes. Despite the conviction of most Germans that they belonged together in a political and psychological entity called Germany, the Reich was a very recent, unstable, and, to a degree, even an artificial creation.

The disjointed state of Wilhelm II's personality made him unusually sensitive to the question of the solidity and durability of German national unity, and he regarded it as his historic mission to increase the cohesion of the German Reich. Wilhelm's concern with national unity was not merely the result of his recognition of Germany's deep internal divisions. Nor was it simply an outgrowth of a general sensitivity to issues of cohesion and coherence. The question of German national unity was so important to the Kaiser because he did not distinguish psychologically between himself and the German nation. In the effort to promote the cohesion of his country, he increased his sense of personal integration; by warding off national fragmentation, he sought to prevent the fragmentation of his self.

As in other areas of his political activity, Wilhelm's promotion of national unity was largely symbolic. With his sensitivity to public opinion, the Kaiser was able to work on several levels to increase the Germans' sense that they belonged together. Recognizing that his subjects needed to have their national identity securely grounded in a sense of historical legitimacy, Wilhelm worked to establish a tradition of a German national monarchy that included the various existing monarchical traditions in a modern national context. The "modern kaiser" as understood and enacted by Wilhelm contained features of the medieval Hohenstaufens, Holy Roman emperors, and Prussian Hohenzollerns. Nevertheless, in contrast to his grandfather, Wilhelm I, who regarded himself primarily as King of Prussia, and to his father, Friedrich III, who thought of the Imperial Monarchy in romantically medieval terms, Wilhelm, as he would stress over and over again, was first and foremost the *German* Emperor.[66] Where no German Imperial tradition existed, he

---

[66]For a discussion of the idea of the imperial monarchy, see Elisabeth Fehrenbach, "Images of Kaiserdom" and particularly *Wandlungen des deutschen Kaisergedankens, 1871–1918* (Munich: R. Oldenbourg, 1969).

attempted to create one by glorifying German military victories (against the French in 1870–1871) and the "pantheon" of national heroes. Despite the fact that Wilhelm I had only reluctantly assumed the imperial crown and had been deeply averse to the subordination of his title of King of Prussia to the imperial title, his grandson glorified "Wilhelm the Great" as German Emperor. Occasions such as the centenary of Wilhelm I's birth were used to celebrate the German character of the Reich and monarchy. Uncomprehending advisors like Chancellor Hohenlohe-Schillingsfürst argued that Wilhelm I's centenary was far less historically important than his accession to the Prussian throne. Wilhelm telegraphed back angrily on December 6, 1896:

> The celebration of the one hundredth anniversary of the birth of the first *German* Emperor of a *German* national Empire from the *German* House of Hohenzollern has a completely different significance for Germany and the whole world than does the coronation of the King of Prussia in 1861.[67]

By communicating to his subjects his sense of personal vulnerability to international "insults," Wilhelm contributed to the climate of anxious and indignant tension in Germany and to the popular perception that Germany was treated with disdain by the other European world powers who were systematically attempting to frustrate Germany's rightful world political ambitions. In no small measure because of the "touchy" and belligerent responses of the Kaiser to these perceived humiliations, Germany came to be viewed in many European capitals as the principal threat to world peace. As England drew steadily closer to France and Russia in their opposition to Germany, Wilhelm and his countrymen began to feel increasingly "encircled" by hostile powers. Although alarmed by Germany's growing international isolation, the Kaiser sought to use the anxiety of his subjects to bring them closer together. In speeches emphasizing the dangers inherent in Germany's geographical position[68] and the need to increase German military preparedness,[69] Wilhelm sought to rally his countrymen behind the defense of the nation's vulnerable independence. In part, the effort to win mass support for the German naval building program was designed to increase national cohesion. "The struggle for the fleet," Wilhelm was utterly convinced, was an ennobling, sustaining, and nationally integrative enterprise: bringing together North and South, Protestant and Catholic, capitalist and worker, and aristocrat and farmer. The navy was modern and liberal (the fleet had been a favorite liberal cause since 1848), in the economic interests of heavy industry and to a degree of the middle class as a whole. The navy was traditional and authoritarian: the arm of the absolutist-militarist state. Above all, however, the navy was national and monarchical-imperialist *(kaiserliche)*. Wilhelm told the British prime minister, Arthur Balfour, in 1902:

---

[67] *Hohenlohe-Schillingsfürst*, 285–286.

[68] See, for example, the Kaiser's Throne Speech of July 4, 1893.

[69] See, for example, the Royal Message of January 18, 1896, on the 25th anniversary of the founding of the German Empire.

Whereas England forms a political totality complete unto itself, Germany resembles a mosaic in which the individual pieces are still clearly distinguishable and have not yet blended together. This is evidenced by the Army which, though inspired by the identical patriotic spirit, is still made up of contingents from the various German states. The young German Reich needs institutions in which the unitary idea of a Reich is embodied. The Navy is such an institution. The Kaiser is its only commander. The Germans from all counties trend toward it, and it is a constant living example of the unity of the Reich. For this reason alone it is necessary and finds a warm supporter in His Majesty.[70]

Ultimately, however, it was less what Wilhelm II did than what he was that made him such a powerful symbolic force for German national unity. As a more psychologically cohesive leader could not have done, the Kaiser was able to personify the often contradictory national aspirations of his subjects. In what Eça de Queiroz described as his "variety of incarnations of Royalty," Wilhelm symbolically represented many different images of Germany which were only united in the national figure of the Kaiser. Specifically, Wilhelm saw it as his task to integrate for his people the conception of a "glorious past" and an autocratic system of government with mass industrial society. "I have been placed in an infinitely difficult period of history," he told Eulenburg in 1903, a period that requires "the reconciliation of traditional society with modern times."[71] The Kaiser dealt with this task by manifesting features of both past and present in his personality and behavior. The glorification of his Hohenzollern ancestors, the court galas, the monumentality of the Siegesallee in Berlin, the restoration of medieval castles, and the spectacular military parades and maneuvers all testified to Wilhelm's reverence for and rootedness in a romanticized past.[72] At the same time, he became the spokesman of his own Wilhelmine epoch. According to the four-volume *Deutschland unter Kaiser Wilhelm II.*, published to celebrate Wilhelm's silver jubilee in 1913:

In our Kaiser the spirit of the new era expresses itself and in the era the spirit of our Kaiser. No matter how stark the contradictions in the nation may be, how violently opinions may clash in parliament and among the people, it remains an unshakable fact that the Kaiser and the vast majority of the German people are united behind the goals of the nation. And in many and perhaps in the most important areas it was the Kaiser who won the nation over to his point of view, who taught the nation to believe in his ideas. Precisely those events of epochal significance: the shift from purely continental policies to *Weltpolitik,* and directly related to this: the supplementation of German armed might on the land with the creation of a battle fleet is based on the idea and determination of Kaiser Wilhelm II.

The author, F. W. von Loebell, insists further that in other areas of contemporary German life—in social, agricultural, commercial, industrial, transportational, artistic, archeological, scientific, technological, medical, and educational developments—the Kaiser had been the dynamic leading force. Von Loebell admits

---

[70]Telegram from Metternich with Wilhelm II in Sandringham to the Foreign Office of November 9, 1902. PA Bonn, Deutschland 138, secr., vol. 5.

[71]"Ein Zwiegespräch." Bundesarchiv Koblenz, Eulenburg Papers, vol. 74.

[72]Fehrenbach, "Images of Kaiserdom," 276. This and the following paragraph generally attempt to paraphrase Fehrenbach's thesis that the Kaiser combined various images of the German Kaiserdom within his person.

that it is difficult to ascribe these advances either to Wilhelm or to the German people. But, he concludes:

> No matter how diverse the achievements in the individual areas of national endeavor may be, the last 25 years have a special character, and that character could scarcely be more tellingly defined than with the name Kaiser Wilhelm II.[73]

Wilhelm saw nothing incongruous about wearing the traditional Prussian spiked helmet to the opening of a technical college in Breslau, and, even more significantly, neither did many of his countrymen. The German historian Friedrich Meinecke, who was not uncritical of the Kaiser, wrote also in 1913 that Wilhelm

> combines the intense actuality, the sharp purposefulness of the modern man with a glowing veneration of the national past. The grand figures and memories of his forbearers, his state, and his people are transfigured into colorful, gleaming symbols of lasting value. One who focuses on the individual features of his being tends to find a contradiction between his determined modernism and romantic traditionalism. In truth, his historical ideals and symbols are the spiritual tools he uses to inspire the energies of his contemporaries and to keep the surging flow of modern life within wholesome limits.[74]

Meinecke was mistaken. Wilhelm's features were in fact contradictory, and he was unable to reconcile the modern and the traditional. He was, however, able to incorporate elements of both in himself and to reflect them back to his subjects—integrated only insofar as they were fragments of the same disorganized personality.

Not only did the Kaiser's lack of self-cohesion enable him to embody the disparate aspirations of his countrymen, but his grandiose and exhibitionistic behavior tended to focus national attention on his person. Wilhelm's perpetual traveling, encountering spectacular receptions everywhere he went, and his countless speeches to enthusiastic audiences kept him constantly—either through the press or directly—in the public eye. As a figure continuously celebrated and attended to by a captivated nation, the Kaiser became the cynosure of nationalistic strivings, the brilliant symbol of a proud, glorious, and united Germany. Wilhelm himself recognized the intersection of his narcissistic needs and those of a people seeking to have their national cohesion affirmed through the "omnipresence" of their emperor.[75] In an interview with the author Ludwig Ganghofer, published in November 1906, Wilhelm praised the optimistic tone of Ganghofer's books and the virtues of an optimistic philosophy of life. "In politics it is no different," Ganghofer reported the Kaiser to say.

> The German people do indeed have a future, and there is a word that always hurts his feelings whenever he hears it: that word is *Reichsverdrossenheit* [weariness with the Reich]. What advantage is there to be had from *Verdrossenheit*? Better to work and be optimistic. I work without weariness *[unverdrossen]* and believe that I do in fact make progress.
>
>   The Kaiser continued by describing in detail the ways and means in which he worked daily and how the profusion and weight of the duties and labors that storm over him are

---

[73] F.W. von Loebell, "Rückblick und Ausblick." in *Deutschland unter Kaiser Wilhelm II*, eds. Philipp Zorn and Herbert von Berger, IV (Berlin: R. Hobbing, 1914), 1698–1699.
[74] Friedrich Meinecke, "Deutsche Jahrhundertfeier und Kaiserfeier," *Logos* 4 (1913): 171–172.
[75] Sombart, "Der letzte Kaiser."

often exhausting. At such times the need always rises up in him to relax and again see a new part of the world, to again meet new people, who again are so stimulating.

The Kaiser described in lively and plastic detail how such a trip gradually has a calming and refreshing effect. "Everything which oppresses Me is gone within a few weeks, and that which gives Me such pleasure other people take amiss frequently. I know that I am called the 'Reisekaiser,' but I have always regarded that as amusing. I don't allow that to take away My pleasure in the world. Travel allows one to make friends, especially in one's homeland. I believe that through travel the feeling of belonging together *[Zusammengehörigkeit]* is strengthened," and, he added, "many Germans do not know at all how beautiful our country is and how much there is to see of it. . . . Such refreshing trips are especially necessary in My serious profession, doubly necessary because one has to fight against many misunderstandings."[76]

From his interview with Ganghofer, one gets a sense of the enormous pressure— both external and internal—on Wilhelm II. Traveling both soothed the Kaiser and allowed him to overcome his underlying depression, the *Verdrossenheit* he was so anxious to deny and allay. The stimulation of new people and impressions restored a measure of psychological balance to the Kaiser and made him feel more internally cohesive. Traveling through Germany, exhibiting himself to his countrymen, increased not only the *Zusammengehörigkeit* of the Germans but that of Wilhelm II as well.

"The German," Wilhelm told Eulenburg in the summer of 1903, "wants to be led."[77] Although the Kaiser does appear to have been in touch with a deeply felt wish of many of his subjects for the autocratic leadership of a great man, it was, as has been discussed at some length, also extremely important psychologically for Wilhelm to appear absolutely sovereign to mask his chronic insecurity. Contemporaries, however, took Wilhelm at his word, and many—both inside and outside of Germany—believed him to be the single most powerful leader in the world. The charismatic and commanding Cecil Rhodes, for example, was fascinated by Wilhelm and recognized a kindred spirit in the Kaiser. After meeting Wilhelm in 1899 he wrote to the Prince of Wales: "the Emperor is really Germany, at least it appeared to me to be so when I was in Berlin, Ministers doing just what he desired and the Reichstag most docile."[78] Instead of appearing increasingly anachronistic, the German absolute monarchy seemed to grow ever more firmly rooted in the national soil, ever more bound up with the national destiny. For many Germans, the kaiserdom appeared to be an institution more of the future than of the past. Writing in 1900, in the psychologically significant first year of the new century, Friedrich Naumann observed:

In present-day Germany there is no stronger force than the Kaiser. The very complaints of the anti-Kaiser democrats about the growth of personal absolutism are the best proof of this fact, for these complaints are not pure invention but are based on the repeated observation that all policy, foreign and internal, stems from the will and word of the Kaiser. No monarch

---

[76]Ernst Johann, ed., *Reden des Kaisers* (Munich: Deutscher Taschenbuch Verlag, 1966), 118–119.

[77]"Ein Zwiegespräch." Eulenburg Papers, Budesarchiv Koblenz, vol. 74.

[78]Letter of late March. George Earle Buckle, ed., *The Letters of Queen Victoria, 1886–1901,* III (New York: Longmans, Green, and Co., 1930), 350.

of absolutist times ever had so much real power as the Kaiser has today. He does not achieve everything he wants, but it is still more than anybody would have believed possible in the middle of the last century. That century, whose middle years echoed with the dreams of a German republic, ended with more power in the Kaiser's hands than even Barbarossa possessed.[79]

The political reality of Wilhelm's sovereignty was rather more equivocal, however, and the historian of the period is confronted with the dilemma of reconciling a Kaiser who could be attacked in a contemporary pamphlet as a "Caligula," that bloodthirsty tyrant who had the audacity to appoint his horse Consul of Rome,[80] with a Kaiser who could feel himself "tyrannized" by his nearly 80-year-old Chancellor Hohenlohe-Schillingsfürst.[81] Historians have long debated the question of Wilhelm's "personal regime," and, as was stated at this chapter's outset, have until very recently tended to play down his actual political authority and significance. Within the limits of the present investigation it is not possible, of course, to provide anything approaching a definitive answer to this extraordinarily complex question.[82] Nevertheless, although in theory Wilhelm was an absolute monarch, as a result of his personality and the nature of his position, in practice his political influence was ill defined and seems in fact to have been rather limited. It would serve no useful purpose at this point to go over once again the various features of the Kaiser's personality that worked to reduce his political effectiveness. In general, it would appear that Wilhelm's impact on the political functioning of government was negative. The Kaiser's absolutist pretensions, his attempt to hold all the reins of power, meant in practice that Wilhelm could only capriciously interfere with the affairs of state. His ready reactive tendencies were exacerbated as, in his effort to stay in charge of everything, Wilhelm would shift his attention from one issue to the next. Unable to have knowledge in depth about those myriad areas over which he claimed authority, Wilhelm's absolutism often took the form of rather sullen and stubborn resistance to the plans and programs drawn up by those expert

---

[79] Friedrich Naumann, *Demokratie und Kaisertum* (Berlin: Buchverlag "Der Hilfe," 1904), 167–68. Translated and quoted in John C. G. Röhl, *Germany without Bismarck: The Crisis of Government in the Second Reich, 1890–1900* (Berkeley, CA: University of California Press, 1967), 279.

[80] Ludwig Quidde, *Caligula—eine Studie über römischen Cäsarenwahnsinn* (Leipzig: W. Friedrich, 1894).

[81] Letter from Chiodwig Hohenlohe-Schillingsfürst to his son, Alexander, of October 31, 1897. *Hohenlohe-Schillingsfürst*, 398.

[82] Those interested in this issue should see Röhl, *Germany without Bismarck*: and Röhl, "Introduction" to *Kaiser Wilhelm II*. Röhl makes a compelling case for Wilhelm's ultimate political importance as well as summarizing the historical debate about the "personal regime." See also the contributions of Paul Kennedy, "The Kaiser and German *Weltpolitik*: Reflexions on Wilhelm II's Place in the Making of German Foreign Policy," 143–168; Kathy Lerman, "The Decisive Relationship: Kaiser Wilhelm II and Chancellor Bernhard von Bülow, 1900–1905," 221–247; and Terence F. Cole, "The *Daily Telegraph* Affair and Its Aftermath: The Kaiser, Bülow and the Reichstag, 1908–1909," 249–268.

in the area in question. Many of his more impetuous orders were never issued, as his aides—recognizing their potentially catastrophic political impact—would delay sending them off until either the Kaiser's impulse had passed or he could be tactfully persuaded to change his mind. In general, Wilhelm's obstinacy interfered with the conduct of government since so much time and energy had to be expended in attempting to "manage" the Kaiser. Still, despite the difficulties involved, Wilhelm's advisors were usually successful at this task. By flattering the Kaiser into adopting their positions as his own or by threatening resignation, chancellors and ministers were in most instances able to get their way with Wilhelm. Even on those rare occasions when Wilhelm was able to formulate a clear political objective, he was not always able to overcome the opposition of those in the government. One of the most telling such examples of the Kaiser's political and personal weakness was his inability either to convince or to compel the chancellor and other top officials to accept the dismissal of Marschall von Bieberstein—a man whom Wilhelm despised—from his position as state secretary in the foreign office for almost 4 years.

Although the Kaiser was far from being a forceful and dynamic political leader, it would be an error simply to dismiss the observations of Rhodes and Naumann. The "personal regime" was not a historically meaningless illusion; it was an emotional and symbolic reality. As the personification of the German nation, as the focus of national pride and popular aspirations, Wilhelm II was truly sovereign. Wilhelm, himself, was certainly aware that as a leader in an age of mass political participation he wielded enormous emotional authority. He wrote to Nicholas II during the waning days of the Russo-Japanese War urging his beleaguered fellow-autocrat to exercise the vast symbolic power at his disposal to mobilize the Russian people and save his crown. "Take your place at the head of your armed forces," the Kaiser told the Czar.

> The European Public as well as the Russian Nation is instinctively looking toward the Zar, and expecting that he will come forth and do something grandly, a great personal act; meant to show that he is the Absolute Ruler of his People and willing to allay their anxieties and pains as far as is in his power.[83]

By communicating symbolically with his subjects, the modern emperor had the ability to mobilize the powerful narcissistic (self-object) bond connecting him with his countrymen. It was this bond that gave a leader his enormous emotional authority, the authority to save a tottering dynasty, to decide the issue of military victory or defeat. For Wilhelm, at least, his symbolic authority seemed to be of greater consequence than the political authority at his command. And indeed in our modern world, the ability of a leader to achieve the emotional mobilization of his nation may perhaps be even more important than the ability to determine who will be the secretary of state.

Once again, there appears to have been an intersection between Wilhelm's narcissistic needs and those of his countrymen. On the basis of his own driven personal

---

[83]Letter of February 21, 1905. *Letters from the Kaiser to the Czar,* 166–170.

agenda and his sensitivity to the wishes of his subjects, the Kaiser sought to focus attention on himself as a symbol of national strength and cohesion. The royal "standard waves high in the breeze," he wrote to his mother in 1898,

> comforting every anxious look cast upwards; the Crown sends its rays "by the grace of God" into Palace and hut, and—pardon me if I say so—Europe and the world listen to hear, "what does the German Emperor say or think"[84]

Through a shared subjugation to and identification with the Kaiser, Germans were to develop a national group identity bridging social divisions. *"Everyone,* without class distinction," Wilhelm told Eulenburg,

> should stand behind me, should fight beside me for the interests of the Fatherland! No matter what class they belong to. On me, no one exerts any influence; and no one will be permitted to exert any influence on me. *I* am to command.[85]

Not only did Wilhelm's assertion of absolute sovereignty bind Germans together by virtue of the fact that all were subject to his authority—that all, in his words, stood *behind* him—but also, through their shared identification with the grand and imposing figure of the Kaiser—through their sense of fighting *beside* him—Germans experienced their own grandiose fantasies about themselves played out on the stage of world history. As was the case with Wilhelm's need to appear to know everything (the Kaiser's omniscience) and be everywhere (the Kaiser's omnipresence), so too was his need to appear omnipotent fundamentally in tune with the need of many Germans to feel themselves defined and represented by a powerful leader who was firmly in control of the national destiny. As Elisabeth Fehrenbach has written, the Germans, lacking a long established tradition of nationhood, came to see Wilhelm II as the embodiment of "the whole spiritual personality of the nation."[86] But, Fehrenbach continues:

> The Kaiser only became the visible and real symbol of the nation-state by virtue of his personal conspicuousness. The identification of the monarch with the nation was not, it is true, manifested in relation to the Reichstag which, owing to constitutional impediments to parliamentary government and the consequent perception which the parties had of their role, was seen more as a forum for the representation of vested interests than the expression of national unity. This identification occurred as a result of the personalization of the image of the Kaiser in "Wilhelminism." The Kaiser made possible the escape from the labyrinths of mass society; he concentrated people's gaze on the great man, the gifted individual, the embodiment of an historical mission.[87]

According to Maximilian Harden, editor of *Die Zukunft* and one of Wilhelm II's fiercest and most effective opponents, "enlightened" critics of the Kaiser were prepared to tolerate his erratic and impulsive conduct in return for the benefits Germany derived from the fact that "the Kaiser is his own Chancellor."

---

[84] Bülow, *Denkwürdigkeiten,* I, 235–237.

[85] "Ein Zwiegespräch." Eulenburg Papers, Budesarchiv Koblenz, vol. 74.

[86] Fehrenbach, "Images of Kaiserdom," 277.

[87] Ibid., 276.

All the important political decisions of the past twelve years have been made by him. Changes in trade policy, the build-up of the fleet, the belief in the German Reich achieving *Weltmacht* on an enormous scale, the friendly relations and secret treaties with England, the military campaign in China, all that and a lot more besides is his work. His objectives have been correct almost without exception, but his chosen ways and means have been unfortunate.[88]

In general, even the most committed adversaries of Wilhelm II tended to direct their criticism at the Kaiser's methods rather than at his goals.[89] It would be difficult, however, to characterize the goals of Wilhelm II's leadership (including those cited above by Harden in *Die Zukunft*) as being circumscribed political objectives in the Bismarckian sense of the term.[90] On sober historical reflection, these objectives were not based upon a clear appreciation of Germany's rational self-interest. They were almost all expressions of Germany's fundamental foreign political ambition before World War I to practice *Weltpolitik*, expressions of the essentially emotional wish that Germany take its rightful place in the world, that it be accorded the international respect that a proud and powerful nation deserved. Harden's "enlightened" critics were correct in attributing these "objectives" to the Kaiser. As has been argued here, Wilhelm's disunity and uncertainty drove him to demand that he be recognized, appreciated, and respected. This goal ultimately formed the basis for his leadership of the Germans. He told Eulenburg in 1903:

> I have never thought about autocracy, but I have long ago made my program of *how* I wanted to be German Kaiser, how I conceived of the German Kaiser: Deep into the most distant jungles of other parts of the world, everyone should know the voice of the German Kaiser. *Nothing* should occur on this earth without having first heard him. His word must have its weight placed on every scale. Well—and I think I have generally held to my program! Also domestically the word of the Kaiser should be *everything*.[91]

The program for the man had become fused with the program for the nation. Internally, the national voice of the Kaiser, it was hoped, would submerge the discordant babble of German voices all speaking at once on behalf of their own narrow interests. It was *Weltpolitik* that provided the principal escape from the domestic din. In this fragmented country, in this recently and insecurely consolidated nation, the emotional goal that the voice of Germany, of the German Kaiser, be listened throughout the world was perhaps the only goal that most Germans could enthusiastically agree upon.

---

[88]"Die Feinde des Kaisers," *Die Zukunft* 40 (1902): 340. Quoted in ibid., 282–283.

[89]Ibid., 269–285. Meinecke, "Deutsche Jahrhundertfeier und Kaiserfeier," 161–175. Meinecke, "Drei Generationen deutscher Gelehrtenpolitik: Friedrich Vischer, Gustav Schmoller, Max Weber," in *Brandenburg, Preussen, Deutschland: Kleine Schriften zur Geschichte und Politik* (Stuttgart: K. F. Köhler Verlag, 1979), 495–505.

[90]With the possible exception of German trade policy, even those goals listed by Harden could hardly be described as being objectives in the Bismarckian sense. In fact they have been considered in the course of this article from the vantage of their emotional meaning.

[91]"Ein Zwiegespräch." Eulenburg Papers, Bundesarchiv Koblenz, vol. 74.

The Kaiser in Psychohistorical Perspective

After World War I, a number of psychiatric studies were published purporting to demonstrate scientifically that Wilhelm II was mentally ill. *Wilhelm II.: Versuch Einer Psychologischen Analyse* (Halle, 1919) by Adolf Friedländer is typical of these attempts to diagnose the Kaiser.[92] The author finds that Wilhelm "shows all the indications of over- breeding *[Hochzüchtung,* in the sense of inbreeding]* and degeneration."[93] Friedländer continues: "Wilhelm II reveals himself to us... as a personality in which the positive and negative hereditary characteristics of his ancestors are present in greatly intensified form."[94] Friedländer's study, like the others published in the aftermath of a bitter defeat, attributes Wilhelm's erratic and extreme behavior to breeding. These studies all share the implicit assumption that part of the blame for the German defeat can be traced to the unstable conduct of the Kaiser, which in turn was a direct result of his hypomania of genetic origin. In the psychiatrist Paul Tesdorpf's *Die Krankheit Wilhelms II* (Munich, 1919), the connection between Wilhelm's "illness" and Germany's loss of the war is made explicitly. "We Germans have lost nothing of our honor and inner greatness. We have emerged internally victorious from this struggle." The author appears to absolve the German people from responsibility for the defeat by attributing it to the Kaiser's sickness:

> The government of Wilhelm II was spurious. It had to collapse. What was to blame for this spuriousness? Was it his will? His will was perhaps noble and pure. But he was sick, sick, as were his thoughts and emotions. . ... For the experienced physician and psychiatrist there can be no doubt that Wilhelm II, already as a youth was mentally ill. . .. The blame for the war which can be attributed to him was the result of this illness.[95]

All the evidence, Tesdorpf concludes, "leads to the natural conclusion that Wilhelm II presents a typical picture of hereditary psychic degeneration."[96]

There are in fact indications that Wilhelm may have had a hereditary predisposition to hypomania, and it is likely that he suffered from congenital hyperactivity.[97] The diagnoses of Friedländer, Tesdorpf, and their colleagues doubtless represent honest efforts to come to terms with a puzzling—and to them historically decisive—personality. Nevertheless, like the veiled ascription of the German defeat to Wilhelm's psychopathology, it seems clear that a diagnosis of inherited "degeneracy" would have suited the needs of many Germans to distance themselves from

---

[92] Adolf Friedländer, *Wilhelm II.: Versuch Einer Psychologischen Analyse* (Halle: Carl Marhold Verlagsbuchhandlung, 1919). See also Franz Kleinschrod, *Die Geisteskrankhejt Kaiser Wilhelm II?* (Wörrishofen: K. Neuwihler, 1919); Herman Lutz, *Wilhelm II. periodisch Geisteskrankheit Ein Charakterbild des wahren Kaisers* (Leipzig: O. Hillman, 1919); H. Wilm, *Wilhelm II. als Kruppel und Psychopath* (Berlin: A. Gerhard, 1920); as well as Dr. Julius Michaelson's article in the *Neue Hamburger Zeitung* of November 30, 1918, Abendausgabe.

[93] Ibid., 44.

[94] Ibid., 48.

[95] Paul Tesdorpf, *Die Krankheit Wilhelms II* (Munich: J.F. Lehmann, 1919), 4.

[96] Ibid., 31.

[97] See T. Kohut, "Kaiser Wilhelm II and His Parents."

their Kaiser after 1919. Sigmund Freud, writing in the summer of 1906, noted that such a diagnosis can often be secretly reassuring to us. In his discussion of Wilhelm Jensen's novella *Gradiva: A Pompeiian Fancy,* Freud asserts that because the hero of the novella, a young archaeologist, had developed a delusion about an antique bas-relief of a young woman, an old-school psychiatrist

> would at once stamp him as a *degenere* and would investigate the heredity which had remorselessly driven him to this fate. But here the author [Jensen] does not follow the psychiatrist, and with good reason. He wishes to bring the hero closer to us so as to make "empathy" easier; the diagnosis of *degenere,* whether it is right or wrong, at once puts the young archaeologist at a distance from us, for we readers are the normal people and the standard of humanity.[98]

Although Freud recognized that the diagnosis of hereditary degeneracy enables us to deny our sense of essential emotional kinship, our empathic bond, with those suffering from psychological disorders, he himself was not immune to the attraction of a popularly held view of the Kaiser that served to increase the distance between the Germans and their leader in defeat. Freud was moved to comment on Wilhelm II's psychopathology by Emil Ludwig's biography *Wilhelm Hohenzollern: The Last of the Kaisers,* which originally appeared in Germany in 1926. For Ludwig, Wilhelm's withered left arm—the result of a birth injury—provided the key to his character:

> Only those who can appreciate this lifelong struggle against the congenital weakness will be fair to him when the future Emperor is seen to strain too far or lose, his nervous energy. The perpetual struggle with a defect which every newcomer must instantly perceive and he, for that very reason, the more ostentatiously ignore—this hourly, lifelong effort to conceal a congenital, in no way repulsive, stigma of Nature, was the decisive factor in the development of his character. The weakling sought to emphasize his strength; but instead of doing so intelligently, as his lively intelligence would have permitted, tradition and vainglory urged him to the exhibition of an heroic, that is to say a soldierly personality.[99]

Wilhelm's blustering bellicosity and inner weakness are directly attributable to his birth defect, according to Ludwig. Indeed, it is implied that a measure of responsibility for both the war and the German defeat can be traced to this "stigma of Nature." The huge success of Ludwig's biography did much to focus attention on the Kaiser's withered arm as a way to understand his personality. It seems likely, in fact, that Ludwig articulated a widely held belief in Germany that attributed the failings and failures of the Kaiser to his physical defect—a defect perhaps the product, according to one popular version of Wilhelm's difficult delivery, of the doctor's having devoted his attention more to the English mother than to her German son. The popularity of Ludwig's biography was such that it came to Freud's attention. Freud invoked it in his *New Introductory Lectures on Psychoanalysis* in 1932 during

---

[98] Sigmund Freud, "Delusion and Dream in Jensen's *Gradiva,*" in *The Standard Edition of the Complete Psychological Works of Sigmund Freud,* ed. James Strachey, vol. IX (London: The Hogarth Press, 1964), 45.

[99] Emil Ludwig, *Wilhelm Hohenzollern: The Last of the Kaisers* (New York and London: G.P. Putnam's Sons, 1927), 30.

the course of his efforts to refute Alfred Adler's theory of the inferiority complex. Specifically, Freud criticized Ludwig for having

> ventured on an attempt to erect the whole of the development of his hero's character on the sense of inferiority which must have been called up by his physical defect. In doing so, he has overlooked one small but not insignificant fact. It is usual for mothers whom Fate has presented with a child who is sickly or otherwise at a disadvantage to try to compensate him for his unfair handicap by a superabundance of love. In the instance before us, the proud mother behaved otherwise; she withdrew her love from the child on account of his infirmity. When he had grown up into a man of great power, he proved unambiguously by his actions that he had never forgiven his mother [in his hostility to her English homeland]. When you consider the importance of a mother's love for the mental life of a child, you will no doubt make a tacit correction of the biographer's inferiority theory.[100]

Freud's interpretation of Wilhelm's psychopathology is important and deserves serious consideration.[101] The subtle shift in emphasis away from Adler-Ludwig's point of view beautifully captures the revolution that Freud brought about in our understanding of human beings. Not the defect of nature by itself, but rather the environment's response to it, is psychologically significant. Nonetheless, Freud has not been able to escape a popular view of the Kaiser in which Germans had an unconscious investment. Freud's interpretation of Wilhelm, while accurate to a degree, is based upon an understanding of the Kaiser derived from the needs of German nationalistic pride, an understanding which again directs responsibility for the Kaiser's psychopathology, for his bellicosity toward Britain, for the lost war, away from Germany, an understanding which attributes Wilhelm II's failings and failures not to his weak and distant German father (or to any other Germans who played a role in Wilhelm's upbringing) but solely to the unempathic responses of the foreign English princess who was his mother.

The diagnoses of the Kaiser suggested by Friedländer, Tesdorpf, Ludwig, and Freud, although explaining circumscribed aspects of the Kaiser's psychopathology, offer a one-sided and convenient picture of his personality and behavior. The continuing popularity of these diagnoses of Wilhelm reflects not only the accuracy of such appraisals, but also their emotional appeal to Germans after the war. By attributing Wilhelm's difficulties to his breeding, his physical deformity, and his English mother, Germans were able to deny their emotional kinship with their Kaiser, their part in influencing and contributing to his actions, and their measure of responsibility for the catastrophe. In the aftermath of a profoundly humiliating defeat, Wilhelm II was made a scapegoat, the target of Germany's own sense of ignominy and helpless anger. In exile in Holland, Wilhelm II in a paradoxical way continued to personify the feelings of Germans about themselves. Now he was not the embodiment of national strength and greatness, but the symbol of national weakness and shame. In a psychological sense, however, the "personal regime" can be said to have continued.

---

[100] Sigmund Freud, "Lecture XXXI. Dissection of the Personality." *The Standard Edition* XXII: 66.

[101] For an extensive consideration of these issues, see T. Kohut, "Kaiser Wilhelm II and His Parents."

In contrast to the diagnoses of Friedländer, Tesdorpf, Ludwig, and Freud, the view of the Kaiser presented in this article makes a direct connection between Wilhelm's personality and behavior and the needs and wishes of his subjects. Of course, the German people were not the cause of Wilhelm's narcissistic psychopathology. His parents and other important caretakers during the Kaiser's childhood, as well as physical and constitutional factors, must bear ultimate responsibility for that. Nonetheless, as a result of the specific nature of his psychopathology, the German nation came to play an important role in determining and directing his attitudes and actions. The weakness and disharmony of Wilhelm's self made it necessary for him to rely on his environment—on self-objects—to supply him with external support and emotional sustenance. The German nation was such a self-object for the Kaiser. Without a firmly consolidated inner program of action or set of guiding ideals, he came to base himself to a significant extent on the ambitions and values of his countrymen. Impelled by a desperate eagerness to please and to find external confirmation, Wilhelm was exquisitely sensitive to the responses of his environment, part of which was public opinion as it was reflected in the press. His extraordinary flexibility, the product of his inner disorganization, enabled him to resonate with disparate segments of German society and generally to assume the roles he sensed that his subjects wished him to play.

The connection between Wilhelm II's disjointed personality and the Germans went beyond his ability to recognize the often contradictory and fluctuating popular mood and to adapt himself to it. There can be little doubt that other manifestations of his narcissistic psychopathology were fundamentally in tune with the needs of his subjects. The Kaiser's restless search for admiration and affirmation, his driven need to exhibit himself and his accomplishments, and his need to be constantly in the public eye served to focus the attention of the nation on his person. Often literally donning the garb of a heroic leader, to cover his inner fearfulness, Wilhelm provided his countrymen with a grand and noble figure with whom to identify and around whom the nation could coalesce. His brittle defensive facade of personal absolutism fulfilled the need of many Germans to have a powerful and independent sovereign, a ruler with perhaps a world-historical mission. In the field of foreign policy, Wilhelm's anxious and belligerent insistence that he be listened to and treated with respect paralleled the widespread sense that Germany was entitled to take its place as a world imperial power. Finally, Wilhelm's inner disharmony and his yearning for increased personal cohesion led him to be particularly sensitive to the issue of German unity and to take steps to promote the consolidation of his young and, in many ways, incoherent nation.

Although Wilhelm's self-pathology allowed him to function effectively as a symbol of the nation and even to be responsive to the emotional needs of his subjects, the Kaiser's central structural weakness and disjointedness made him a singularly ineffective politician. Here, the manifestations of his narcissistic psychopathology—his impressionability, his labile dependence on others to supply him with ideals and directions (on self-objects that supplied him with conflicting ideals and impelled him in different directions), his tendency to understand and respond to everything personally, his extreme vulnerability, his inability to tolerate criticism or take advice, his impulsive emotionality and reactive character, and his lack of diligence and persistence—all prevented him from being able to chart and maintain a steady course. It would be a mistake, however, to assume that because of his political ineffectiveness the Kaiser was politically inconsequential. In domestic affairs, his influence was mostly negative in the sense that his capriciousness and constant meddling interfered with the consistent conduct of government. In foreign affairs, his political impact was even more deleterious. Wilhelm's precipitous shifts in direction and his flamboyant reactive bellicosity alarmed a watching world and contributed directly to Germany's ultimate diplomatic and military isolation. Wilhelm's inability to define a personal self-interest, to decide who he was and what he wanted, found political expression in his inability to determine the self-interest of the nation and to take steps to realize it. In sum, the very psychological incoherence that accounted for the success of the Kaiser's symbolic leadership of the Germans also accounted for his failure as the political leader of his country.

Although we shall never know whether a more psychologically cohesive leader could have created a truly cohesive German national self-interest, it is clear that the Kaiser personified the German nation not only through his effective symbolic leadership but also by virtue of his very political incompetence. As a total personality, in other words, Wilhelm II characterized a nation and a historical epoch. There is a striking psychological and historical parallel between this youthful, energetic emperor whose internal psychic disjointedness prevented him from defining a coherent personal self-interest and the newly formed, dynamic nation whose economic, social, regional, political, and intellectual disjointedness seems to have precluded the definition and realization of a national self-interest. There is a striking psychohistorical fit between an emperor who covered his profound inner disharmony with a layer of flamboyant, provocative, and even bellicose self-aggrandizement and a nation that covered its profound lack of domestic consensus with a foreign policy of *Welt politik*—a policy of flamboyant, provocative, and even bellicose national self-assertion. Both Wilhelm and Germany during his reign sought to escape from internal contradictions with a *Flucht nach vorn,* a "flight to the front." According to a number of thoughtful contemporary observers, the Kaiser as a total personality reflected the "personality" of his countrymen and of his times. Egon Friedell wrote in 1927:

> Wilhelm the Second did in one sense actually fulfill the task of a king completely in that he almost always was the expression of the overwhelming majority of his subjects, the champion and executor of their ideas, the representative of their outlook on life. Most Germans were nothing more than pocket editions, smaller versions, miniature copies of Kaiser Wilhelm.[102]

In his successes and failures, Wilhelm II represented the successes and failures of his countrymen. In their adulation of the Kaiser and in their irritation with him, the Germans were expressing in part their feelings about themselves. As Elisabeth

---

[102]Egon Friedell, *Kulturgeschichte der Neuzeit,* III (Munich: C.H. Beck, 1931), 421.

Fehrenbach has written, "criticism of [Wilhelm's] personal rule was usually in evidence when the fiction of the glorious Kaiser threatened to crumble."[103] On the one hand, Wilhelm was criticized when he failed to live up to the idealized expectations of his subjects—when he was unable to realize their glorified image of themselves and of their country. Wilhelm's shortcomings frustrated the wish of many Germans to be led and represented by a monarch who was omnipresent, omniscient, and omnipotent. On the other hand, as was clearly revealed by the reaction of the Germans to Wilhelm after the war, the Kaiser was most bitterly condemned when he personally manifested those features of his countrymen of which they themselves were most ashamed. Wilhelm was adored when he reflected back an image of German national greatness. He was reviled when he reflected back an image of German national disharmony, ineffectuality, and weakness. In their reactions to the Kaiser, the Germans were on some level reacting to an image of themselves.

It is tempting at this point to speculate about the narcissistic disturbance of the Kaiser as a definition of the narcissistic psychopathology of a nation, of a people, and of an era. Despite the host of psychological and historical problems with such generalizations, Nicolaus Sombart's judgment on the relationship between Wilhelm and the Germans should not simply be dismissed out of hand:

> If one wishes to label Wilhelm II as a psychopath, to charge him with Caesarian madness, this conclusion is only correct insofar as the psychopathological features of the age found precise expression in the figure of the Kaiser. Every society has not only the government it deserves but also the systems of insanity and representative psychopathological figures.[104]

These fascinating and complex issues lie at present on the border of our historical and psychological knowledge. What can be said with confidence today only echoes the voices from Wilhelm's own time, the voices of Walter Rathenau and Friedrich Naumann quoted at the outset of this chapter. Wilhelmine Germany could hardly have had a more fitting Kaiser than Wilhelm II. Both as a leader and as a man, Wilhelm II was indeed the "mirror image" of his nation. Herein lies his principal historical significance.

Acknowledgments This essay owes its inspiration and many of its conclusions to a lengthy and intense collaboration with an experienced psychoanalyst, Dr. Nathaniel London, and to the Kaiser Colloquium, a gathering of Kaiser Wilhelm II scholars on the island of Corfu in September 1979. The spirit of that meeting on Corfu is captured in an article on the Kaiser Colloquium by Jost Nolte in *Die Zeit Magazin* of October 26, 1979, titled "Der Kaiser, der em Spiegel seines Volkes war" (a title very similar to that of this chapter) and by the book *Kaiser Wilhelm II: New Interpretations* edited by John C. G. Röhl and Nicolaus Sombart (Cambridge, 1982), which contains the papers presented on Corfu. To Dr. London and the members of the Kaiser Colloquium this chapter is affectionately and gratefully dedicated. I also want to thank Otto Pflanze, Lamar Cecil, and Robert G. L. Waite for their help in preparing this article for publication, as well as the fund which provided for the typing of this article and the Department of Psychiatry of Michael Reese Hospital and Medical Center for help provided in preparation of this manuscript.

---

[103] Fehrenbach, "Images of Kaiserdom," 282.

[104] Sombart, "Der letzte Kaiser."

Chapter 6
Osama Bin Laden: The Man and the Myth

Bruce B. Lawrence

It was Fall 2006, less than five years ago. George Bush was President of the USA. The war on terror was full throttle forward. The October issue of *US News & World Report* had the following insert box in its "Washington Whispers" Section:

> There has been a lot of recent talk about whether President Bush tried as hard as President Clinton to nail OBL. That got us wondering how bad the prez wants the terrorist. Real bad, it seems. One key insider says that Bush is nearly obsessed with "OBL" as he's called. "He's very taken with the hunt, and it is very much a priority on his mind," says terrorism adviser Frances Townsend. "He has an extraordinary memory for detail. He has an extraordinary ability to recall particular details, plots, and individuals, to ask questions about it. And I will tell you that he asks very specific questions on the hunt for bin Laden on a regular basis."[1]

Contrast former President Bush's obsession to hunt down OBL, with this sober assessment of al-Qaeda: "Al-Qaeda," writes British insider Paul Grieve, "is now an all-consuming idea, a Salafi rallying cry across the Muslim world that will never be suppressed. Al-Qaeda is a franchise, and not the worldwide organization sought by the American government as an ideological opponent to replace communism... Global events, especially the running sore of Iraq, have demonstrated that this phantom will never be destroyed, even if the personal inspiration of Osama bin Laden or OBL were to be eliminated."[2]

As of early May 2011 OBL is no longer an active agent of terror. He was killed in a US military operation as effective as it was stealthy. Now that President Obama has succeeded in doing what neither President Clinton nor President Bush could do – kill Osama bin Laden, not in Tora Bora or the Hindu Kush but in a military town near the Pakistani capital, Islamabad, what can we say and how must we reckon with OBL as an historical figure? Is OBL now reduced to a mere myth, or does he remain

---

B.B. Lawrence (✉)
Duke University, Durham NC, USA
e-mail: bruce.bbl@gmail.com

[1] *US News & World Report*, 9 Oct 06:16.

[2] Paul Grieve, *A Brief Guide to Islam – History, Faith & Politics* (London: Running Press, 2006): 314.

C.B. Strozier et al. (eds.), *The Leader*, 2nd ed., DOI 10.1007/978-1-4419-8387-9_6,
© Springer Science+Business Media, LLC 2011

a lodestone of symbolic hope and enduring resistance for future jihadis? These are the questions we will attempt to answer in the essay that follows.

The Man

Let us examine the first three decades of his life. From his birth into a wealthy Yemeni-Saudi family to his mediocre career as an engineering student to his early adventures with Muslim radicals, Osama Bin Laden was not an exceptional figure. But in the 1980 s he embraced the Afghan resistance, framed as a defensive struggle, or jihad, against Soviet invaders. Several Saudis, and the American government, supported him at this time. In a 2005 interview, Prince Turki al-Faisal, former Saudi ambassador to the USA, who had met OBL five times during the '80s, described him as "a very shy person, very self-effacing, extremely sparse in his words and generally a do-gooder, someone who brought financial and medical and other support to the Afghan mujahidin."[3] OBL expected to play a role in the Saudi response to Saddam Hussein's invasion of Kuwait in 1990, but he was rebuffed. He then moved to Sudan, where he spent nearly five years before returning to Afghanistan in 1996. In that year, through a juridical decree known as the Ladinese Epistle, he became a more widely regarded public figure. Some Saudis welcomed his attack on the continuing American presence in the peninsula, but few paid much attention to the subsequent decree issued as a joint statement under the World Islamic Front. In 1998 the bombings of American embassies in Kenya and Tanzania actually gave him a negative image, since many of those killed were Muslims. But because they were followed by retaliatory American bombings, OBL was spared further criticism. Indeed, he turned the American bombings to his advantage since many Muslims felt that the attacks had been indiscriminate. No one believed that he would be able to execute a 'counter-attack' on the magnitude of 9/11. Once again, many in the Muslim world did not approve of this attack, but in the aftermath of further American military strikes, this time against Afghanistan and Iraq, OBL's stature as the symbol of resistance to American hegemony and Arab perfidy grew, and it was enhanced by media coverage of his every word, at least until the election of President Obama and the subsequent political move to deemphasize 'the war on terror'.

Yet till May 2011 OBL persisted as a complex, even wily character. Like a sphinx or a riddle, OBL defied easy description, and eluded procrustean labels. The more written about him, it seems, the less he was understood. He circulated beneath the radar screen of even the most dogged researcher and the most adroit analyst, and continues to do so in the flurry of commentaries churned out since the successful Navy Seal attack in Abbottabad on 2 May 2011. A leading British journalist once depicted him as "the standard bearer for the radical extremist fringe of the

---

[3]"New Saud in the House", interview with Deborah Solomon, *The New York Times Magazine* August 28, 2005,11.

broad movement that is modern Islamic militancy." In other words, Bin Laden the man was inseparable from Bin Laden the ideologue, and the ideology he projected, according to this same journalist, was "a debased, violent, nihilistic and anti-rational millenarianism".[4]

For the general public two labels seemed to stick: fundamentalist and terrorist. Each located OBL in a generic profile with identifiable antecedents and cohorts. As a fundamentalist, he elided with other text-riveted Islamic activists, from the Pakistani Mawdudi to the Egyptian Qutb to the Sudanese Turabi. As a terrorist, he joined other kill- and-destroy ideologues, religious and secular, whether from the Middle East (Palestine, Israel and Lebanon) or from Europe (Ireland, France, Italy, Germany and Russia).

The two labels conflated in the persona of OBL. He was a Qur'an quoting, gun toting warrior defending a violated sacred domain, the super-nation of Islam, against both vile infidels (with the US at the head of the list) and traitorous apostates (including the Muslim leaders of Jordan, Syria, Palestine, Pakistan, the Gulf states and, of course, Saudi Arabia). But do the labels of terrorist and fundamentalist go any further toward understanding him than qualifiers such as 'debased, violent, nihilistic and anti-rational'?

Was he a fundamentalist? Yes, if one reckons that he was guided by scriptural mandates which he felt have but one, valid interpretation and one, necessary application. By his own reckoning, however, a fundamentalist was simply a true believer, one who seamlessly invokes God, the Book and the Prophet on his own behalf. 'Fundamentalist' may help to describe him to outsiders, but it does not help to understand him from his own worldview or that of his followers. Indeed, OBL fit better into the binary mindset of an apocalyticist, well described in a recent book by Charles Strozier et al.[5]

Was he a terrorist? Yes, if one considers how he attracted a cadre of likeminded dissidents, at once educated in technical skills and angry at the asymmetry of power, with the will and the means to wreak havoc by destroying urban structures and killing non-combatants on a massive scale. To many Western observers, OBL was the quintessential terrorist, but to non-Western others, he loomed as a valiant defender of the Islamic super-nation, one who assessed the enemy accurately: it was "the Zio-Crusader alliance", at once intrusive, disruptive and ruthless in its attack on the Islamic super-nation. From his perspective, he was not a terrorist seeking a target, but a leader avenging his victimized community. 'Our' terrorist becomes 'their' freedom fighter, so terrorist, like fundamentalist, does not help to understand OBL.[6]

---

[4]Jason Burke. *Al-Qaeda: The True Story of Radical Islam*, xxiii-xxiv.

[5]Charles B. Strozier et al., *The Fundamentalist Mindset: Psychological Perspectives on Religion, Violence, and History* (New York: Oxford University Press, 2010).

[6]Beyond this oft-repeated contrast of opposites, there is the simple definition offered by Louise Richardson: "Terrorism simply means deliberately and violently targeting civilians for political purposes". Louise Richardson, *What Terrorists Want: Understanding the Enemy, Containing the Threat* (New York: Random House 2007), 4. Yet as Richardson herself goes on to note, it

One label alone seems to take the measure of the man, and to offer some insight into his public persona as well as his enduring appeal. He was a polemicist – indeed, a dogged, razor-edged polemicist advocating an anti-imperial ideology. OBL was committed to seeing and arguing and defending a single, inevitable outcome to the current struggle between faith and unbelief: the world order as we now know it must come to a violent end, until and unless imperialists are able to reform, not just reform but retreat from Muslim territory that they now occupy. Such full-scale reform was not only an unlikely prospect, it was so wild and grandiose as to be preposterous, redoubling OBL in his commitment to pursue his polemical cause with a laser-like intensity.

Since 9/11/2001 and until 5/2/2011, he eluded capture. As recently as January 2010, he continued to project himself through strategic pronouncements recorded on videotapes, and then delivered to stations that broadcast them to diverse audiences.[7] It was the same message, deftly packaged to appeal to Muslims across a broad spectrum. There are five genres of public political discourse that he negotiated: the declaration, the juridical decree, the public lecture, the written reminder, and the epistle. OBL was not concerned to obey the rules of each genre. Instead, it was his ability to "maneuver between these genres which enabled Bin Laden to legitimate himself in relation to different traditions of political authority."[8] It was this uncanny skill at manipulating the expectations of his audience that set OBL apart from other polemicists who advocated defiant struggle, or jihad, in the name of Islam. His decrees were more formulaic and general in tone, while the declarations and epistles addressed specific groups, explaining what he intended to do - or more often, how he hoped to motivate others to act on his behalf. Muslims, especially Arabic speaking Muslims, were his primary but not his sole audience. He also refined his message in addressing Europeans as well as Americans. He resorted to numerous rhetorical strategies, including a slippage of language and a shift of registers that enshrouded rather than illumined the intent of his message. Indeed, OBL's vivid presence existed in a kind of virtual ether that served his heroic status. He was immanent, known but not seen, felt but not touched. His expulsion from Afghanistan after 9/11 and his mysterious but miraculous survival actually increased his majesty and power to influence others, not in operational terms, but as inspiration, which is of course exactly how Al-Qaeda has worked in local cells throughout a networked information circuit. In OBL's view, it was the leadership style of God that has been

---

is reversible, and it also can have government, intelligence and military as well as civilian targets. Most analysts, even the most astute, such as Marc Sageman, focus on terrorists or terror networks rather than terrorism per se. See also Marc Sageman, *Understanding Terror Networks* (Philadelphia: University of Pennsylvania Press, 2004).

[7] See the html: http://www.dailymail.co.uk/news/worldnews/article-1245650/Osama-Bin-Laden-tape-warns-Barack-Obama, with the racy title "From Osama to Obama". We now know that it was his reliance on courier service to provide him information, and also to deliver his messages to the world, that finally allowed the US Intelligence Services to track him down to his latest, and last, hide out, in the Abbottabad compound, where he was killed on 2 May 2011.

[8] W. Flagg Miller, "On 'The Summit of the Hindu Kush': Osama Bin Laden's 1996 Declaration of War Reconsidered", unpublished talk delivered at University of Michigan in March 2005. Cited by permission of the author.

forced upon him by circumstance but perfectly suited to his remote, quiet, serene, religious self.[9]

The inverse side to OBL's anti-imperial polemics was its impracticality as a pragmatic strategy. On the one hand, he claimed to be directing his followers to attain immediate goals, yet he announced a future ideal that has no precedent. Indeed, because it was apocalyptic and imagined an idealized past projected forward into a mythical future, it could not have either a timetable or a concrete outcome.[10] The power of his speech derived in part from his deployment of the empty signifier. He appealed to a perfectly rational, Arab anti-imperialism, yet he deftly concealed the lack of any pragmatic plan of action within an Islamist rhetoric. He quoted the Qur'an repeatedly but always piecemeal and selectively. Pursuing what Emmanuel Sivan terms a strategy of selected retrieval, he overlooked the norms and values of Islam, such as generosity, hospitality and peace, which have been central to the Qur'an, Islamic civilization and current Muslim societies.[11]

The larger purpose of this essay is to make sense of OBL in terms of his family. This close reading of his genealogy becomes even more important as speculation mounts about his legacy following the May 2011 successful attack on his Abbottabad compound, which not only resulted in his death but also yielded a large cache of intelligence re both OBL and al-Qaeda. As valuable as may be the new treasure trove of information, it is no substitute for sustained attention to the oddities of OBL's birth and early family life. His father, Muhammad bin Laden, wasn't just a wealthy Yemeni contractor who made his fortune in KSA in the first years of the Aramco-KSA relationship that began in late '30s and gave Saudi ruling elites a new window of opportunity, both for themselves and for the kingdom. Instead, he was one of the inner circle of King Abdul Aziz. Abdul Aziz was shrewd enough to deal almost entirely in ready cash, rather than institutional banking structures, but he also had to trust others to do what neither he nor either Saudis could do. The one group of Arabs that provided the most consistent labor pool came from south of the border: Yemenis from the Hadhramaut region comprised one of the poorest of Saudi Arabia's southern neighbors. But none of those Hadhramaut Yemenis did as well as

---

[9]See Sageman, *Understanding Terror Networks*, 173. OBL seems to be "the opposite of a narcissist. He is publicly self-effacing and seems content to relinquish control of an organization (which would have implied a hierarchial structure) for the sake of efficacy. He shows his disapproval not by killing his potential rivals but simply by withdrawing funds from them until they come back to his fold. This type of leadership is rare and may well account for the robustness of the global Salafi jihad, its ability to respond to changing conditions, and its widespread appeal to (some) Muslim youths." Michael Scheuer has similarly accented OBL's flexibility and his ability to survive against all odds as major measures of his heroic stature. "As each year passes," wrote Scheuer just months before May 2011, "his status as a contemporary Islamic hero grows, as does the Saladin-like legend he will eventually leave in the annals of Islam's history." (Michael Scheuer, *Osama bin Laden* (New York: Oxford University Press, 2011): 133.

[10]See Strozier, *The Fundamentalist Mindset*, for elaboration of this mindset as a psychological reflex.

[11]Emmanuel Sivan, "The Enclave Culture" in Martin Marty and Scott Appleby, eds., *Fundamentalism Comprehended* (Chicago: University of Chicago Press, 1995):11–68.

Bin Laden's father, Mohammed. He was an illiterate immigrant who was working as a bricklayer and jack of all trades even before oil was discovered. He observed well the double facet of Saudi elites: they did not like to work with their hands, but they needed, and remunerated, those who did. Mohammed bin Laden became one of Abdul Aziz's closest advisors from the early 1930s when he started his own construction company. He was awarded major contracts for internal road construction. It was construction that linked the port city of Jeddah to the Prophet's second home, Medina, and also linked Jeddah to the mountain resort of Taif.

Mohammed succeeded in earning the King's trust because of his hard work, his efficiency and, above all, his loyalty. He became so wealthy that he was able to marry not one, two, three or four wives but multiple wives. He would divorce one of the canonical four before marrying another in her stead, as was the case with Alia Ghanem, OBL's mother. She was from a working class Syrian family. Mohammed had met her in Latakia in 1956, and Osama was born the next year. He became the 17th of the 24 sons whom Mohammed sired. Mohammed had three 'permanent' wives, all of them Saudis, and by them he produced the sons who became, and remain, the successors to his lucrative and far flung family business.

Mohammed left Alia Ghanem soon after Osama was born, but he did not abandon her. She, like all of his wives or concubines, was provided with a fine home, allowances, and opportunities for remarriage after he had divorced or ceased to be interested in them. In Alia Ghanem's case, she remarried another Yemeni from the Hadhramaut, Mohammed al-Attas. By him she had three more sons and a daughter. It was Mohammed who saw that Alia was introduced to her new husband, and also that she continued to have a salaried position in the bin Laden construction firm.[12]

OBL's own account of his life glosses his Yemeni origins at the same time that he emphasizes his intimate connection to the spiritual lifeline of KSA. It is provided in the Nida'ul Islam interview of October 1996.[13] It concludes with this phrase:

> I studied economics at Jeddah University and I began working in my father's company and on roads from an early age, even though my father passed away when I was 10.

The death of his father meant that the vast family business had to be taken up by siblings, and two of the oldest, Salem and Baker, succeeded their father while also maintaining occasional ties with their other half-brothers, including Osama. But he spent most of his time with his mother. It was she who selected a first cousin from Syria as his first wife. Osama married Najwa when he was but 17 (in 1974) and she 14 years old. By her he had 11 children. After marriage, he remained attached to his

---

[12] Both Lawrence Wright and Steve Coll hint at the impact that an absent yet idealized father had on the young OBL. See Lawrence Wright, *The Looming Tower – Al-Qaeda and the Road to 9/11*(New York: Knopf, 2006), 71–74, and Steve Coll, *The Bin Ladens – The Story of a Family and Its Fortune* (London: Allen Lane, 2008), 137–140.

[13] This and all subsequent references are to Bruce B. Lawrence, ed., *Messages to the World: The Statements of Osama Bin Laden* (London & New York: Verso, November 2005). Hereafter abbreviated as MW, it is the first comprehensive collection of interviews, pronouncements, and legal directives made by the now deceased Saudi fugitive/terrorist/global jihadist. The current reference is to MW # 4.

mother. He stayed in Jeddah and went to university there. A mediocre business student at King Abdul Aziz University, he pursued work with the family construction firm and never finally graduated from the university.

By his mid-20s he had already become interested in Muslim causes abroad - Afghanistan in 1979, and then in the local Mecca mosque incident of 1979. OBL never seemed to address directly the question of how to mediate the fine line between corrupt Muslims and corrupt infidels. That has been the issue bedeviling all strict Wahhabis,[14] yet it did not greatly exercise the young OBL in his pursuit of "truth". Though he failed as an engineering student, he imbibed from his university experience a commitment to the Wahhabi-Salafi model of Islamic rules. He also achieved a range of engagement with traditional Arabic literature, Qur'an and tradition but also commentaries and poetry, that was uncharacteristic of most engineering students.

Few of his early associates saw Osama as a potential leader, most suspecting him of indirect influence through backdoor funding of anti-regime activities. Yet he generated an appeal precisely because he did not parade grasp of Qur'anic subtleties that marked either a Wahhabi scholar from Medina/Mecca or an Azhari scholar from Egypt. He adopted instead an easeful reference to the Qur'an as though it were a book of day-to-day guidance, a place where even the illiterate, like OBL's father, could function as both pious Muslims and advocates of radical change within the world they uneasily inhabited with other, less avid believers.

OBL was as much a risk taker as his father. He understood the notion of zeitgeist, grasping the spirit of a time then committing oneself to challenging and changing how others lived. Mohammed was content with making his own fortune in the shadow of untold affluence for newly petro-rich Saudis, while Osama saw himself as coming out of the shadow of docile Muslim believers within a West dominated world order and remaking a new world through global jihad in the name of "revenge". His "father" was both MBL and the Abraham of lore, a prophet-like figure who confronted his own society in the name of a higher principle linked to a clearer, overriding insight into the Great One, the Creator and Terminator of all life. Like his forefathers, OBL sensed how the tide of affairs – commercial, political and also religious – was changing. While his father had served and bested the royal family and Saudi elites, his son took on a larger, less defined cohort: wannabe resisters/fighters defending Islam against their religious foes, those who invaded, occupied and destroyed the sacred lands of the Islamic supernation. One might surmise that OBL not only admired his father but also wanted to best him. Beyond his father there was only the distant Almighty, God Almighty, to confront, and that confrontation was deferred till Judgment Day.

OBL projected himself as genuinely humble and submissive, almost feminine and soft in his endeavor to be a true servant of God Almighty, and follower of His

---

[14]See Vincent Olivetti, *Terror's Source: The Ideology of Wahhabi-Salafism and its Consequences*: 21–48. Despite the overgeneralizations of the author, the frame of his analysis is correct, his insights helpful.

Prophet Muhammad. Time and again in his speeches, he removed himself from central stage except as an observer or arbiter or visionary. But his very self-effacement was at the same time an act of self-promotion, the subtlest of ways to project his own worldview as "Islamic truth" no matter what the consequences for others, whether family members or fellow believers. The humility, in other words, was strategic. Because it also fit his personality, he could pull it off without appearing inauthentic— a trait crucially important for any successful leader. Impressed by his father's ability to will his way to great fortune, he saw his own fortune to be in the way of jihad, attracting other 'Muslim' professionals beyond the allure of prosperity, professionalism, and familial comfort.

OBL embraced a militant anti-imperial view of the Arab/Muslim world at the same time that he became a religious zealot. A dissident from his homeland, a renegade in his faith community, a terrorist in the eyes of his enemies, he became an anti-imperial polemicist intent on seeking his fortune through religious ardor and rhetorical deftness.

The one constant element in his outlook was the deep conviction that a crossroads had been reached in the modern world, that two resolute and irreducible enemy camps had taken shape, that their war would be ongoing, that only one could prevail, that Islam was destined to be first the victim, then the victor in a protracted, divinely refereed contest.

In both forms of the defining Ladenese epistle of August 1996,[15] the theme of two opposing camps comes up again and again. One is the Zionist-American Crusaders. In varying forms, this phrase becomes a trope for everything that is unbalanced, oppressive and wrong between West and East, between the US and the Muslim world. It is they who are responsible for "the attacks and massacres committed against Muslims everywhere, the latest and most serious of which – the greatest disaster to befall the Muslims since the death of the Prophet Muhammad – is the occupation of the Land of the Two Holy Sanctuaries, cornerstone of the Islamic world, place of revelation, source of the Prophetic mission, and home of the Noble Ka'ba where Muslims direct their prayers."

That occupation, of course, was the 1990-91 US-led intervention to evict Saddam Hussein from Kuwait and to retain the independence of KSA (but to maintain the Saudi royal family as leaders of KSA and the king as "Protector of the Two Holy Places"). But more than the shame of Muslims and the profanation of Islamic holy places resulted from the Second Gulf war. There was also the systematic harassing and often the outright murder of some leading Muslim voices:

> They killed the holy warrior Sheikh 'Abdallah 'Azzam, they arrested Sheikh Ahmed Yassin at the scene of the Prophet's night journey to the seven heavens, and they killed the holy warrior Sheikh 'Omar 'Abd al-Rahman in America, as well as arresting – on the advice of America – a large number of scholars, preachers and the youth in the Land of the Two Holy Sanctuaries. The most prominent of these were Sheikh Suleiman al-'Auda and Sheikh Safar al-Hawali and their brothers."

---

[15] See MW # 3.

It was Suleiman al-'Auda, the dean of a major Islamic college in Mecca, who had signaled back in September 1990 that the real infidels were internal, that they had to be fought and defeated before the external enemy – the West, including the US and Israel – had to be confronted. He had been removed from his post, and arrested, along with another strident academic opponent of the ruling family, Safar al-Hawali, a teacher at the major Islamic university in Riyadh.

What these passages, and others like them, illustrate is the extent to which OBL remained a product of the environment of KSA during the second half of the twentieth century but especially during its final, critical decade. The unspoken but crucial factor is the culture of labor in KSA: do not do what you can employ others to do, and pay them not just for their labor but also for their loyalty. The key element of trust pervaded all of MBL's dealings with King 'Abd al-'Aziz and his successors, and the same was true for OBL: he paid others, first in Afghanistan, then in Sudan, then back in Afghanistan, but he paid them for loyalty as well as for labor. Their loyalty had a double coin: it required dedication and efficiency.

But equally important was how his own familial dispossession left him in a relationship of anxiety vis-à-vis his homeland. One might even speculate that his banishment from his original homeland contributed to his radicalism. He suffered in exile and yearned always to be home; the longer he was forced to remain abroad and unable to return to Arabia, the more committed he became to violence and destruction, denying others the safety of their homeland.

The breaking point for OBL was not the US invasion of Lebanon in 1982. That only seemed so in retrospect. What really mattered was 1990-91. After the glow of having defeated the Soviet forces in Afghanistan, why were Saudi elites unwilling to allow him to confront the atheist Saddam once he had invaded Kuwait and threatened to take oilfields in eastern Saudi Arabia? Their weakness led to their betrayal of him, a near native son. Saudi elites were unable to defend themselves except through foreign help. Just as they had minimal stake in creating a petro-dollar kingdom of modern splendor hallowed, and also concealed, by an ethos of ascetic piety, so they had almost no ability to repel a foreign invasion apart from the help of foreign others, whether paid mercenaries like the Pakistanis, or allies intervening on their behalf, as with British and Americans in the First Gulf War.

OBL's disgust for the Saudi elite fueled his determination to oppose them and the entire Saud family. He became a tireless yet adaptive polemicist, first against the Saudis and then against their American allies and then finally against the Zio-Crusader alliance that fuels incessant warfare in the name of religion. He took his cue from a particular, but also a peculiar, reading of scripture. He believed that the end time was near because Islam was threatened with annihilation and must fight to preserve its very existence. Islam could not, and would not, survive in the world of the 21st century unless Muslims united in defense of their faith. He reckoned the present conflict to be nothing less than the Third World War.[16] It was an ongoing

---

[16] See below MW Fragment # 2 from 27.12.2004.

war – at once necessary and ceaseless - between two combatants, the evil other, who is Western, and the good self, who is Muslim.

By OBL's calculus, the war has only just begun. Nor will it end soon. It is a war to be fought not in days, weeks, months or years but over decades, engaging generations to come. This grand scale war is not just the Third World War but also the final war of humanity. It has a plan that goes beyond the intention or the deed of enemy combatants. It is divinely sanctioned; God will decide its outcome. Muslims, if they are loyal to God as defenders of the faith, and if they persist as combatants on behalf of global jihad, will win.

But what does victory mean? It is never hinted at, much less spelled out. The Islamic supernation is constantly invoked but as an empty signifier. Its vagueness reflects, even as it redirects, its age-old sanctity. The absence of detail is deliberate, to magnify its appeal by mobilizing the greatest number in a cause for which the outcome can never be specified, but where the implication is that the world as we know it will end. It remained the leitmotif of OBL as an apocalyptic fighter in exile; it guided him from his earliest pronouncement on 29 December 1994 to his pronouncement one decade later on 27 December 2004. Only through this lens, the lens of the arch-apocalypticist who drew on scriptural fundamentals and exercises terror in the name of God, can we hope to understand him.

Mediating the Cosmic Warrior

There is probably no aspect of OBL's profile that is more critical nor less understood than his use of the media, especially *al- Quds al-'Arabi* and al-Jazeera. One episode from late 2003 illustrates how intertwined were the interests of the Saudi dissident and the major Arabic language media. On 10 December 2003 the London-based Arabic daily *Al-Quds Al-Arabi* reported that Al-Qa'ida, headed by Osama bin Laden, "is gearing up for a big operation to coincide with Eid Al-Adha [February 2, 2004]... a new videotape of bin Laden will be circulated shortly before the holiday... it will surface in conjunction with 'a great event that will shake the region,' and it will be broadcast by *Al-Jazeera* television.' The source explained that al-Qa'ida had an agreement with *Al-Jazeera* by which it was committed to broadcast any videotape that the Sahab Institute provides about Al-Qa'ida. He pointed out that the Institute would sever its relations with the station if it refused to broadcast a videotape, and reiterated that "the station is obligated to broadcast any videotape we send to it."[17]

In the several messages included in my collection of Bin Laden's writings, the relationship of OBL to al-Jazeera proves to be almost as important as his decision to wage jihad. Prior to December 1998, when the US and Britain launched an attack on

---

[17]See the (too) brief reference to Al-Sahab in Hugh Miles, *Al-Jazeera: How Arab TV News Challenged the World* (London:Abacus, 2005), 180. Other sources are equally dismissive or neglectful of this crucial conduit to the OBL media strategy.

Iraq, called Operation Desert Fox, al-Jazeera had been a local satellite news service. Founded in February 1996 by the Emir of Qatar, its goal was to promote freedom of information among Arabic speaking citizens of the Gulf and its neighbours. In 1998, the Baghdad office got the big break when they filmed the missiles launched against Iraq from British and American airplanes. OBL gave an interview that was broadcast on al-Jazeera in December[18] and he became an instant international attraction. So significant was the impact of this interview that nine days after 11 Sept 2001 it was rerun by al-Jazeera. Accompanying the 90-minute video were pictures of OBL firing a gun. The message, in images as well as in words, was: the war is religious, the war is between aggressive crusaders and defensive believers, and Muslims have a stark choice, either to side with the infidel oppressors or to support the beleaguered but pure and resolute Muslim defenders.

The same message was articulated in all OBL's subsequent epistles that were broadcast via al-Jazeera. Each was tailored to the audience whom he addressed. Jason Burke observed that "bin Laden seemed to show an incredible instinctive grasp of modern marketing techniques."[19] Flagg Miller goes further, explaining why the genre of epistles may be one of the best marketing techniques for OBL's message. "Epistles became a defining medium of eloquence in the 9th-century Abbasid court of Baghdad. In epistles colorful pleasantries, competitive verbal jousts, and political wrangling are all of a piece. Bin Laden deploys the genre with his own rhetorical flourishes. As pious public lecturer, militant *jihadist*, and now enfranchised literate scribe, Bin Laden excoriates ruling Saudi leaders for corruption, fiscal mismanagement, human rights abuses, and especially for their alliance with 'American Crusader forces' since the Gulf War of 1990. Such accusations gain religious significance for Bin Laden as apostasy (*shirk*) insofar as Saudi leaders are represented as recurring to man-made state law instead of to true Islamic law (*shari'a*), the latter of which remains confidently underspecified. Overall, the pious tenor of Bin Laden's epistle is consistently maintained as an act of remembrance (*dhikr*), so central to Islam's message that mankind is essentially forgetful, and is thus in need of constant reminding."[20] Indeed, the epistles function as sermons, delivered from on high, and projected globally in ways that enhance OBL's charismatic stature.

His epistles to the Iraqis were elaborated with scriptural and historical citations and also with poetic verses, some from his own pen. His epistle to the Afghans flowed with cascades of Qur'anic citations as he reminded them of his struggle on their behalf against the Soviets. His letter to the Americans and Europeans, by contrast, contained an unadorned accusation: they were blindly following leaders who were dooming them to an endless war of attrition. In every instance, he was an

---

[18] See MW # 7.

[19] Burke, *Al-Qaeda*: 175.

[20] W. Flagg Miller, "On 'The Summit of the Hindu Kush': Osama Bin Laden's 1996 Declaration of War Reconsidered", unpublished talk delivered at University of Michigan in March 2005. Cited by permission of the author.

anti-imperial polemicist on behalf of global jihad, shaping the message to reach the audience.

In the sermon he delivered in 2003 on the holiest day in the Islamic calendar, Id al-Adha, he combines elements from all his letters and declarations to address Muslims around the world. He talks to individuals directly, commending each one's worthiness to participate in global jihad and accusing their leaders of criminal corruption. Like the first encounters that the 7th century Arabs had with unbelieving Persians, the current jihad pits absolute good against absolute evil. Psychologically speaking, it is as though OBL is charged with a paranoid certainty about the end time, the apocalyptic moment in which all are living but only he, and the guided warriors from al-Qa'ida, understand fully. Numerous Qur'anic citations and prophetic traditions weave his fervent appeal to believers to take up arms against the US, UK, Israel and their collaborators in the Arab world. Like the Prophet Muhammad's followers, his Muslim armies will prevail. They have a recent history of victories over the superpowers. Who was it that defeated the Soviet Union in Afghanistan and the Russians in Chechnya if not the Afghan-Arab mujahidin? Was it not they who conquered the Americans in Lebanon, Somalia, Aden, Riyadh, Khobar, East Africa, at home and, most recently, in Afghanistan? The myth of American democracy and freedom has been shattered, thanks be to God! And then, remarkably, he concludes with his own poem in which he vows to fight until he is granted martyrdom. Those who join his jihad and are martyred will be with him forever. He concludes his sermon in the accustomed way by praising God.

Alas, due to the dizzying shifts of technology in the Information Age, one loses all sense of just how dramatic are OBL's moves as a risk taker. "Bin Laden's bald comparisons between hallowed personages of early Islamic history and contemporary actors and events," explains one analyst, "subject him to decided risks. Not only does he hazard alienating Muslim listeners by compromising the unique role that the Prophet played in Islam; he also risks becoming a poor historian, one whose antiquarian zeal fails to re-connect narrated events with present concerns. It is precisely here that Bin Laden adopts an entirely new tactic, one that moves him from his role as pious public lecturer to the roles of tribesman, poet, and ultimately cosmic warrior. In the midst of this set of transformations, the temporal distinctions of 'then' and 'now' become entirely blurred, and listeners are invited, through the most sonorous and impassioned portions of the cassette, to mobilize as eternal holy combatants."[21] The oracle who speaks has recast himself as a cosmic warrior, auguring both the end time and its 'certain' outcome.

If the evidence so far presented suggests that OBL not only mastered modern media but was also its primary beneficiary, another lesson needs to be added. No one should assume that OBL benefited from his use of the media in general and al-Jazeera in particular without some cost to his project. The channel of influence and of risk taking was two way. OBL advocated the maximal response to imperialism.

---

[21] Ibid.

He constantly called on sacrifice, especially of youths through martyrdom for a greater cause, yet he gave no hint of a future frame beyond the shibboleth 'Islamic state' or 'rule of God on earth'. The emptiness of his political vision was made clear in the Taysir Alluni interview in October 2001 (MW # 11), when he declared that jihad will continue till "we meet God and get His blessing!" Yet earlier, in the Ladenese Epistle of August 1996 (MW # 3), he had seemed to call for a deferral of apocalyptic rewards, insisting on the value of oil revenues for a near term Islamic State:

> I would like here to alert my brothers, the Mujahidin, the sons of the nation, to protect this (oil) wealth and not to include it in the battle as it is a great Islamic wealth and a large economical power essential for the soon to be established Islamic state, by the grace and permission of God.

Still later in his second letter to the Iraqi people (11 Feb 03; MW #18), he calls again for establish(ing) the rule of God on earth, but only through incessant warfare against multiple enemies, with no agenda for a structure or network that will replace the current world system.

While there are many ways to connect OBL to the early generation of Islam, perhaps the crucial move is to see how he contrasts the perfection of early Islam with the desecration of the 21st century. In the same way that former President Bush saw freedom and democracy as standards of global virtue, projecting both holistic soundness and indivisible oneness for 'the axis of good', so OBL saw sacrifice and war as the dual emblems of early Islam that persist till today as the axis of hope for all committed Muslims who recognize the seriousness of the moment. Yet it is a hope that can never be realized under the current world order because all are living in an end time of total crisis. There is no rush to restore the Caliphate, nor to remake the Ottoman Empire in the pre-WWI image of a pan-Islamic Muslim polity. No, the ultimate criterion is "meeting God and getting his blessing". That is a deferred hope, one that will not be achieved in this world during the lifetime of Muslim martyrs but soon for all humankind in the terrible reckoning that God Almighty has prepared.

The great unaccounted for in this scenario are those Muslims who still consider themselves custodians of the faith and followers of the Prophet yet do **not** see perpetual warfare in the name of jihad as the only measure of Islamic loyalty. Instead of opposing perfections, they try to see the will of God in this age through different instruments, affirming the current world order, at once trying to maximize its benefits while curbing its excesses. They need more than scriptural dictates, poetic balm or binary shibboleths to chart their everyday life, whether as individuals or as collective members of local communities, nation-states and the world at large. For them, OBL's legacy will be one of deviance and damage rather than persistence and profit in the cause of Islam. The world is not coming to an end, and other means have to be found to advance Islamic principles and the well being of the Muslim supernation (*ummah*).

The Future

In the aftermath of his May 2011 death, there are two opposite resources for understanding OBL's future legacy: polls and videogames. Most pollsters believe that to understand Bin Laden is not to approve him or to support al-Qaeda but rather, to fathom the depths of a worldview that produced him and that continues to generate support for al-Qaeda in some quarters of the Arab/Muslim world. The June 2005 survey conducted by the Pew Charitable Trusts was undertaken as part of a new national project to survey global attitudes toward the US and also US foreign policy. The Pew Trust Global Attitudes survey found that while Muslims are worried about consequences for them of the war on terror, a surprising number still had confidence about OBL in world affairs, but when this same survey was conducted five years later, in 2010, the results were drastically different. Two cases may be cited to show the precipitous decline of OBL's stature as a world leader. In Jordan his ratings fell from 61% approval to 14%, while in Pakistan the fall was from 52% to 18%.[22]

Yet there is another gauge of his legacy, and it comes from Genghis Khan. Genghis Khan understood that military conquest brought limited gains: while you may defeat an enemy with superior tactics and weapons, you can conquer a nation only by conquering the hearts of its people. If the war of weapons, launched against Afghanistan and Iraq, is to succeed, there must also be a war of words where the options are clear, the stakes known, and the attraction of Western ideals – democracy and prosperity - compelling. In that decisive war, neither Afghanistan nor Iraq will be the ultimate theatres for measuring the success or failure of al-Qaeda, much less the final legacy of Bin Laden. There must be a reckoning with the leitmotif that guides Bin Laden and projects his image as charisma for some, cataclysm for others. And it must address the challenge thrown down by OBL in all his addresses, but especially the 14 February 2003 Feast of Sacrifice sermon:[23]

> America is a great power possessed of tremendous military might and a wide-ranging economy, but all this is built upon an unstable foundation which can be targeted, with special attention to its obvious weak spots. If it [America] is hit in one hundredth of those spots, God willing, it will stumble, wither away and relinquish world leadership and its oppression.

The strategies of American and Allied military forces will have to reckon with the symbolic power of words and deeds in the Information Age. The conduits of instant information and multiple images come not just through the Internet but also through videogames. In the same way that the Christian right has mobilized and marshalled young people to support its apocalyptic vision through Crusader videogames, so Islamic 'fun' has now taken a commercial turn towards videogames where the images are equally violent but the outcome differs. There are videogames

---

[22]http://pewglobal.org/reports/pdf/247.pdf, a survey of sixteen nations, released on 23 June 2005, and then the sequel from 2011: http://pewresearch.org/pubs/1977/poll-osama-bin-laden-death-confidence-muslim-publics-al-qaeda-favorability.

[23]MW # 19.

showing Hamas fighters in southern Lebanon succeeding against Zionist invaders, but there also are other videogames that feature Ummah Defense, that is, Defense of the Islamic Supernation so central to OBL's polemical diatribes against the US and other infidel/apostate enemies. One takes place in 2114 when the Earth is united under the banner of Islam. As a member of the intergalactic Muslim Council, your job is to help coordinate Dawa efforts on other planets. A robot invasion threatens the earth, and you must defend it.[24]

Fanciful? No more than its hyper-Christian counterparts, and what it projects is a long-term legacy of OBL's polemical project: to mobilize all Muslims on behalf of the Islamic supernation and to struggle patiently for that outcome until, by God's will, it happens. And happen, it will, if God wills, in the year 2114. Why 2114? Almost no prospective Muslim buyer would miss the irony, or deny the fascination, of that year. In the traditional or Christian calendar, it calculates a divine reckoning by the chapters of the Holy Qur'an. They number 114, and so the ultimate triumph and further test for Islam will come 114 years after the 19 martyrs of al-Qaeda, inspired if not directed by OBL, made plans to attack America on 9/11/2001 initiating what became the Third World War.

If OBL survives beyond death as the ultimate risk taker, wagering that his dystopic view of a polarized, warring world will prevail, then 2114 will be the virtual pay off for that investment. It is a dystopia now overshadowed by the euphoria of the Arab spring, set in motion across North Africa and the Middle East since December 2010, but the first signs of "spring" are still tentative. The ultimate jihadist may be dead, but for his vision to die requires an equivalent imagination, and steely resolve, in global planning of the 21st century and beyond.

One must admit that whatever his shortfalls, Osama bin Laden did not paint himself into a corner as did Saddam Hussein or before him Khomeini. The latter had to reverse his stand in ending the First Gulf War in 1989, while the former became a sudden advocate of the Palestinian cause and the Iraqi people when he found himself in the docket for war crimes. OBL did not end his life in obscurity. Though he died by American bullets in Abbottabad, his own verse immortalizes him as:

> a martyr,
> dwelling in a high mountain pass
> among a band of knights who,
> united in devotion to God,
> descend to face armies.

Victim or martyr, he remains the purveyor of irony. The greatest irony is that others, future Muslim knights or warriors, would have to risk their lives or give their lives for the cause of jihad that OBL emblazoned. As a Yemeni by lineage and a Saudi by birth, he gambled his legacy on delegating to others the work that no longer suited

---

[24]See *The Independent* Wednesday 17 August 2005, for a two page spread in the Science & Technology subset of Life & Culture: 38–39. "Jihad: play the game", by Rebecca Armstrong. The subtitle reads: "Western PC games feature US forces destroying Arab enemies. Now Islam is fighting back."

him. Former President Bush did not catch him, but President Obama did, and one can dare to hope that in the aftermath of OBL's death and with the continuance of an Arab spring into summer, fall and beyond, there will emerge a brighter Muslim world that may yet outdistance his dystopia and replace his nightmare with real hopes. Indeed, it must, for only two outcomes are possible: either the world will come to a horrific, near term end, or else it will not. Most would wager against OBL that the world will not come to an end, at least not in the near future. For such folk, the pragmatists, Muslim as well as non-Muslim, the real work is to prepare for an eventuality beyond the diatribes of apocalyptic doomsayers, and in response to the pragmatic soothsayers of the Arab spring from Tunis, Cairo and Benghazi.

Chapter 7
Redemptive Narratives in the Life and the Presidency of George W. Bush

Dan P. McAdams

In *Leading Minds: An Anatomy of Leadership*, Howard Gardner writes: "Leaders achieve their effectiveness chiefly through the stories they relate."[1] Leaders express stories in the way they live their own lives, and they aim to evoke stories in the lives of those they lead. "The artful creation and articulation of stories constitutes a fundamental part of the leadership vocation," Gardner claims. Further, "it is *stories of identity*—narratives that help individuals think about and feel who they are, where they come from, and where they are headed—that constitute the single most powerful weapon in the leader's literary arsenal."[2]

Whether drawing upon stories from their own lives or invoking stories that are widely recognized and shared among their respective constituencies, effective leaders may employ narrative to guide, motivate, persuade, control, or inspire those whom they are entrusted to lead. In the same vein, leaders use stories to explain their own positions and policies and to justify both what they aim to do and what they urge others to do. In many cases, stories may serve as a moral justification for a leader's agenda. People will commit their hearts and their souls to narratives. They will fight hard to enact the plots and affirm the values that their stories exemplify. They will even die for a story they believe in.

In this chapter, I will consider the role of one particular story in the life and the American presidency of George W. Bush.[3] Around the age of 40, George W. Bush developed a narrative that conferred upon his own scattered and chaotic life a sense of personal mission and purpose. In the manner of many successful and admired American adults who explicitly aim to leave a positive legacy for future generations, Bush constructed a personal narrative of *redemption*, a story about the deliverance from suffering to an enhanced status or state. Psychological research

---

D.P. McAdams (✉)
Department of Psychology, Northwestern University, 2120 Campus Drive, Evanston, IL 60208, USA
e-mail: dmca@northwestern.edu

[1] Howard Gardner, *Leading Minds: An Anatomy of Leadership* (New York: Basic Books, 1995), 9.

[2] Gardner (1995), 43.

[3] The argument in this chapter is spelled out in more detail in: Dan P. McAdams, *George W. Bush and the Redemptive Dream: A Psychological Portrait* (New York: Oxford University Press, 2011).

C.B. Strozier et al. (eds.), *The Leader*, 2nd ed., DOI 10.1007/978-1-4419-8387-9_7, © Springer Science+Business Media, LLC 2011

shows that redemptive personal narratives among midlife American adults are positively associated with mental health, well-being, and a generative perspective on life.[4]

As governor of the state of Texas from 1994 to 2000 and as the 43rd president of the United States (2001–2009), George W. Bush projected his redemptive story onto those whom he was elected to lead, for better and for worse. Bush's own unique brand of personal redemption—a story about the restoration of goodness through self-discipline—may have served the president and his American constituency well in the dark days after 9/11. The same redemptive narrative, however, provided the president with his deepest justification for the American invasion of Iraq in the spring of 2003. Whereas the Bush administration publicly justified the war as an effort to find and eradicate weapons of mass destruction, the invasion served the psychological function of playing out the president's private narrative quest. No weapons of mass destruction were ever to be found. Thousands of American troops were to die. Even as Iraq descended into chaos, the president never lost faith in the war, for he never lost faith in the redemptive story that served to animate both his own life and the American invasion. The United States would stay the course in Iraq, Bush insisted, and the United States would prevail, no matter what, for Bush's redemptive story would allow no other plot and no other outcome. The case of George W. Bush, then, illustrates how a leader first articulated an inspiring story of personal redemption to integrate his own life and how he subsequently came to employ that same story, albeit in an unconscious and starkly inflexible manner, to inform and support a controversial decision to wage war, with fateful consequences for millions of people.

Life Stories and Personality

Philosophers, poets, and storytellers have long observed that human lives resemble stories, with beginnings and endings, plots and scenes, and characters and themes. Freud saw in dream narratives clues to the broad psychological motifs that run through people's life stories. Many psychoanalysts have traditionally viewed their craft as a kind of narrative intervention—the systematic effort to assist their patients in the construction of better stories to live by, stories that expose and work through problematic dynamics in a person's life and promote coping, adaptation,

---

[4]The link between generativity and mental health on the one hand and personal redemptive narratives on the other, and the cultural meaning of these narratives, is the main theme in this book: Dan P. McAdams, *The Redemptive Self: Stories Americans Live By* (New York: Oxford University Press, 2006). See also: Dan P. McAdams, Jeffrey Reynolds, Martha Lewis, Allison Patten, and Philip J. Bowman (2001). When bad things turn good and good things turn bad: Sequences of redemption and contamination in life narrative, and their relation to psychosocial adaptation in midlife adults and students. *Personality and Social Psychology Bulletin* 8: 593–603. And also: Dan P. McAdams, Anne Diamond, Ed de St. Aubin, and Elizabeth Mansfield. "Stories of Commitment: The Psychosocial Construction of Generative Lives." *Journal of Personality and Social Psychology* 72: 678–694.

satisfaction, social engagement, and meaningful relationships with others.[5] It was not until the 1980s, however, that behavioral scientists began to develop formal theories and undertake systematic empirical research on the stories people construct to make sense of their lives. Over the past 25 years, narrative has gone from being a peripheral and fanciful idea in psychological science to secure a central position for empirical inquiry. Today, neuroscientists examine narrative processing in the brain; cognitive psychologists examine the narrative structure of autobiographical memory; developmental psychologists trace the origins of story comprehension in children; social and personality psychologists explore the ways that stories integrate lives and shape relationships; and scholars in the social sciences more broadly consider the role of stories in the psychology of groups and organizations, political discourse, social change, and culture.[6]

An organizing concept for contemporary research and theorizing on the psychology of life stories is *narrative identity*. Drawing from narrative theories of the self as well as the classic writings of Erik Erikson, a number of contemporary researchers conceive of narrative identity as an internalized and evolving story of the self that people begin to construct in late adolescence and young adulthood to provide their lives with some degree of unity, purpose, and meaning.[7] A person's narrative identity explains, for the person and for the society within which the person lives, how he or she came to be, where his or her life may be going in the future, and what his or her life may mean in broad terms within a given cultural and historical context. As such, narrative identity combines the person's selective reconstruction of the past and imaginative anticipation of the future to create a story about who I was, who I am now, and who I will be, and how the three are causally related in time.[8] According to many contemporary scholars of narrative identity, it is the particular story of life that a person begins to formulate in the emerging adulthood years that ultimately brings that sense of inner sameness and continuity that Erikson famously

---

[5] On the role of narrative in psychoanalysis see especially: Paul Ricoeur, *Freud and Philosophy: An Essay on Interpretation* (New Haven, CT: Yale University Press, 1970). See also Donald P. Spence, *Narrative Truth and Historical Truth: Meaning and Interpretation in Psychoanalysis* (New York: Norton, 1982).

[6] On the upsurge of interest among behavioral scientists in the topic of narrative see especially: Dan P. McAdams, "The Psychology of Life Stories," *Review of General Psychology* 5 (2001): 100–122.

[7] McAdams introduced the concept of narrative identity in this book: Dan P. McAdams, *Power, Intimacy, and the Life Story: Personological Inquiries into Identity* (New York: Guilford Press, 1985). See also: Dan P. McAdams, Ruthellen Josselson, and Amia Lieblich, eds., *Identity and Story: Creating Self in Narrative* (Washington, DC: American Psychological Association Press, 2006). And see: Kate C. McLean, Monisha Pasupathi, and Jennifer L. Pals, "Selves Creating Stories Creating Selves: A Process Model of Self-development," *Personality and Social Psychology Review* 11 (2007): 262–278.

[8] Although children begin to tell stories about their experiences around the age of 2 or 3 years, it is not until adolescence that individuals have the cognitive wherewithal to understand their entire lives—reconstructed past, experienced present, and anticipated future—as evolving stories. See especially Tilman Habermas and Susan Bluck, "Getting a Life: The Emergence of the Life Story in Adolescence," *Psychological Bulletin* 126 (2000): 748–769.

deemed to be at the heart of ego identity. Life stories, furthermore, situate a person in the adult world of work and love, specifying what kinds of roles the person will assume and what kinds of commitments the person will make over time. In Eriksonian terms, a person's narrative identity spells out a particular psychosocial niche while providing a coherent understanding of what a particular adult life means in the mind of that particular adult.

Within the field of personality science, researchers have developed reliable methodologies for collecting life-narrative accounts and coding salient psychological themes. A growing body of research explores how different forms and features of life narratives relate to basic personality traits, goals and values, developmental tasks, political orientations, mental health and psychopathology, and the course of psychotherapy.[9] A growing consensus among personality psychologists suggests that narrative identity is itself an integral component of a person's developing personality. According to this view, narrative identity is the third of three layers that make up human personality.[10]

The first layer of personality, which begins to manifest itself soon after birth, consists of those broad dimensions of temperament style that eventually develop into full-fledged dispositional traits. After 50 years of statistical research on the topic, personality scientists now generally agree that the many traits that might be invoked to describe individual differences in social behavior may be grouped into five broad dispositions: extraversion (social dominance, energy), neuroticism (anxiety, depressiveness), conscientiousness (dutifulness, competence), agreeableness (altruism, tender-mindedness), and openness to experience (curiosity, innovativeness).[11] Individual differences in these broad dimensions describe personality from the standpoint of the social *actor*.

Beginning in mid-childhood, a second layer of goals, values, and personal strategies begins to emerge, as selves begin to be defined from the standpoint of the motivated *agent*. To be an agent is to pursue self-chosen goals in a planful manner. Personal goals and the full superstructure of associated values, plans, projects, and strategies that form around them in mid-to-late childhood come to layer over basic dispositional traits, even as those traits continue to develop. By late adolescence and young adulthood, personality adds a third layer, as persons begin to develop narrative identity. The third layer is about the person as an autobiographical

---

[9] For a review of contemporary research on life stories in personality science see: Dan P. McAdams, "Personal narratives and the Life Story," in *Handbook of Personality: Theory and Research,* eds. Oliver P. John, Richard W. Robins, and Lawrence Pervin (New York: Guilford Press, 2008), 3rd ed., 241–261.

[10] See Dan P. McAdams and Bradley D. Olson, "Personality Development: Continuity and Change over the Life Course," in *Annual Review of Psychology,* eds. Susan Fiske, Daniel Schacter, and Robert Sternberg, vol. 61 (Palo Alto, CA: Annual Reviews, Inc., 2010), 517–542. See also: Dan P. McAdams and Jennifer L. Pals, "A New Big Five: Fundamental Principles for an Integrative Science of Personality," *American Psychologist* 61 (2006): 204–217.

[11] Robert R. McCrae and Paul T. Costa, Jr., "The Five-Factor Theory of Personality," in *Handbook of Personality: Theory and Research,* eds. Oliver P. John, Richard W. Robins, and Lawrence Pervin (New York: Guilford Press, 2008), 3rd. ed., 159–181.

author. The stories that people begin to author about their own lives—their narrative identities—eventually layer over goals and values, which themselves layer over traits. Personality in adulthood, then, may be seen as a dynamic and evolving pattern of dispositional traits (the person as actor); characteristic goals and values (the person as agent); and integrative life narratives (the person as author) situated in a complex interpersonal, social, cultural, and historical context.

When it comes to the personality of President George W. Bush, dispositional traits and characteristic goals and values may have played important roles in his decision to launch a military invasion of Iraq. A very strong trait of extraversion, traceable even to descriptions of his behavior when he was 4 years old, may have predisposed him as president to act boldly and aggressively on the world stage, in keeping with empirical research on extraversion. What was likely to be his very *low* standing on the dispositional trait of openness to experience, moreover, predisposed him to base his decision on gut feelings rather than reasoned argument. Research shows that adults low on openness to experience brook no disagreements and tolerate little ambiguity with respect to the decisions they make. Evaluating all the American presidents (going back to George Washington) on the five basic traits, a team of psychologists and historians recently rated Bush as near the top on extraversion (along with Teddy Roosevelt and Bill Clinton) and dead last on openness to experience.[12]

From the perspective of the person as a motivated agent, Bush set as one of his lifelong personal goals defending his beloved father against his most hated enemies. In Oliver Stone's movie, *W*, and in a number of books on Bush, biographers have intimated or asserted that George W. Bush invaded Iraq to prove himself a better and stronger man than his father. According to this line of thinking, George W. spent the first 50 years of his life in the shadow of his esteemed father, resentful and frustrated because he never measured up. As president, he was finally positioned to kill off the father, in an unconscious Oedipal sense.[13] The Oedipal argument sounds good, but the hard evidence for it is lacking. A careful analysis of Bush's motivational agendas—going back to his grade-school days—suggests instead that defeating his father's enemies, rather than defeating his father, was a prime motivator throughout much of his life. Going back to the 1991 Gulf War, Iraq's Saddam Hussein represented George Bush Senior's most despised enemy in the world. A few years later, when the Kuwaiti government and the Federal Bureau of Investigation (FBI) exposed an alleged Iraqi plot to assassinate George Bush Senior, his firstborn son and future heir to the presidency developed an even greater hatred for the "guy who

---

[12]Steven J. Rubenzer and Thomas R. Faschingbauer. *Personality, Character, and Leadership in the White House: Psychologists Assess the Presidents* (Washington, DC: Brassey's Inc., 2004) See also: Chapter 1 ("The Actor's Traits") in McAdams (2011).

[13]For Oedipal arguments on George W. Bush and his father, see for example: Justin A. Frank, *Bush on the Couch: Inside the Mind of the President* (New York: Harper, 2007). Oliver Stone (Director) and S. Weiser (Writer), *W*. [Motion picture] (United States: Liongate, 2008). Jacob Weissberg, *The Bush Tragedy* (New York: Random House, 2008). See also: Stanley A. Renshon, *In His Father's Shadow: The Transformation of George W. Bush* (New York: Palgrave Macmillan, 2004).

tried to kill my dad at one time."[14] In that Saddam Hussein was generally viewed, furthermore, as a tyrant who enslaved his own people, Bush's goal to defeat Hussein dovetailed with the neoconservative political value system he developed in the years leading up to his presidency, which sought to spread democracy and freedom to the Middle East.

The 9/11 terrorist attacks provided a once-in-a-lifetime opportunity to exact revenge on his father's greatest enemy while advancing the neoconservative value agenda, and in a manner so nicely simpatico with the dispositional traits that had been developing in George W. Bush's personality since childhood. Psychologically speaking, however, he still needed a personal story to justify the act and the goal and to give personal meaning to the values. He found that story in his own narrative of personal redemption.

Redemptive Narratives in Life and Culture

When people construct stories to make sense of their lives, they assimilate their remembrances of things past and their anticipations of what may lie in the future to the models for storytelling that prevail in their own culture. A person's culture, broadly construed, provides the acceptable metaphors, images, plots, conflicts, quests, and character types that can be used in that culture to make a life sound sensible—sensible both to the ear of the audience and the sensibility of the self.[15] In one way or another, all life stories reflect the culture wherein they are made and told. Yet some stories may be more paradigmatic, more representative of dominant cultural themes, than others. In particular, some life stories may approximate, in their structure and content, what a given society idealizes as an especially good life, a story worthy of emulation. It follows, therefore, that these exemplary stories might indeed be those lived and told by a society's healthiest, happiest, most successful, or most admired members. Acknowledging that exemplary life narratives are likely to come in a multitude of forms, life-narrative researchers have paid particular attention to the narrative identities of American men and women who score especially high on well-validated measures of psychological well-being and *generativity*. Considered a hallmark of psychosocial adaptation in midlife, generativity is an adult's concern for and commitment to promoting the well-being of future generations.[16] Findings from life-narrative research show that a central feature of the

---

[14]Quoted in Craig Unger, *The Fall of the House of Bush* (New York: Scribner, 2007), 264.

[15]On the cultural contouring of life narrative, see especially: George C. Rosenwald and Richard L. Ochberg, eds., *Storied lives: The Cultural Politics of Self-understanding* (New Haven, CT: Yale University Press, 1992). See also: Dan P. McAdams, "The Problem of Narrative Coherence," *Journal of Constructivist Psychology* 19 (2006): 109–125.

[16]Erik Erikson introduced the concept of generativity in this landmark volume: Erik H. Erikson, *Childhood and Society* (New York: Norton, 1950). For an overview of contemporary theory and research on generativity, see Dan P. McAdams, "Generativity in Midlife," in *Handbook of Midlife Development*, ed. M.E. Lachman (New York: Wiley, 2001), 395–443. See also: Ed de

narrative identities constructed by well-functioning generative adults in American society is the theme of redemption. In its most general sense, redemption is the deliverance from suffering to an enhanced status or state.

Employing objective content-analytic procedures, researchers have repeatedly shown that highly generative American adults express more incidents of redemption in their life stories than do less generative, less psychologically healthy American adults. In construing negative events as opportunities for further growth and positive outcomes, generative adults develop life narratives that affirm hope and progress. As such, redemptive stories of the self help to promote generativity. Research shows that the redemptive life narratives constructed and told by highly generative American adults at midlife often express a variation on this common pattern: *I am the gifted protagonist who journeys forth into a dangerous world. Blessed with special advantages and sensitive to the suffering of others, I make it my mission in life to make the world a better place, in keeping with my own strong values and beliefs. Bad things happen in my life, but good things often follow, for I am able—through my own efforts and the help of others—to overcome adversity. I will continue to give back for the blessings I have received and in accord with my personal calling to do good.* The story is as American as apple pie and the Super Bowl, a tale of how I have been chosen to be a light unto the world, the personification of a city on a hill, a beacon of hope, and a force for good in the world. It is my personal manifest destiny to give back for the blessings I have received—American exceptionalism writ small, packaged this time in an individual American's story of personal redemption.

Therefore, whereas redemptive life narratives may support psychological adaptation and generativity among midlife American adults, these same stories reflect cherished and contested themes in American culture. As reflected in Hollywood movies, American political discourse, folk conceptions of American history and heritage, and many other cultural expressions, Americans love redemptive narratives, even when they sense how limiting and unrealistic these stories can sometimes be. Among the favorites in the American pantheon of redemptive tales are stories of atonement, upward social mobility, liberation, and recovery. Going back to the Massachusetts Bay Puritans and forward to the born-again tales of Christian evangelicals, stories of atonement trace the redemptive move—sometimes sudden, sometimes gradual—form sin to salvation. Canonized as the American Dream, stories of upward mobility find their earliest expression in Benjamin Franklin's iconic autobiography, reworked ever since in Horatio Alger stories, immigrant narratives of aspiration, and countless other tales about how America is the land of boundless opportunity. Contemporary tales of personal liberation have their deepest cultural roots in the nineteenth-century narratives of escaped African-American slaves, an extraordinarily powerful line of discourse that may be traced forward to movements for civil rights, women's liberation, and the rights of gays, lesbians, and other oppressed groups. Finally, stories of recovery describe how protagonists have lost

St. Aubin, Dan P. McAdams, and Tae-Chang Kim, eds., *The Generative Society: Caring for Future Generations* (Washington, DC: American Psychological Association Press, 2004).

some kind of valued quality—health, wholeness, purity—and now seek to get it back. As expressed in 12-step programs, tales of psychotherapy, recidivism, and a host of other popular forms, recovery narratives chart the move from sickness, addiction, crime, or abuse to the restoration of the good inner self. Once upon a time, I was good and pure. And then the bad things happened. And now I am seeking to recover the goodness that was lost.[17]

Around the age of 40, George W. Bush transformed his life into a narrative of personal redemption. In line with the kinds of narrative identities that many highly generative American adults construct in their midlife years, Bush drew mainly from the American redemptive discourses of atonement and recovery. His was to be a life story wherein the protagonist *atoned* for the squandered years of young adulthood by finding God and committing himself to the disciplined life of conventional generativity. In so doing, the protagonist of this redemptive quest would *recover* the sobriety, goodness, innocence, and freedom of his childhood years, as he reconstructed them in his cherished memories of growing up in Midland, Texas. As president, the narrator would project the same narrative frame onto America and the world. In the narrator's mind, his own redemptive journey would become ours.

George W. Bush's Redemptive Journey

As a story to live by, narrative identity is an artful coming-to-terms of imagination and reality. Developing a coherent and affirming narrative of the self involves a good deal of editing, embellishment, selective forgetting, and other forms of authorial work aimed at making meaning out of a life that may, on first blush, seem mean-ing*less*. Lives do not come in prepackaged narrative form; instead, authors make their lives into stories, and their readers give them some authorial leeway to do so. But if one's story is to be credible in the communities wherein it has its meanings, then the author cannot ignore the facts on the ground. My friends and neighbors will reject my rags-to-riches narrative if they know that I grew up as the son of a wealthy investment banker. If I claim to have attended Princeton but no grade transcripts can be found, I will likely lose credibility with the people who count most in my life, to say nothing of losing credibility with myself. Human beings are social animals, and their stories are negotiated and evaluated in a social context. For social animals, narrative identity does not (usually) work well when it turns out to be complete fiction. Social reality matters.

Social reality was the big problem for the 20-something George W. Bush when he first set out to construct his own narrative identity. As a young boy, he fantasized that he might become a great baseball player, like Willie Mays, the star centerfielder

---

[17] For a full discussion of the varieties of redemption to be found in the life stories of highly generative American adults and in a range of American cultural forms, see McAdams, *The Redemptive Self: Stories Americans Live By* (2006).

for the San Francisco Giants. By the time he was a freshman at Yale, however, the paradigmatic story he imagined for his own life was that of his famous father, George Bush Senior. Like his father, he attended Andover for high school and then Yale for college. Like his father, he was inducted into Skull & Bones, Yale's prestigious secret society. Like his father, he proposed marriage at the age of 20 to a woman from Smith College (yes, the very same college that Barbara Bush—his mother—attended). When he applied for the Texas Air National Guard, he told the officers that he wanted to be a fighter pilot, as his father was. In his late 20s, he tried to make a go of it in the Texas oil industry, where his father made his fortune. But reality kept undermining the anticipated plot. At Andover and Yale, the father was a star athlete and top student; the son never made the teams (though he organized a stickball league and was a cheerleader at Andover). The son pulled mediocre grades. The father was a decorated war hero, bailing out in the nick of time when his plane went down over the Pacific; the son sat out the Vietnam War. The son's engagement to the girl from Smith (Cathy Wolfman) eventually fell apart, and he never turned a profit in the oil business.

The most glaring feature of social reality differentiating the father from the son, however, was the son's abuse of alcohol. The Delta Kappa Epsilon (DKE) fraternity parties at Yale were like the movie *Animal House*, and George W. Bush regularly played the role of John Belushi. As one fraternity brother recalled those times, "we drank heavily at DKE. It was absolutely off the wall—appalling. I cannot for the life of me figure out how we all made it through."[18] Beginning in college and running through age 30, George W. Bush was arrested three times for alcohol-related activities. Driving his 17-year-old sister home after 3 hours of heavy drinking in 1976, he was pulled over in Kennebunkport, Maine, and given a sobriety test. His blood alcohol level registered 0.12; he subsequently pleaded guilty to a driving under the influence (DUI) charge.

The years between his Yale graduation in 1968 and the arrest in Maine correspond roughly to what George W. Bush later characterized as his "nomadic period." Lacking a clear direction in life, he moved from one job to another, served in the Texas Air Guard, and eventually attended Harvard Business School. He drank heavily throughout. At the Chateaux Dijon apartment complex in Houston's Galleria district, George W. hung around the pool on Mondays through Thursdays, awaiting his regular weekend duties as a pilot, chain-smoking Winston cigarettes and downing one Budweiser after another. Or else he tooled around Houston in his blue Triumph, looking for a good party. During this period, his social activities were dominated by what he called "the 4 B's" in life: "beer, bourbon, and B & B."[19] He returned nightly to a disheveled bachelor apartment, stumbling over dirty laundry, unread magazines, empty bottles, and beer cans strewn about the path to his bed. On one particular night of heavy partying, he needed badly to relieve himself on

---

[18] Quoted in Christopher Andersen, *George and Laura: Portrait of an American Marriage* (New York: William Morrow, 2002), 64.

[19] Quoted in Andersen (2002), 106.

the way home. A woman reported that she observed him urinating on a car in an Alabama parking lot.[20]

Even as he began to turn his life around in his 30s, George W. Bush continued to drink to excess. He took an early step toward rehabilitation in 1977 when he met, and then married 3 months later, Laura Welch. Concerned family members noticed that the quiet but steady Laura seemed to be the first person in a decade to have a positive influence on prodigal George. The couple gave birth to twins in 1981, shortly after George Bush Senior assumed the office of Vice President of the United States, under Ronald Reagan. George the younger relished his new role as father and spoke about it often in highly generative terms. But he continued to drink throughout this period, even as he charged off to work every morning, faithfully attended civic events in Midland, Texas, and taught Sunday school at the local Methodist church. He often came home drunk at night, falling asleep on the living room couch. On more than one occasion, Laura threatened to leave him.

Bush took a second critical step toward rehabilitation in the spring of 1984, when the evangelist Arthur Blessitt brought his traveling salvation show to Midland. For seven evenings, Blessitt held Christian revival rallies at the Midland Chaparral Sports Center. Intrigued by Blessitt's message, Bush asked friends to arrange a private meeting with the evangelist. On April 3, Blessitt and a local businessman met with Bush in a coffee shop at the Midland Holiday Inn. The three men shared stories and prayed together. Bush told Blessitt that he desired to have a closer relationship with Jesus Christ. Blessitt led him through a conversion prayer, proclaiming love for Jesus and asking Jesus to "come into my heart." When the prayer was finished, Bush smiled broadly, and Blessitt began to rejoice in the power of the Lord. That evening, Blessitt wrote this in his diary: "A good and powerful day. Led Vice President Bush's son to Jesus today. George Bush, Jr.! This is great! Glory to God."[21]

Bush's commitment to an evangelical brand of Christianity intensified in the months that followed. He became a regular participant in a community Bible study. In 1985, he met with the Reverend Billy Graham in Kennebunkport to discuss his life and his faith. Although he continued to drink regularly, he began to believe that alcohol abuse and his rejuvenated Christian faith were fundamentally at odds with each other. Finally, just short of his 40th birthday (in the summer of 1986), Bush quit drinking, cold turkey. After going for his customary morning run following a night of drunken revelry, he announced to Laura that he would never touch alcohol again. If the public record is to be believed (and there is no reason not to believe it) he kept his promise. In later years, Bush offered a number of different reasons for giving up alcohol. About to turn 40, he worried that drinking was slowing him down, physically and mentally. He worried about the effects on his family. He may have

---

[20]Unger (2007), 82.

[21]The account of Blessitt's meeting with George W. Bush on 3 April 1984 comes from a number of sources, including especially: Stephen Mansfield, *The Faith of George W. Bush* (Lake Mary, FL: Charisma House, 2003), 61–66.

worried that his drunken antics could jeopardize his father's upcoming campaign for president. But George W. Bush typically gave the lion's share of redemptive credit in his life to God. As president himself two decades later, he once told a group of White House visitors: "There is only one reason why I am in the Oval Office and not in a bar. I found faith. I found God. I am here because of the power of prayer."[22]

The Restoration of Goodness through Self-Discipline

By the time he turned 40, George W. Bush had taken the necessary behavioral steps to turn his life into a story of redemption. He had married a mature and serious-minded woman. He had begun to raise a family. He had taken on an array of generative roles in the church and the community. He had experienced a religious conversion and renewal of his personal faith. He had finally given up drinking. For the first time, he could discern an overall pattern for his life that might provide a coherent and satisfying narrative identity. His story was not to be his father's. It was instead to be a self-defining and forward-looking story of redemption. Around age 40, George W. Bush finally became the *author* of his life. He began to reconstruct his past and imagine his future as a grand narrative in which a flawed protagonist endures years of waywardness and depravity only to emerge, at midlife, as a generative man on a mission.

The new story became the implicit frame within which George W. Bush came to understand the subsequent accomplishments, triumphs, and challenges in his life. His father enlisted his firstborn as a top aide in the 1988 presidential election. George W. proved especially effective in helping his Episcopalian father relate to the Christian evangelicals, who were becoming an indispensible part of the Republican political base. In the business realm, George W. became part-owner of the Texas Rangers baseball team, fulfilling a lifelong desire to have a meaningful role in professional baseball. In his new position, George W. hobnobbed with the Rangers players and fans, and he was instrumental in raising funds to construct a new stadium for the team, which gave him positive visibility throughout Texas in the late 1980s and early '90s.

In 1992, George Bush Senior failed to win a second term as president, losing to Bill Clinton. Shortly after his defeat, his namesake announced he would run for governor of Texas, against the popular incumbent Ann Richards. To most people's amazement, including his parents', he defeated Richards in the 1994 race. On that fateful night, second-born Jeb Bush (whose childhood dream was to be president) lost his initial bid to become governor of Florida. In the next few years, George W.'s star continued to rise. Republicans and even many Democrats in Texas came to see him as a relatively effective and bipartisan governor. By the late 1990s, Republicans

---

[22]Quoted in David Frum, *The Right Man: The Surprise Presidency of George W. Bush* (New York: Random House, 2003), 283.

nationwide began to consider him as a potential contender for the presidency. After listening to Pastor Mark Craig's inspiring sermon in 1998, George W. phoned James Robison, a Southern Baptist evangelist, and told him: "I've heard the call. I believe God wants me to run for president."[23] Of course, it was not only God's voice that Bush was hearing. From the moment he beat Ann Richards, George W. became the darling of many Republicans, especially those on the right wing. Among other strategic advisors, Karl Rove helped to portray Bush as a principled, serious, and electable Republican on the national scene. At the urging of George Senior, Condoleezza Rice and Paul Wolfowitz schooled Bush on foreign policy, inculcating the values of neoconservatism.

As part of his push for the presidency, Bush collaborated with his close aide Karen Hughes as authors of *A Charge to Keep*, which became his campaign autobiography and a public telling of his own life story. The book begins with the promise of redemption:

> Most lives have defining moments. Moments that forever change you. Moments that set you on a different course. Moments of recognition so vivid and so clear that everything later seems different. Renewing my faith, getting married, and having children top my list of those memorable moments.[24]

In the first sentences of *A Charge to Keep*, then, the author informs the reader that the story about to be told will feature life-changing moments. The three examples given—renewing faith, getting married, having children—suggest that these moments will feature redemptive moves wherein the hero of the story consolidates his generative commitment. The author follows through on his promise. Each of the

---

[23] The story of Pastor Mark Craig's sermon and its alleged effect on George W. Bush's decision to run for president is told in many places. Whereas Bush himself argued that the sermon convinced him to make a presidential bid, others have suggested that his mind was made up long before he heard Craig's sermon. See, for example, Weissberg (2008). See also: David Aikman, *Man of Faith: The Spiritual Journey of George W. Bush* (Nashville, TN: Thomas Nelson, 2004).

[24] George W. Bush, *A Charge to Keep: My Journey to the White House* (New York: Harper, 1999), 1. Although Karen Hughes may have penned most of the words that appear in *A Charge to Keep*, the sentiments clearly belong to George W. Bush. Hughes developed an astute psychological understanding of Bush, and she was able to convey clearly the contours of his life story and his vision for America. At the same time, Hughes was also cognizant of how a campaign autobiography needs to take advantage of the political moment, for the ultimate goal here is to get her man elected, rather than merely to tell his story for the sake of the telling. Hughes knew that as a politician Bush had everything to gain and nothing to lose by accentuating his small-town, West Texas experiences and downplaying the fact that he was the privileged son of an elite Eastern family. But George W. Bush knew the very same thing, ever since he lost his first election campaign (for Congress, in 1978) to a Texas good old boy. He knew it so well, in fact, that it became an authentic and intrinsically motivating part of his narrative identity. George W. Bush certainly made good use of the nearly limitless social capital with which his eminent family provided him throughout his life. But in the redemptive story that he authored for his own life around the age of 40, he is the redeemed sinner who seeks to recapture the all-American goodness of a wholesome, small-town childhood. The estate on Kennebunkport, the years at Andover and Yale, the Harvard MBA—all of these are mere footnotes. They do not play major roles in the basic arc of his narrative identity.

first four chapters is structured as a redemption sequence, a move from suffering to enhancement. Chapter 1 (entitled "A Charge to Keep") begins with an account of political defeats—George W.'s own loss in a 1978 congressional race, his father's loss to Bill Clinton in 1992, and his brother Jeb's loss in the Florida governor's race in 1994. The chapter ends hopefully with George W.'s decision to run for president upon hearing Craig's sermon. Chapter 2 ("Midland Values") begins with an account of the death of his little sister Robin when George W. was 7 years old and ends with an evocative description of the happiness, security, and freedom he felt growing up in Midland, Texas. Chapter 3 ("What Texans Can Dream Texans Can Do") begins with an account of the long odds he faced when he decided to run for governor. The chapter is structured like a David-defeats-Goliath narrative; the underdog who faces an overwhelming challenge at the outset emerges the victor at the chapter's end. Chapter 4 ("Yale and the National Guard") begins with a vaguely negative description of campus unrest and the general chaos, as George W. reconstructed it, of the late 1960s. It ends with his flying a jet plane high above the clouds. Sharply disciplined and in perfect control, he soars free and clear above the turmoil on the ground.

Chapter 10 ("The Big 4-0") describes Bush's renewal of Christian faith and his resolution to quit drinking. "Faith changes lives. I know because faith changed mine."[25] The redemptive power of faith runs throughout the campaign autobiography, and is captured in the book's very title. A Charge to Keep is named, in part, after a Methodist hymn written by Charles Wesley. The hymn's first two verses suggest that God redeems Christian lives so that men and women will follow their generative calling to serve Him:

> A charge to keep I have,
> A God to glorify,
> A never dying soul to save,
> And fit it for the sky.
> To serve the present age,
> My calling to fulfill;
> O may it all my powers engage
> To do my master's will!

Broadly structured as a redemptive story of atonement and recovery, the narrative identity that George W. Bush eventually constructed in his mind and portrayed for the world featured themes that recent empirical research has shown often run through the life stories of especially generative American Christians who also happen to espouse strongly *conservative* political viewpoints. Compared to their more liberal and equally generative Christian counterparts, conservative Christians are more likely to describe their lives as stories in which protagonists struggle against

---

[25] George W. Bush (1999), 159.

chaos (sin, conflict, temptation, disorder in the world) and, with God's help, achieve redemption through *self-discipline*. When asked to imagine a life without God, for example, American Christian conservatives describe a chaotic world in which impulses run rampant and institutions crumble, whereas Christian liberals imagine a barren and lifeless landscape with nothing to sustain its inhabitants.[26] In describing key scenes in their own life stories, Christian conservatives highlight the redemptive power of following rules and summoning forth self-discipline, whereas liberals tend to accentuate themes of empathy for others and personal fulfillment.[27] When they pray to their respective Gods, Christian conservatives pray for forgiveness for their sins and ask for strength and guidance to make it through a dangerous world; Christian liberals pray for provision, asking God to meet their needs and fill up their empty souls.[28]

There are conservative and liberal variations on redemptive stories in American lives, and George W. Bush's story was, not surprisingly, a decidedly conservative one. Again and again in the narrative accounts he constructed for his life in midlife, Bush highlighted the power of self-discipline to overcome chaos. The protagonist in his story led a tumultuous and chaotic life for much of his early-adult years, but with the help of a steady woman, a good family, and God, he managed to summon forth the steely discipline needed to foreswear alcohol and focus his attention unswervingly on generative goals in his life. As governor and president, Bush was famous for his nearly obsessive self-discipline, reflected in everything from his personal habits to the fact that White House meetings always started and ended on the precise minute scheduled. More important, self-discipline became the mechanism whereby the protagonist in his story might *recover* the goodness that, once upon a time, was experienced, subsequently lost, and now re-found. As with many men and women who abuse alcohol, that goodness was sobriety. But in the life story that came to define George W. Bush in midlife, that goodness also represented the sense of control, security, and freedom that the protagonist knew and enjoyed once upon a time, as a child growing up in Paradise. Conservatives often look back in history and in life to an imagined or experienced golden age.[29] For George W. Bush that golden age was the reconstructed world of his own childhood—the control, security, and freedom he knew, once upon a time, growing up in Midland, Texas. In *A Charge*

---

[26] Dan P. McAdams, and Michelle Albaugh, "What if There Were no God? Politically Conservative and Liberal Christians Imagine Their Lives without Faith," *Journal of Research in Personality* 42 (2008): 1668–1672.

[27] Dan P. McAdams, Michelle Albaugh, Emily Farber, Jennifer Daniels, Regina L. Logan, and Bradley Olson, "Family Metaphors and Moral Intuitions: How Conservatives and Liberals Narrate Their Lives," *Journal of Personality and Social Psychology* 95 (2008): 978–990.

[28] Kathrin J. Hanek, Bradley Olson, and Dan P. McAdams, "Political Orientation and the Psychology of Christian Prayer: How Conservatives and Liberals Pray," *International Journal for the Psychology of Religion* 21 (2011): 30–42.

[29] See for example: Andrew Sullivan, *The Conservative Soul* (New York: Harper, 2006). See also Patrick Allitt, *The Conservatives: Ideas and Personalities throughout American History* (New Haven, CT: Yale University Press, 2009).

to Keep, Bush makes it clear that in the beginning, there was Midland, and it was good:

> Midland was a small town, with small-town values. We learned to respect our elders, to do what they said, and to be good neighbors. We went to church. Families spent time together, outside, with grown-ups talking with neighbors while the kids played ball or with marbles and yo-yos. Our homework and schoolwork were important. The town's leading citizens worked hard to attract the best teachers to our schools. No one locked their doors, because you could trust your friends and neighbors. It was a happy childhood. I was surrounded by love and friends and sports. . ... Everyone played together. Everyone's parents watched out for everyone else's kids. Midland was a place where other people's mothers felt it was not only their right, but also their duty, to lecture you when you did something wrong, just as your own mother did.[30]

Remarking on several idyllic passages regarding Midland that can be found in *A Charge to Keep*, biographer Stephen Mansfield asserts that "the Midland of memory is the core image" of George W. Bush's life, "his West Texas version of a New Jerusalem."[31] This is a keen psychological insight. His nostalgic memory of Midland captures perfectly George W. Bush's image of how people—all people everywhere—should live together. Like most utopian visions, there is peace, harmony, happiness, and love. But in his deeply conservative version of utopia, there is also security, discipline, and freedom. People are safe in Midland because they are disciplined, because God and the rules and the good authorities in this small town keep the world's chaos at bay.

And so we flash forward to the days following 9/11, when America and her president faced the terrifying prospect of chaos. With fear spreading in the wake of the terrorist attacks and the autumn's subsequent anthrax scare, President George W. Bush found the perfect historical and psychological opportunity to project his own redemptive story onto the nation and the world. Beginning on September 14, 2001, with a powerful address at the National Cathedral and an impromptu speech to firefighters at the site of the fallen twin towers, President Bush and his administration began to articulate a story of national redemption—the restoration of goodness through self-discipline. Like all redemptive narratives, the president's story for the American people begins with suffering. "We are here in the middle hour of our grief," the president announced at the National Cathedral prayer service. "It is said that adversity introduces us to ourselves. This is true of a nation as well." In order to find redemption in the adversity, the American people need to summon up their self-discipline, the president said, and re-focus on their historical charge to keep, the calling to secure freedom. "In every generation, the world has produced enemies of human freedom. They have attacked America because we are freedom's home and defender, and the commitment of our fathers is now the calling of our own time."

In the redemptive story that George W. Bush projected onto America and the world, security and freedom were God-given, universal values, available to all

---

[30]George W. Bush (1999), 17–18.

[31]Stephen Mansfield (2003), 35.

people and felt most deeply for the president in his recollections of growing up in the small town of Midland, Texas. In *A Charge to Keep*, Bush explicitly labeled these values "Midland values."[32] In the wake of 9/11, Bush saw an opportunity to defeat those evil forces who threatened to undermine Midland values, and that threatened to destroy the Paradise of social life that (in George W. Bush's redemptive story) God has promised all the world's people. Even the people of the Middle East deserve to live in Midland, Bush believed—a sentiment that resonated with the neoconservative agenda for foreign policy espoused by many of Bush's advisors. Therefore, America's redemptive response to 9/11 could and, if the narrative is to be played out, *should* target the worst enemies of freedom in the Middle East. In his 2002 State of the Union address, Bush famously identified Iraq as part of the world's "axis of evil." To the extent he harbored terrorists and developed weapons of mass destruction, Iraq's Saddam Hussein became a mortal enemy for America. But even if he did none of the above, the president believed, the ruthless Iraqi dictator was an enemy of freedom, just like the al-Qaeda operatives who took the towers down. And we should never forget, for indeed President Bush never forgot, that Saddam was that very same man "who tried to kill my dad at one time."

Conclusion

From a psychological standpoint, why did President George W. Bush invade Iraq? His decision was driven by an array of mutually reinforcing personal factors that managed to come together and achieve activation at a singular moment in history. Dispositional personality traits of sky-high extraversion and rock-bottom openness to experience set the *actor* up to perform boldly on the world's stage. Energetic, restless, socially dominant, supremely confident, narrowly focused on a few key ideas, unwilling to entertain many dissenting points of view, he was dispositionally primed to do something like an Iraq invasion. His all-consuming hatred for Saddam and his personal goal to defend his beloved father's greatest enemies helped to focus his energy on the Iraqi dictator, at a time when that dictator could be readily perceived by Americans as a clear and present threat to security and freedom. As a motivated *agent*, then, the president found a way to achieve a personal goal while accomplishing strategic national goals regarding security and American influence in the post-9/11 world.

The deepest psychological source for the invasion of Iraq, however, and its most compelling justification in the mind of the president was George W. Bush's own redemptive story for his life. In the particular narrative identity he *authored* for himself at midlife, George W. Bush was the gifted protagonist who squandered much of his youth only to find focus and generativity in his middle years, with the consolidation of a stable marriage, renewal of his Christian faith, and commitment to lifelong sobriety. The midlife hero is called to a redemptive mission that cannot fail.

---

[32]George W. Bush (1999), 14–22.

He will turn sorrow into joy, chaos into Eden. For better and for worse, the president projected his personal redemptive story onto the American people and the world in the days after the 9/11 attacks. He knew deep in his bones that the story must end happily. He was convinced that the mission would be accomplished, victory would be assured, and Midland would be restored. He knew this all because that is how his own life narrative had worked out.

Chapter 8
Paranoid Leadership

David M. Terman

Richard Hofstadter's astute analysis of the paranoid style in American history—
from an eighteenth-century group of New England clergy who feared a massive
subversion from a small European enlightenment group, the Illuminati through the
many nativist movements and virulent hate groups in the nineteenth and twentieth
centuries, along with, one might add, the activities of right-wing extremists since
the election of Barack Obama—notes the significance of the paranoid theme from
the very beginnings of our political and cultural experience.[1] This troubling tendency in human affairs is not, as some authors have said, characteristic of modern
times—especially the twentieth century. I believe we can even see evidence of it
in ancient Egypt, while perhaps the urtext of the paranoid organization is the book
of Revelation, written in 95 AD, that concludes the New Testament. Such paranoid
thought that I have called the "paranoid gestalt" has since arisen in large groups and
small throughout Western history, and we have seen it in other cultures as well. That
gestalt is a cognitive-affective structure that can be found in both individuals and
groups. In individuals it presents in a range of states, from the mild, fleeting feeling that "the world is against me" through the conviction that an amorphous "they"
have control over one's life, jobs, status, money, power, and so on to, finally, the
psychosis of delusions of persecution. Over the whole range of these states, there
is the conviction that someone or some group is very powerful and malevolently
intended. Distrust is the hallmark of most relationships, for even apparent surface
benignity or neutrality masks underlying malevolence. When the source of hostility
and threat is seen to be a group, then the belief is that there is a group of individuals
who are not only malevolently intended but are also interconnected in their activities
and intentions against the victim, that is, they share a conspiracy in which the chief
object is to harm the victim.

D.M. Terman (✉)
Training and Supervising Analyst, former Director, Chicago Institute for Psychoanalysis
e-mail: dmterman@comcast.net

[1] Richard Hofstadter, "The Paranoid Style in American Politics," in *The Paranoid Style in American
Politics and Other Essays*, ed. Richard Hofstadter (New York: Alfred A. Knopf, 1965), 3–40.

C.B. Strozier et al. (eds.), *The Leader*, 2nd ed., DOI 10.1007/978-1-4419-8387-9_8,
© Springer Science+Business Media, LLC 2011

The perception of an imbalance of power is a very important part of the gestalt, for the malevolent forces are always very powerful, and the victim is undeservedly and unjustly weak. The persecutor is only and always concerned with increasing his or her power at the expense of the victim. In groups the pattern is even more stereotypic. There is an aggrieved, in group, the group that is organized by the paranoid gestalt, and there is a feared, hated group that is seen as destructive, which is the paranoid object. The paranoid group is suspicious of the destructive group's intentions and purposes in a fashion analogous to that in the individual. The designated destructive group is the chief source of danger to the paranoid group's well-being or welfare. Even more crucially, the destructive group is the chief and determined obstacle to the achievement of the ideal state that the paranoid group is trying to establish.

This ideal state is a very important element of the gestalt for the paranoid group. It is the carrier of the moral superiority of the group, and serves as a cohesive force binding the group together. But inextricably intertwined with the ideal state is the destructive force that opposes it, and that usually is seen to be demonic. The ideal state can be achieved only with the destruction of the destructive force, almost always the members of the destructive group. It is a moral virtue to eradicate, kill those who want to prevent or destroy the establishment of the ideal condition; in fact, that destruction, itself, is often seen to lead to the ideal state. Like the individual, the paranoid group believes itself far superior morally but far weaker physically than the destructive group. This moral quality to the paranoid gestalt has some other dimensions that relate to violence: That evil other deserves to be dispensed with, which in its more extreme forms requires annihilation through murder, mass killings, ethnic cleansing, or genocide.

This schema characterizes many political, social, and religious groups throughout history. In addition to the contemporary activist fundamentalist groups today, many revolutionary movements follow this prescription. The French and Russian revolutions, for example, fit this model well. Each had its version of the perfect society. The French believed that they would establish the perfect Enlightenment state that would be liberal and absolutely egalitarian. The communists in Russia believed they would establish the worker's paradise. And each had its destructive group. Among the French, Marat, Robespierre, and the Committee of Public Safety saw the aristocrats and the Royalists trying to subvert and undo their new order and saw them in ever-widening groups, and the Bolsheviks targeted all the wealthy and privileged groups in Russia, from the aristocrats to the capitalists to the rich peasants. Each group was driven to self-righteous excess in its will to exterminate the evil members of the group they designated as demonic and destructive.

The traditional emphasis on projection in the psychological literature on paranoia may well cloud our appreciation for what motivates the projection, namely the interrelated issues of shame and humiliation that profoundly affect self-esteem. There is an interesting homology in this connection between the damage to an individual's self-esteem that is so important in understanding the forms of paranoia that emerge from it, and the collective experiences of shame and humiliation that serve as preconditions for the appearance of the paranoid gestalt. It is in the context of that gestalt—and I would argue, only within that context—that paranoid leadership emerges.

The psychology of the group, in other words, is essential to the existence of paranoid leadership. In a sense the group finds its leaders. That fact does not preclude the interaction between the group and its leader in forging the psychological organization of the group, but I contend that the group cannot have a paranoid organization unless the group has been stressed in the ways I outline in this chapter. A leader who has a paranoid personality organization cannot impose himself or herself on the group, unless the group is predisposed toward such leadership because of its own paranoid orientations.[2]

How can one understand the underlying psychology that leads to the formation of this gestalt? Contemporary theories of a particularly intense, unforgiving and unrelenting anger offer some clues.[3] Called narcissistic rage by Heinz Kohut, this kind of rage occurs when an essential part of the person's psychology is felt to be endangered or destroyed. For the individual, such parts of the person are his or her ambitions or ideals. Each of these qualities depends on the capacity of the caretaker to respond in a way that enables the child to develop and integrate those parts of the personality. When the caretaker is unable to respond in such a fashion, the experience of the child may be one of helplessness and powerlessness. It is like being unable to move a part of one's body, a finger or a leg. Such lack of power over the essential other may lead to catastrophic, relentless, and boundless rage.[4] A person so traumatized by his or her lack of control over the essential other must maintain one's sense of total control over all others. Then his or her own failures and weaknesses become intolerable. As a result he or she surrenders his or her reasoning and rationalizes these failings as caused by the malevolence and corruption of the unwilling or uncooperative other.

---

[2] An example of a paranoid leader who did not impose his paranoia on the social or political group of which he is head may be Richard Nixon. Nixon's obsession with enemies, and his pursuit of them in an effort to thwart activities that he deemed destructive to him led to the Watergate break-in and the violation of American laws. Rather than stimulating support, these actions and the Nixon paranoid view of the world alienated the people and led to his resignation. In his case, the paranoid gestalt concerned only his own person; it was not cast in larger social terms. And rather than make it part of his overt political position, he hid it. So he made no attempt to use it as a basis to mobilize and organize the group. And at that time, there was no group need for such a psychological organization. Nixon was aware enough of the needs of the political group to hide his personal paranoid organization. I would infer that he sensed that it would alienate the group rather than mobilize it—as it did.

[3] Erich Fromm, Anthony Storr, and Heinz Kohut each began to single out this particular form of anger or rage. Fromm labeled it "malignant aggression" and Storr described a "thirst for vengeance" that is "cruel, lustful and insatiable." See Erich Fromm, *The Anatomy of Human Destructiveness* (New York: Holt, Rinehart and Winston, 1973), 271; and Anthony Storr, *Human Destructiveness* (New York: Basic Books, 1972), 108.

[4] See Heinz Kohut, "Thoughts on Narcissism and Narcissistic Rage," *The Psychoanalytic Study of the Child* 27 (1972): 360–400 for a full discussion of the mechanism of narcissistic rage.

I have added several ideas to fill out an explanatory framework for the paranoia.[5] One is the importance of the experience of power in itself as a source of self-esteem. Children naturally feel pride in their capacity to develop skills, to master the world around them, to have a sense of power and mastery over the things and people in their world. Such pride in power may be emphasized by the particular family or cultural milieu in which the child is raised. Power becomes especially important in situations in which authorities use it harshly and arbitrarily in ways that emphasize the helplessness and inferiority of those under their control. Paradoxically, the greater the power of the parent or person in authority and the more helpless the child feels under that power, the more important the attribute of power is to the child and the more humiliated and traumatized the child becomes with the frustration of its own power. Such disparity in power relationships is humiliating. It defines the weaker as weak and contemptible. In the course of numerous struggles over power in the context of the child's relationships with caregivers or in competitive situations with stronger adversaries, defeat can be crushing to a sense of pride or dignity. There is also often a moral dimension to childhood defeat or limitation at the hands of a forceful or angry caretaker—and certainly at the hands of a brutal one. Then one is not only weak, one is bad. And since children are crucially defined in such transactions, the badness becomes intrinsic to one's being, one's sense of self. The combination of these factors leads to an overwhelming sense of humiliation and defeat.

The step from humiliation and defeat to the paranoid gestalt is relatively small. The experience of weakness or defect is so intolerable that it cannot come from oneself; it must come from the outside (as it did, in fact, in the initial traumas). The transfer of blame for the defect or weakness is to the other. Any subsequent situation that might lead to the experience of weakness or defect cannot be permitted or endured. It is the doing of the "other." This becomes the gestalt of "I am not weak or defective; it is others who prevent my strength and success" or, in more archaic terms, "my greatness and omnipotence." Further, my self is not defective; it is perfect. The narcissistic rage, on the other hand, that is mobilized in this situation is expressed in the hatred and wish to destroy the malign other. The stance toward the other is not to see him or her as separate and with complex sets of motivations and needs, but as a being who is organized only around the destruction of one's self and whose essence is essentially evil. So the paranoid object is not just a flaw in the narcissistic universe that must be obliterated, but an evil whose existence threatens one's destruction.

When we turn to understanding the group, we can apply these ideas in a useful way. Mindful that the group is not the individual writ large, and that groups have neither childhoods nor parents, one cannot postulate the traumata of a vulnerable child as the nucleus around which later injury and the gestalt arises. However, there is a way in which the group can be thought of as having a "group self." The group has a shared history and develops collective perceptions of its characteristics. These include its power vis-à-vis other groups, its notions of greatness and goodness, and

---

[5] See David Terman, "Fundamentalism and the Paranoid Gestalt," in *The Fundamentalist Mindset,* ed. Charles Strozier, David Terman, and James Jones, with Katharine Boyd (New York: Oxford University Press, 2010), 47–61.

its values. All these are sets of qualities that the group may see as uniquely its own and that give it a sense of continuity with itself. Corresponding to the "grandiose self" of the individual is the group's sense or experience of power, and corresponding to the individual's need for both ideals and idealizable figures are the ideal visions of the group and the need for idealized leaders.

Ideologies are largely the embodiment of the group's ideals, and they are extremely important to the group.[6] Part of most ideologies is the vision of the perfect society. Corresponding to the need for the "perfect self" of the narcissistically injured individual is the perfect self of the group—the utopian ideal. A number of authors have shown that damage or threats of damage to ideologies in the perception of the group or its members is a key source of terrorism.[7] Some of the injury and rage of the Muslim Middle East, for example, arises from their perception that the erosion of the most central values and tenets of Islam are being undermined and destroyed by the secular, materialist West.[8] Clearly, damage to the group's ideology is a serious narcissistic injury, and is an important source for the stimulation of the paranoid gestalt in the group with its compensatory emphasis on the utopian state.

Damage to the group's sense of power and greatness also engenders humiliation and the need for revenge. There are numerous examples of such traumata throughout history. Two widely documented instances are the Germans after World War I and the Treaty of Versailles, and the Muslim Middle East after the nineteenth-century decay and collapse of the Ottoman Empire. The Germans felt humiliated by the terms of the Versailles Treaty, which stripped them of all their colonies, imposed heavy sanctions, and forbade them from having an army. After the crushing and humiliating military defeat, these decrees further destroyed central sources of pride and power as it had been so fervently pursued throughout the nineteenth century. The humiliation of the state could not have been more complete. The economic collapse that followed also left individuals feeling defeated and helpless. These were the perfect conditions for the development of the paranoid gestalt by the country, as it did. The paranoid organization offered by the Nazis reclaimed German glory and power and proposed an evil "other" to blame for their collapse and to see as the barrier to the establishment of the German millennium.

---

[6] See Terman, *The Fundamentalist Mindset*, Chapters 2 and 4 for the function of ideology in groups.

[7] There are a number of authors that have shown the importance of ideology—and especially, perceived injury to the group ideology. See Nehemia Friedland, "Becoming a Terrorist: Social and Individual Antecedents," in *Terrorism: Roots, Impact, Responses*, ed. Lawrence Howard (New York: Praeger, 1992), 81–93; Mark Juergensmeyer, *Terror in the Mind of God* (Berkeley: University of California Press, 2000); and Martha Crenshaw, "How Terrorists Think," in Howard, *Terrorism*, 71–80.

[8] Bernard Lewis has extensively studied Islam and its relation to the West. A particularly succinct account of the sources of the injury and rage of the Muslim world can be found in his article in the Atlantic Monthly some 20 years ago. See Bernard Lewis, "The Roots of Muslim Rage," in *The Atlantic Monthly* (September, 1990). Lewis enumerates the ways the Muslim community has been traumatized especially by the challenge to their traditional values and beliefs—and in the end, their dignity and even their livelihoods—by the force of Western values. This perspective has been expressed repeatedly in the works of Sayyid Qutb, whose life and thought are discussed in the chapter. For example, in *Milestones* (Damascus: Dar Al-Ilm, n.d.), Qutb inveighs against the West in calling for jihad against all that is deemed *jahiliyyah*, impure and ignorant of divine guidance.

The story of Nazi Germany—which is discussed in much greater detail below—is a most perfect illustration of the issues of paranoid leadership. First, there is the state of the group—and here one probably oversimplifies to speak of a whole nation as a single group, but that not withstanding for purposes of our discussion—that is the group self as a whole. Second, there is the ideology of the group that is an expression and embodiment of its goals and ideals and that provides a cohesive meaning structure and places goals and ideas in a context. Finally, there is the all-important leader who directs the course of events and makes manifest what is otherwise latent and mere potential. In what became Nazi Germany, there was a remarkable convergence of all these elements, each of which took the form of the paranoid gestalt provoked by profound narcissistic injury. In considering the nature of paranoid leadership—or any leadership—one has to take into account the nature of the group, for the leader reflects the psychological organization of the group. Different groups with different psychological structures require different leaders.

II

I begin the story of Nazi Germany with an excerpt.

> The Jews have gained control of the press, and through Palestinization of universities, of the law, of medicine, and of the state they control all thought. Jews and capitalists should be destroyed. The state should at once seize all credit and banking facilities thus depriving the Jews of their means of existence. With this usurious vermin no compromise is possible: with trichinae and bacilli one does not negotiate, nor are trichinae and bacilli subjected to education; they are exterminated as quickly and as thoroughly as possible.

An excerpt from the Wansee conference when the final solution was formulated in 1942? A passage from Mein Kampf? No. These sentiments were expressed in 1853 in the work later published in the 1878 as *Deutsche Schriften* by a German cultural critic named Paul de Lagarde. Described in a fascinating and famous study by the German cultural historian, Fritz Stern, de Lagarde's life history well illustrates the link between personal character—in this case paranoid—and the creation of an ideological system.[9] The following account will give the flavor of his life and mind.

De Lagarde was born in 1827 into an old Saxon family who had sent its sons into the Protestant ministry for generations. That family's name was Botticher. (The fact that his name was de Lagarde is a story that I won't detail here. Simply, as an adult, he changed it to the name of an aunt, Ernestine de Lagarde, who left him a sizable inheritance.) His mother died 12 days after he was born, and his father went into prolonged and bitter grief and mourning, hating his son and blaming him for his mother's death. There were two maternal aunts who cared for him and were said to love him. His father, however, in addition to the proximate reasons for his harsh and negative attitude toward his son, was characterized as a "bigoted, cheerless Christian, who thought that unmitigated gloom was the proper mood for a religious

---

[9]Fritz Stern, *The Politics of Cultural Despair* (Berkeley: University of California Press, 1961).

home. This devoutly pious egoist terrorized his son just as he did his students at Friedrich-Wilhelm's Gymnasium where he taught Greek and Latin." The poisonous relationship with his father was worsened by the father's remarriage when Lagarde (Botticher) was four. "Within two years he had two stepbrothers. . . . Within the new family Paul seems to have been treated as an outsider, an interloper. . . Nor did the elder Botticher relent; as Paul grew older, his father became more tyrannical still."

This experience of grinding humiliation at the hands of his father was the ground out of which the paranoid character grew. His adult life showed that character vividly. Lagarde went into the family business of theological studies. He specialized in Old Testament studies, learned Arabic and Persian, and published philological subjects that showed Arabic and Persian influences on Aramaic, and his work set standards in the field.[10] However, he had a terrible time establishing himself as an academic for reasons of his resentment and arrogance. Stern writes, "From the very beginnings of his career, Lagarde loathed the guild, as he called it, and in time his contempt hardened into a somewhat paranoid fear of a professional conspiracy directed against himself. Most of his colleagues, he thought, either plagiarized or traduced him, and all sought to block his advancement. . ...[however] his belief in a conspiracy against himself had no foundation." As Stern added, "Lagarde stood squarely in his own way. His failure to obtain a university appointment was not due to a conspiracy of frightened colleagues, as he assumed. . . He had his share of pro-fessional breaks. . .., and he had his successes, but he fostered in the guild a sense of himself as a rash, querulous man of principled unreliability."

During this time in his life, indeed, throughout his life, he wrote a series of cri-tiques of German culture, society, and government that were assembled in 1878 as the *Deutsche Schriften*. In addition to the anti-Semitic location of the evil other in his thought, de Lagarde fulminated against the nature of German Protestantism. Its Christianity had been Judaized—especially by the Jew, Paul—and was a "spiritu-ally bankrupt shell over a materialistic secularism." Lagarde further declared that there should be a "new, heroic faith that would have to be a cleansed version of Christianity, appropriate at last for the German character. Even some of the old pagan rites would have to be revived. . . the essence of the religion of the future would be a fusion of the old doctrine of the Gospel with the national characteristics of the German. . . .The new religion would have to arrest [the decline of German independence and moral austerity] and recover and preserve the old Germanic virtues. It would have to propagate Germany's cultural uniqueness and her imperial destiny." As with other such ideologies, there was an appeal to return to a mythical, purer past. Lagarde promised a redeeming superiority to those shamed by a corrupt society.

Lagarde was actually one of three such critics who, remarkably, presaged what became the Nazi ideology. The others were Julius Langbehn and Moeller van

---

[10]Thomas Mann maintained that de Lagarde was one of the most productive and influential German thinkers of the nineteenth century and compared him to Nietzsche and Wagner. See Robert G.L. Waite, *The Psychopathic God: Adolph Hitler* (New York: Basic Books, 1977), 274.

den Bruck. Langbehn was 30 years younger than de Lagarde, was also personally paranoid, was equally anti-Semitic, and also wanted to return to a mythic volk. The one difference of his thought from Lagarde was that he hated and demonized modern science as well as the Jews. The third of Stern's trio, Moeller van den Bruck, was not personally paranoid, nor was his thought, and interestingly was dropped from the Nazi canon in 1939. Abundant evidence attests the direct influence of Lagarde and Langbehn on the most important National Socialist ideologists. Alfred Rosenberg, the chief ideologist of the Hitler movement, considered himself Lagarde's disciple. The National Socialists celebrated the pair as their forebears and, although at one time or another they repudiated every other influence, they never wavered in their loyalty to these two.

The works of Lagarde and Langbehn created quite an éclat among the critics and intellectuals of the time, and they became part of an ideological stream that attracted the attention of many German intellectuals.[11] But Germany was on a triumphant rise. It had united under Bismarck in 1871, and was proclaimed a unified German nation at the Palace of Versailles after the Franco-Prussian War. Germany was the leading power in Western Europe. It had a rising and prosperous middle class. Its achievements in science and the arts—especially music—were unrivalled in the world. And the majority of the population could feel considerable pride in Germany's power and its place in the world (even if its pride had the somewhat uncertain ring of a parvenu). So the receptivity of the majority of the German people to de Lagarde's angry and injured view of the world at this point in German history did not translate into any meaningful political action.

Of course, we all know what disaster lay before it after World War I. Versailles, the site of the apogee of its glory, became the perigee of its shame. In this case, the history of the group bears the analogous form to one of the conditions for the development of the paranoid gestalt in individuals. That is, the stripping away of all that the Germans took particular pride in as a group is like the exultation of the victor at the expense of the vanquished in the experience of the individual. For the Germans it appeared to be the triumphalism of the victor at the contemptible weakness of the loser. The terms of the treaty also emphasized the disparity in power between the winner and the loser.

It was easy for many Germans who returned from the war to believe that the destruction of their military might and their position as the strongest power in Europe could only be the doing of an evil other. David Redles, in an excellent chapter in our book, *The Fundamentalist Mindset*, chronicles the disorientation and disillusionment of the returning soldiers. Everything they had believed in was gone. They did not know what to make of the world. It was with great relief, then, that they encountered Adolph Hitler and the Nazi party. Here was the explanation of their failure, and here was the vision of the new Germany that could inspire them.

---

[11] Waite, *The Psychopathic God,* comments that Langbehn's work on Rembrandt in which he glorified art, denigrated modern science, and held Jews responsible for all German ills had 40 printings in the 1890s.

With huge relief, they became enthusiastic and dedicated members of the Nazi party especially as it was embodied in the inspiring figure of Adolph Hitler.

Hence, we must turn now to a brief examination of perhaps the quintessential paranoid leader, Adolph Hitler. There has, of course, been a vast amount written about him and a considerable amount of research done on his life beginning with our own Office of Strategic Services (OSS) during the war.[12] Hitler's father was Alois Schicklgruber, the illegitimate son of Maria Anna Schicklgruber. He had his name changed as an adult to that of an adopted father, Johann Georg Heidler, which the clerk misspelled as "Hitler," and so Alois Schicklgruber became Alois Hitler. Though raised with the stigma of illegitimacy, he became a member of the Austrian Civil Service and was able to elevate himself to quite respectable middle-class status. His climb was not without the scars and their sequelae that reflected the earlier damage to his self-esteem. In his attempt to overcome his shameful origins, he became martinet at work. He insisted that his employees report for work within minutes of their required time, for example. And though he, himself, was an addicted pipe smoker, he permitted no one else to smoke. He demanded that everyone address him by his official title—Herr Senior Official Hitler. His insistence on respect extended to his family and was accompanied by his arbitrary and brutal treatment of his family. Although there is no evidence that he was a drunkard as Hitler alleged in *Mein Kampf,* there is plenty of evidence that he was demeaning and abusive. He beat his children, and demanded that they call him Herr Vater and be silent in his presence unless bidden to speak. He beat the family dog until it wet the floor, and often summoned Adolph with the same whistle that he used for the dog. Hitler's mother, Klara Potzl, was Alois's third wife and had been employed as a maid before Alois got her pregnant with Adolph and then married her. She was 23 years younger than her husband and was quite subservient to him. Though she was quite indulgent of Adolph, she was powerless to protect him from his abusive father.

In addition to the humiliation Hitler suffered at the hands of his father, he was genitally defective. Though first disputed, the accuracy of the Russian autopsy on his burned body confirmed that he had a missing left testicle.[13] His behavior in his life

---

[12] See Walter C. Langer, *The Mind of Adolph Hitler and the Secret Wartime Report by Walter C. Langer* (New York: Basic Books, 1972). I have used several biographies of Hitler to extract the data about his life. Robert G.L. Waite's *The Psychopathic God: Adolph Hitler* provided important information about Hitler's early life and childhood. Norbert Bromberg and Verna Small, *Hitler's Psychopathology* (New York: International Universities Press, 1983) also offered some additional points of view. Ian Kershaw's *Hitler 1889–1936: Hubris* (New York: W.W. Norton, 1998) was helpful in providing a contemporary evaluation of the scholarship on Hitler. The account of August Kubizek, *The Young Hitler I Knew* (London: Greenhill Books, 2006), offered an invaluable peek into Hitler's adolescent mind, and Hitler's own *Mein Kampf,* translated by Ralph Manheim (Boston: Houghton Mifflin, 1999), with appropriate caution can sometimes help reconstruct aspects of his inner world.

[13] There is an extensive discussion of the evidence for the missing testicle in Waite, *The Psychopathic God,* 150–162, which I have excerpted. I find Waite's full discussion of the evidence quite persuasive. The combination of the lack of motivation for falsifying a report of a missing testicle on autopsy and the behavioral symptoms cited in his latency and adolescent years make a

further confirms the experience of defective male genitalia. Compensatory behaviors in childhood that are found in other monorchid boys were also present in Hitler's life. For example, he was quite hyperactive and relentlessly played war games— long after his peers grew tired of them. He was never seen naked by his valet or any intimate. He would not wear a bathing suit. And from all available evidence, it is likely that he never had genital union with a woman. Rather, he subjected them to perform perverse excretory actions that excited him to climax.

By age 11 or 12, he began to do poorly in the Realschule in Linz, to which he was sent. He had to repeat the first year. Until he dropped out of the school at 16, he never was able to bring his work up to standard. His father died when he was 13. After he dropped out of school at 16, he led a rather pampered life in which he lived out grandiose fantasies of artistic and cultural attainment supported by his mother's funds. At 18, in September 1907, he moved to Vienna to apply to art school. He failed the examinations for admission to the Academy of Art in Vienna and was rejected, though he told no one. His mother died of breast cancer in December of that year. He was left with both an orphan's pension and various inheritances. These funds permitted him to live very frugally but without working until he was about 20. However, after that he slid into a semi-impoverished state, but not into total penury as he began selling pictures he had painted of scenes of Vienna.

Out of this matrix of events arose his anti-Semitic beliefs and evidence of his messianic self-conceptions. We have the memoirs of August Kubizek to thank for the record of these episodes. Kubizek was an alter-ego soul mate to Hitler from his 16th to 19th years, and he remained totally adoring of Hitler (in spite of being abruptly deserted when Hitler was 19). He wrote of these adolescent years with him and unwittingly recounted some of his most pathological behavior and attitudes. The messianic strain was vividly recorded by Kubizek after a performance of Wagner's *Rienzi* they had attended when Hitler was 17.

"I was struck by something strange, which I had never noticed before. . .. It was as if another ego spoke from within him, and moved him as much as it did me. . .. it was a state of complete ecstasy and rapture, in which he transferred the character of Rienzi, without even mentioning him as a model or example with visionary power, to the plane of his own ambitions. . .. Hitherto I had been convinced that my friend wanted to become an artist, a painter or perhaps an architect. This was now no longer the case. Now he was talking of a mandate which, one day, he would receive from the people to lead them out of servitude to the heights of freedom. . . He spoke of a special mission which one day would be entrusted to him."[14]

---

quite plausible case for such a condition. Though one does not need such a physical defect to feel a sense of shame and humiliation, and there was ample cause for such an inner state from Hitler's experiences with his martinet father, this defect would have compounded such an inner conviction and help account for the intensity of his rage and the consequent violence of his paranoid structure.

[14] August Kubizek, *The Young Hitler I Knew* (London: Greenhill Books, 2006), 117–118. This edition of Kubizek's memoires was translated by Geoffrey Brooks and has an introduction by Ian Kershaw. In his introduction, Kershaw cautions against taking Kubizek's account too literally.

There is some dispute about the precise timing of the onset of his anti-Semitic beliefs, which was, of course, a crucial element of his paranoid gestalt. He was known to be an enthusiastic follower of Georg Schonerer whose violent anti-Semitism had created it as a political force in late nineteenth-century Vienna, but whether his beliefs were as immovable and virulent in 1908 as they clearly were by 1919 when he got enthusiastic approval from the veterans of World War he lectured is less important than the evidence of the psychological structure that made them the "evil other."[15] However, both his rejection from art school and his mother's death help lay the groundwork of humiliation and the inability to experience blame or responsibility for one's own failures or experiences of defect. Kubizek wrote of Hitler's finally revealing to him in the spring of 1908 that he had, in fact, been rejected from the Art Academy.[16] He recorded that Hitler exploded in a diatribe against the Art Academy, "This Academy, he screamed, is a lot of old-fashioned fossilized civil servants, bureaucrats, devoid of understanding, stupid lumps of officials. The whole Academy ought to be blown up! 'His face was livid, the mouth quite small, the lips almost white. But the eyes glittered. There was something sinister about them, as if all the hate of which he was capable lay in those glowing eyes!'" Hitler then revealed the truth that he had held back for months, "They rejected me, they threw me out, they turned me down." There were further outbursts and harangues.[17] "He cursed the old-fashioned bureaucracy of the Academy where there was no understanding for true artistry. He spoke of the trip-wires which had been cunningly laid—I remember his very words—for the sole purpose of ruining his career."And rather than take realistic steps toward realizing an ambition to become an architect, he engaged in "private studies."[18] Hitler persisted only at his self-training in drawings of architecture, avoiding any contact with practical steps toward that profession. At the same time, he became increasingly preoccupied with political issues, often in the form of hate-filled harangues. Kubizek observed, "The

---

However, the basic tenor of the account is quite plausible. Grandiose visions of himself were evident in his activities as they constituted grand plans without any real, concrete actions that might be a step to actuate such ambitions.

[15] Ian Kershaw, *Hitler 1889–1936: Hubris* (New York: W.W. Norton, 1998). Kershaw points out in his biography that Kubizek's contention that Hitler joined the Antisemitic League after revealing the fact that he was rejected from the Art Academy could only have been false because the League was not formed until 1918. Kershaw also dismisses Hitler's contention in *Mein Kampf* that he had developed his anti-Semitism in 1908 in Vienna. Though there may be some reasons to doubt Hitler's accuracy about the precise date, the assertion makes great psychological sense. Hitler's subjective sense of the origins of his anti-Semitism may be more trusted than apparent external reasons that Kershaw summons to refute it.

[16] Kubizek, *The Young Hitler,* 160

[17] Kubizek, 174

[18] Kubizek, 175, "Personally, I doubted if, indeed, anything would ever come of my friend's private studies. Admittedly he studied with incredible industry and a determination which one would have thought beyond the strength of his undernourished and weakened body. But his pursuits were not directed towards any practical goal. On the contrary, every now and again he got lost in vast plans and speculations."

most difficult problems became easy when they were transferred to the political plane."[19]

Here, then, we have the paranoid psychological organization. As he had to confront and admit a failure, he could not own its origin in himself. The blame lay with the malevolent others. And very quickly those malevolent others were symbolized in the political realm. The other elements of the gestalt that we see in groups—the combination of the utopian ideal with the obstruction of the evil other—are already present in his mind, but not yet linked. They were, of course, linked in the work of de Lagarde and other radical cultural critics, and that thought—as well as violent anti-Semitism of Georg von Schonerer and the Vienna of the late nineteenth century—easily became Hitler's own as everything was "transferred to the political plane."

I want to underline the narcissistic injury in Hitler's life that I believe is the source of his paranoia. First, there was the demeaning behavior of his father. It was designed to enforce the father's superiority both by insisting on being treated in an exaggeratedly deferential way, and by making Adolph feel inferior and helpless at his hands. He was at times, literally, treated like a dog. Alois's treatment of Adolph is parallel to Botticher's treatment of Paul de Lagarde. But in addition, Hitler probably suffered the experience of defect that was embodied in his absent testicle. There were some questionable assertions by some who had seen him in the context of the German army that his genitals were grossly deformed. Whether they were in fact or not, his behavior indicated that he felt they were deformed. These injuries laid the psychological groundwork for the step into the paranoid gestalt—I am not to blame for any defect or failure—it is the others, the evil others, who are to blame. The episode recorded by Kubizek of his enraged, shame-filled revelation of his failure to be admitted to the Art Academy vividly reveals this mechanism. The codification of the evil other into the Jew, whenever it precisely occurred, and the centrality of anti-Semitism in his ideology was the elaboration of his personal psychology.

The power of this construct was quite astonishing, as we all know. I wonder if part of the force of this phenomenon was not only the congruence of the personal histories of narcissistic injury in all the components of the triad—the ideological creators, the group, and finally the leader—but the depth and intensity of those injuries. The grotesqueness of the person of this paranoid leader and the monstrousness of the Nazi regime may have come from both the extent and intensity of the narcissistic injury to each.

III

The extremity of this example, however, illustrates a more universal, if less dramatic and sometimes less horrendous, tendency. The psychologies of the creators of paranoid ideologies, the groups that adopt them, and the leaders that espouse and

---

[19]Kubizek, 223

personify them all show the congruence that we have seen in Nazi Germany. The Muslim Middle East illustrates a similar congruence. One of the most important creators of the Jihadist ideology was Sayyid Qutb, an Egyptian civil servant. His personal history was also marked by what I infer to be adolescent narcissistic injury that led him to a paranoid narcissistic organization by the time he was in his early 20s.[20]

His route to the personal paranoid organization was quite different from that of Paul de Lagarde, and it is interesting to compare them. Rather than having been an unloved child of a martinet, he was the oldest, favored son of a declining, formerly prosperous and prestigious family of the village of Musa, 235 miles south of Cairo. His father was a farmer who became progressively more impecunious during the course of his life and had to sell off parcels of the family patrimony to stave off bankruptcy. Qutb was made aware of his father's failures at age 10 when his weeping mother told him about it and impressed on him that he must restore the family's honor and fortune when he grew up. In this situation, Qutb had to deal with a traumatic disillusionment with his father and a grandiose demand from his mother while simultaneously being deprived of the capacity to use a healthy identification with his father to achieve such a task. He was both inflated and weakened at once.

The effects of this toxic brew would not be evident until he became an adult and had to confront the issue of sexuality and his capacity to have a sexual or intimate relationship with a woman. For many years, he did very well as an inflated child and a favorite of his mother, indeed, the whole village. He was quite intellectually gifted, and he came to be so regarded by the village. At the time of his mother's burdensome charge he also memorized the Qur'an, read to the village, and was consulted by others for his wisdom.

At 15, he left his village to study in Cairo at his uncle's house. Eventually, he became part of a sophisticated literary movement. When he was 27, his father died, and then his mother and three younger siblings moved to Cairo to be with him. Poetry written at that time seem to signal a change in his inner life with great preoccupation with questions of sin and the quest for an eternal beloved.[21]

Qutb's mother died in 1940 when he was 34. Only after that, when he was 36, did he attempt a serious relationship with a woman. This was a serious, unhappy affair that ended in a traumatic rupture. The inner state was recorded in an autobiographical novel titled *Ashwak* (Thorns), which he wrote shortly after the affair ended.[22]

---

[20] Much of the biographical material on Qutb's early life comes from the PhD dissertation of Adnan Ayyud Musallam, "The Formative Stages of Sayyid Qutb's Intellectual Career and His Emergence as an Islamic Da'iyah. 1906–1952" (PhD diss., University of Michigan, 1983).

[21] Musallam quotes a number of his poems that reflect these themes, ibid, 85.

[22] Though the novel has not been translated into English, we have Musallam's précis of its contents. Musallam describes the novel as follows: 150–151 "This romantic novel portrays the stormy relationship of Sami and Samirah, an engaged couple, following Samirah's confession to Sami of a love affair she had had with a young army officer before meeting Sami, coming at a time when he had pinned his hopes on settling down with her to build a family life. This confession leaves

His description of the cancellation of an engagement because of the man's inability to accept the fact of his fiancée's previous romantic affair and the chronic, obsessive suspiciousness of her fidelity that the fact engendered is quite probably a description of his own feelings and is the evidence of what is becoming a paranoid obsession with women's sexuality, purity, and betrayal. Qutb never married, and his attitudes spread to the culture at large. He began to be highly critical of Egyptian public life. In 1940, he inveighed against "sick singing on the Egyptian public radio. He said that these songs were more dangerous than any "fifth column." They were a "poison running through the essence of the nation." He advocated forming groups to combat the "sick singing which... destroyed Egypt's pride, manhood and femininity, excited the basest instincts, and anesthetized its nerves like narcotics."[23]

These attitudes hardened into the condemnation of all Western cultural influences and, finally, of the "impure" Arab governments that did not abide by Islamic law. By the mid-1940s, his anger at the West became political as well as cultural. He attacked Britain and France for their suppression of revolts and the USA for its supporting Jewish immigration to Palestine.[24]

The other side of the demonization of the West as the evil other was the vision of the perfect world. The full articulation of the utopian fantasy was in one of his central works, *Social Justice in Islam* [25], and in it, he describes a world in which the material and spiritual are united. However, this beguiling vision, open only to those who adhere to the Qur'an, became a statement of superiority in his last work written while he was imprisoned and tortured by the Egyptian government. For example:

> The Believer is most superior in his values and standards, by means of which he measures life, events, things and persons. The source of his belief is the knowledge of God and His attributes as described by Islam, and the knowledge of the realities prevalent in the universe at large, not merely on the small earth. This belief with its grandeur provides the Believer with values which are superior to and firmer than the defective standards made by men who

---

Sami bewildered and in doubt about his idealized fiancée and her moral standards. Sami's suspicions bring their relationship to the verge of collapse, but Sami's deep love for Samirah continues. Desire for her happiness motivates his decision to search for her previous lover in order to arrange for his reunion with Samirah—even if that would mean the demise of Sami's own future with her. But his conversation with the army officer is fruitless and only leaves him more suspicious of Samirah's moral standards.... The vicious circle of suspicions continue to haunt the couple's relationship. Even though Sami tries repeatedly to forge ahead with their wedding plans, his suspicions have already done permanent damage. Three days before the wedding a misunderstanding causes Samirah and her family to break off the engagement. Sami tries to restore the relationship, but to no avail."

[23] Musallam, Dissertation, 158.

[24] Incidentally, the full paranoid attitude toward the West long antedated his visit to America in 1948–1950. His visit to America only confirmed what he had come to believe as a result of his personal development more than a decade prior to his visit.

[25] Sayyid Qutb, *Social Justice in Islam,* ed. John Hardie (Oneonta, NY: Islamic Publications International, 2000).

do not know anything except what is under their feet. They do not agree on the same stan-dard within the same generation, even the same person changes his standard from moment to moment.[26]

Unlike the West, which divides secular and sacred, Islam reunites these in service to and as part of God as revealed in the Qur'an. The faithful will return to this state of belief and the adherence to all the laws of Shar'ia, but the demonic "other" is not absent. With imprisonment and torture in 1954 under Nasser, the demonic "other" is believed to gain more prominence. Muslim countries will also become the source of impurity and evil that must be destroyed. They are *jahiliyyah* ("pagan igno-rance and rebellion against God"). As a result, the world will be divided absolutely in two.[27]

> The callers to Islam should not have any superficial doubts in their hearts concerning the nature of *jahiliyyah* and the nature of Islam, and the characteristics of *Dar-ul-Harb* and *Dar-ul-Islam*, for through these doubts many are led to confusion. Indeed, there is no Islam in a land where Islam is not dominant and where its Shar'ia is not established; and that place is not *Dar-ul-Islam* where Islam's way of life and its laws are not practiced. There is nothing beyond faith except unbelief, nothing beyond Islam except *Jihiliyyah*, nothing beyond the truth except falsehood. Further, the aim of *jahiliyyah* society is to block Islam. Hence, true Muslims and believers must work to abolish the *jahili*—the corrupt, unredeemable West that opposes the virtuous and righteous Muslim world.

As Qutb was imprisoned and tortured, his writings became more vehement about the necessity of exterminating the Western Infidels, the Jews, and the corrupt Arabs.[28] They became the basic texts of the Muslim Brotherhood and the jihadist movement, and they have since been the framework in which numerous alienated, depreci-ated enraged young Arabs in the Middle East and young men of Arab extraction in Europe coalesce into terrorist groups. Though each of these groups are said to have a leader, the ideology and the shared narcissistic injuries seem to be enough to make the groups into groups and organize their lives and activities.

Of course, the focus of the movement and the leader of al-Qaeda is Osama bin Laden, whose rhetoric is in the classic paranoid gestalt. However, the spirit and writ-ings of Qutb are easily seen. Bin Laden's development as the leader of what became al-Qaeda is well chronicled by Lawrence Wright.[29] Though Qutb's influence is striking as it shaped the jihadist movement, bin Laden's espousal and articulation of

---

[26] *Milestones*, Chapter 11, 143

[27] Qutb, ibid, Chapter 9, 127

[28] Sayyid Qutb wrote three books that are the basis of jihadist ideology: *In the Shade of the Qu'ran, Social Justice in Islam*, and finally, *Milestones* (Damascus: Dar Al-Ilm, year of publication and translator unknown).

[29] For a very interesting and informed account of the development of Osama Bin Laden's life and terrorist career see Lawrence Wright, *The Looming Tower* (New York: Alfred A. Knopf, 2006). Wright has traced the background and interrelationships of the central and influential people in bin Laden's life. The complex web of associations spring from those associated with Sayyid Qutb. Also see Steve Coll, *The Bin Ladens: An Arabian Family in the American Century* (New York: Penguin Press, 2008) for an account of the family and a picture of the hedonistic, Western-oriented Bin Laden brothers.

the paranoid ideology also arrived by a route that was different from the German's and, in some ways, quite similar to the development of Qutb's character. I will qualify the speculations about bin Laden with the caveat that we do not yet have access to material that reveals his inner world. There are no letters, poems, or writings from which one might infer his inner state. We do have information about his actions and his public statements, as well as portraits of the significant figures in his life, and from these one must be very tentative.

Osama bin Laden had always been a somewhat passive member of the 54 bin Laden children and especially compared with his dominant, older half brothers who eventually managed and controlled the bin Laden empire. He was the son of an inferior wife who was divorced by Mohammed bin Laden, his father, when he was five. The mother was given to one of bin Laden's employees, and Osama was raised in a separate, more modest house. Shortly after the divorce, his father was killed in an airplane crash. His older half brothers dominated the family, ran the businesses, and led very opulent, secular lives. Unlike them, who were educated in the West, he had been educated in fundamentalist-dominated school in Syria, and he became quite religious as an adolescent—much more than the rest of his family. As part of his adolescent religiosity, he was attracted to jihad. Some have noted that he might have been so motivated by a charismatic Syrian gym teacher who was part of the Muslim Brotherhood.[30] Certainly, he showed a lifelong pattern of association with very motivated, ruthless, injured, and enraged men. As he matured, he became a rather feckless worker in his family business and quite an ineffective warrior in the Afghan war that drove out the Soviets in the 1980s. However, he allied himself with driven jihadists who were impecunious and became dependent on his wealth.

One of the most salient of such figures is Ayman al-Zawahiri. Zawahiri is an Egyptian who comes from one of the most prestigious families of Egypt. An uncle was also an intimate of Qutb whom he admired greatly. Zawahiri was raised in Cairo, however, as socially second class. He is highly intelligent and well organized and became a doctor. Numerous experiences of humiliation led to his radicalization long enacted as plots to overthrow the Egyptian government and substitute the perfect Islamic state—as Qutb had urged. He formed a terrorist group called al-Jihad, which the Egyptian government tried to exterminate, and he lived a ruthless, violent, and revenge-filled life. He was also an excellent organizer. He became allied—uneasily—with bin Laden in their first Afghanistan fight, and even became Osama's doctor. His fierce hatred of the *jahiliyyah*, his ruthless, self-righteous violence, and his organization helped bin Laden gain focus. Finally, in the late 1990s, he helped make al-Qaeda an effective terrorist organization.

Earlier, other such men helped bin Laden consolidate his role as an avatar of Muslim and Arab resurgence. Although his participation in the Afghan war was minor and ineffective, he came back to Saudi Arabia with a myth that he had driven

---

[30]Wright, *The Looming Tower*, 75.

out the Soviet forces and hence radiated a heroic aura. There is evidence that he believed in his powers, as well. When Saddam Hussein invaded Kuwait in 1991, he was enraged and humiliated that the Saudi government should turn to the United States for help. He seriously proposed to the Saudi defense minister and then to Prince Turki, head of Saudi intelligence, that he could defend the Kingdom and raise an army of 100,000—though he barely had several thousand in Afghanistan. Wright writes about Turki's reaction to bin Laden's proposals that, "...he was alarmed by the 'radical changes' he saw in bin Laden's personality. He had gone from being 'a calm, peaceful and gentle man' whose only goal was to help Muslims to being 'a person who believed that he would be able to amass and command an army to liberate Kuwait. It revealed his arrogance and haughtiness.' " I infer that an important determinant of his later rage at the presence of American troops on Saudi soil, though part of the ideology of the Qutb and the jihadists—another instance of colonial "occupation" of Muslim land, was the narcissistic injury that the ministers' rejection of his pretensions created. They did not see him as a grand and glorious defender of the faith. The injuries to his grandiose vision of himself multiplied in his misadventures in the Sudan in the early 1990s where he lost all his money in poorly planned and diffuse business ventures and, finally, in his repudiation by his family and the revocation of his Saudi citizenship in 1995.

I would also speculate that the grandiose vision that bin Laden had for himself was a brittle, psychological construction in place of a weak, humiliated child who, though inflated by both his radical religiosity and his later inherited wealth, felt weak without a father and in comparison with his confident, older half brothers, and who longed for the strength that he saw in such figures. Hence, his espousal of the paranoid ideology was both an attempt at reversing and denying the felt humiliations and a connection with powerful and effective masculine figures whose strength he might then experience.

The convergence of an aspect of character and development between Qutb and bin Laden is interesting. I would speculate that both men had to deal with compensatory inflated selves that rested on a sense of defective strength and masculinity, and that later humiliations that led to the paranoid gestalt involved the blows to the compensatory, split-off grandiosity. There may be a further correspondence with the group self of the Muslim Middle East. Perhaps there, too, the Arabs have a sense that the power and wealth that oil has brought to their societies are also fragile and hollow. The real strength of an effective society with governmental, commercial, and financial institutions in which citizens can do meaningful work is absent. Though their history and their decline and exploitation over the recent centuries give ample cause for humiliation and rage—and hence, the grounds for the development of the paranoid gestalt—would this aspect of the central hollowness of the group and individual self make these particular figures most congenial? Like the Germans, there is a psychological congruence between the creators of the ideology, the leaders, and the political group. In the Muslim Middle East, that congruence has a somewhat different cast.

IV

There are numerous other examples of paranoid leadership in history. The point of this essay is not to be complete in naming those many examples but rather to indicate the conceptual contours of a psychology of paranoid leadership. But even within my circumscribed ambitions, there are many questions that beg for further exploration. One is the interesting question whether a paranoid leader can enact the gestalt without the psychological readiness of the group, so to speak. I think the answer is no. Richard Nixon seems to be an example of that. Conversely, can a leader help a damaged group into a nonparanoid organization? The Black Civil Rights Movement may be an example of the latter. Though there were certainly paranoid elements of the movement—the Black Muslims—the dominant strain was Martin Luther King's integrationist, nondemonizing view of the world. It may also be that King did, in fact, reflect the dominant nature of the black population; for though they had ample reason to be both narcissistically damaged and enraged—as many were and are—their own ideology was the Christian ideal of the brotherhood of man.

Finally, I must note that once a paranoid organization becomes the structure of a nation, the ruthlessness of the force exerted against any who would differ is a factor in maintaining the power of the paranoid group. That ruthlessness is born of both the self-righteousness of the rulers and the concomitant demonization of any opposition. Hence, change or modification of the structure is very difficult. Change sometimes comes from outside force or with the decay of the belief in the perfection of the utopian state.

To summarize: Paranoid leadership cannot be considered apart from the condition of the group and the guiding ideology of the group and the leader. The peculiarity of paranoid leadership is that it springs from severe narcissistic injury that results in the cognitive-affective structure that I have called the paranoid gestalt. This gestalt offers a utopian vision—either secular or religious—together with the need to exterminate the evil other. The frequency of this political and social organization in history suggests that it is a kind of attractor state, a default organization, that emerges under stress.

Subject Index

A

Abolitionism, 58, 60
Abolitionist movement (1830), 68–69
Abolitionists, case of, 67–68
Absolute monarch, 88, 90, 107–108
Absolutism, 108
Agreeableness, 138
Alcibiades, 8–11
  in Athens, 10–11
  early life, 9–10
  gifted leader/military genius/impulsive,
    9–11
  and Hipponides, 10
  public life, 10–11
  vanity and ambition, 10
Al-Jazeera, 128, 130
  relationship to bin Laden, 128
Al-Qaeda, 119, 122, 128–129, 131–133, 150,
    167–168
Al-Quds al-'Arabi, 128
American Crusader forces, 129
Analysis of the Ego, 25, 29
Annihilation, 127, 154
Applied psychoanalysis, 13
Aristocracy, Plato's theory, 6, 8
Armenian crisis, 85
Aryans, 52
Ashanti campaign, 93
Ashwak, 165
9/11 attack, 120, 122, 133, 136, 140,
    149–151
Ayman al-Zawahiri, 168
  al-Jihad, formation of, 168

B

Bible
  Bush as participant in community Bible
    study, 144
  Egyptians, 5

excessive reading by Lincoln, 74
  Jacob, 3, 5, 25
  Joseph, story of, 3
  Moses, story of, 23
Bismarck, Otto von, 23, 52, 84–85, 96,
    111, 160
Björkö Treaty, 97
Black Civil Rights Movement, 170
*Blind Trust: Large Groups and Their Leaders
  in Times of Crisis and Terror*, 43
Bodily symbolism, 34
Boer Republic's act, 93, 99
Boxer Rebellion, 97, 101
Brzezinski, Zbigniew, 39–40
Bush, George W.
  conservative and liberal variations,
    148
  life stories and personality, 136–140
    narrative identity, 137
  as motivated agent, 139–140
    personality traits, 139
  redemptive journey, 142–145
    alcohol abuse, 143–144
    commitment as evangelist, 144–145
    Midland values, 149
    nomadic period, 143
    power of self-discipline, 148
    redemption sequence in '*A Charge to
      Keep*', 146–147
    rehabilitation in 1977, 144
    social reality, 142
    speech to firefighters, 9/11,
      148
    "the 4 B's," 143
  redemptive narratives, 140–142
  restoration of goodness through
    self-discipline, 145–150
    neoconservatism, 146
    Senior's defeat, 145

C.B. Strozier et al. (eds.), *The Leader*, 2nd ed., DOI 10.1007/978-1-4419-8387-9,
© Springer Science+Business Media, LLC 2011

Business
    Bernard Shaw's success in, 33
    family business of bin Laden, 123–124
    Wilhelm's presentation as a businessman,
        94

C
Carter, Jimmy, 37–38
Central Intelligence Agency (CIA), 38
A Charge to Keep, 146–147, 149–150
Chinese cultural revolution, 45–46
Churchill, Winston, 53
    calm certainty of victory, 53–54
    childhood, 53
Civilization and Its Discontents, 25
Civil rights, movements for, 141
Collective experiences
    of childhood, 6
    of shame and humiliation, 154
    of we-ness, 47
Collective patienthood, 35
Communist revolution, 52
Conflicts, drive related, 27
Conscientiousness, 138
Crisis
    Iran hostage, 38
    of the 1850s, *see* Lincoln, Abraham
Cubism, 49

D
Da Vinci, Leonardo, 17, 25
Death in Venice, 50
Death symbolism, 45
Declaration of Independence (US), 57–58, 60,
        62, 70–71
De Lagarde, Paul
    as critic, 158
    humiliation, source of paranoid
        character, 159
    influence on socialist ideologists, 160
    studies, 159
Delta Kappa Epsilon (DKE) fraternity
        parties, 143
Democracy, Plato's theory, 6–8
Depression, 30, 34, 79, 89,
        97, 107
Despotism, 7–8, 58
Die Krankheit Wilhelms II, 112
Dimensions of a New Identity, 34, 36
Drive theory
    conflicts, drive related, 27
    drives, according to Freud, 28
    Kaiser's driven display of himself, 82

oedipal drives, 22
Wilhelm's driven need for recognition/
        appreciation, 97

E
Ego personality
    controlled and adaptive ego strengths, 8
    ego ideal, 30, 47
        in Freud, 15
    ego identity, 138
    Henry, egotistic desires, 21
    Kubizek, alter-ego soul mate to Hitler, 162
    person's own ego, 30
    superego, 50
        formation in girls, 28
Erik Erikson
    bodily symbolism, 34
    Childhood and Society, 31, 33
    "collective patienthood," 35
    developmental progress chart, 32
    diversity of applied analytic work, 32
    Gandhi's midlife crisis, 32
    George Bernard Shaw, 33
    on Hitler, 31, 33–34
    Martin Luther, 32, 35
    on Thomas Jefferson in *Dimensions of a
        New Identity*, 34, 36
    Young Man Luther, 33
Extraversion, 138–139, 150

F
Family model for leadership, 25, 28
Feast of Sacrifice sermon, 132
Fliess, Wilhelm
    cubism, discovery of, 49
    "transference of creativity," 49
Franco-Prussian War, 160
Franklin, Benjamin, 141
French Revolution, 20–21, 154
Freud
    family issues with father cluster, 27
    family model for leadership, 25–28
    father in *Totem and Taboo*, 27–28
    group behavior, 29
        ego ideals, 30
        libidinal ties among individuals, 30
    Interpretation of Dreams, 25–26
    libidinal attachment for mother, 26
    'return of the repressed', 27
    rivalry with father, 26–27
    self-analysis, 25–26
    spread of psychological symptoms, 69

Freud and followers
  common ego ideal, 15
  Fliess, Wilhelm, 13
  limits to psychoanalytic theory, 17
  *Minutes of the Vienna Psychoanalytic
    Society*, 13
  monopolizing discussion, 15
  Otto Rank, 13
  paper on Tatjana Leontiev (Wittel), 16
  pathography, 17
  sexual and emotional pathology of
    poets, 17
  Stekel about Grillparzer, 14
  tyranny of Freud's leadership role, 16
  "tyranny of the urn," 15
  Vienna group's discussion, 16–17
Fugitive Slave Law, 58, 61, 65
The Fundamentalist Mindset, 160

G

Gandhi, Mohandas, 32, 34–35
  ashram, 35
  bodily symbols, 35
  Brahmacharya, 35
  Gandhi's Truth, 35
  learning from mistakes, 32
  personality, 35
  satyagraha, 32
Generativity, 32, 140–142
Glad, Betty, biographies of Jimmy Carter, 38
Government, forms of, 6
Gradiva: A Pompeiian Fancy, 113
Graf, Max, 13
Grashdanin (Russian paper), 85
Greece
  biographies of 51 of noblest Greeks, 8
  Persian and, 10
Group
  behavior, 29
    ego ideals, 30
    libidinal ties among individuals, 30
  damage to ideology of, 157
  damage to sense of power, 157
  ideals/ideologies, 157–158
    See also Ideals
  narcissistic leader and injured group, 38
  paranoid gestalt, 156
  psychoanalytic group cohesion, 47
  regression, 43
  self, concept of, 47–48, 52, 57–76, 156,
    158, 169
    See also Lincoln, Abraham
  understanding, 156

The Group Mind, 29
Group Psychology and the Analysis of the Ego,
    24–25, 29
Group self, 47–48, 52, 57–76, 156,
    158, 169
  See also Lincoln, Abraham
Gulf War
  First, 127, 133
  Second, 126, 129, 139

H
Hereditary degeneracy, 112–113
*High Hopes: The Clinton Presidency and the
    Politics of Ambition*, 41
History/historical
  of abuse by "Crusaders and Zionists," 52
  actor, 45–46
  American history, 73, 141, 153
    around issues of health of the leader, 40
  case history and psychological portrayal, 17
  circumstances, 30
  figure, 17
  German history, 77, 79, 160
  group's shared, 156
  humiliation in Serbian population, 42
  and issues of leadership (*Imago*), 18
  Kohut's contribution to, 47
  methods, 98
  model, 6
  Napoleon's personal, 20
  phases in political realities, 21
  powerful social change (Mazlish), 37
  process, 30
  psychism, interface of leader, group and, 46
  and psychology (Erikson's theory), 35
  reality, 28
  See also Psychohistory/psychohistorical
Hitler, Adolph, 160
  anti-Semitic beliefs, 162
  compensatory behaviors in childhood, 162
  element of paranoid gestalt, 163
  humiliation at hands of father, 161
  Kubizek's note, 162–163
  movement, 160
  narcissistic injury, 164
  paranoid psychological organization, 164
Holocaust, 52
"Holy Crusade" on slavery, 73
Homesickness, 75
Homosexuality, 24, 30
Hubris, 8, 83
Hypnosis, 30

I

Ideals, 40, 50, 58, 67, 78, 81, 99, 101, 115,
        132, 155, 157
    as "direction settings symbols of
        perfection," 50
    ego, 30
    group, 157–158
    life, 58
    narcissistic rage, 155
    of nation, 67
    need for, 157
    self from, 40
    "selfobjects" to determine, 81, 115
    subjects as embodiment of, 99
    superego, 58
    "symbolic leadership," 78
    Western, 132
Identity crisis, 32–33
Ideologies, 157
    See also Ideals
Imago, leadership into, 18
    Amenhoteps reign/religious activities,
        18–19
    Bismarck, dream of (Hans Sachs), 23
    life of Henry VIII (Flugel), 21–22
    Napoleon, life of, 19–20
        ambivalence, 20
        Louis, favorite brother, 23–24
        Paoli, 20
        patriotism, 20
        political mythology (Lorenz), 18
        Totem and Taboo, 18
The Immortal Ataturk: A Psychobiography, 44
Inferiority complex, theory of (Adler), 114
*In His Father's Shadow: The Transforming of
        George W. Bush*, 41
The Interpretation of Dreams, 25–26, 47

J

Jacksonian era, 66
Jacob, 3, 5, 25
Jefferson, Thomas, 31, 34, 36, 58, 73
Jihad(ist), 52, 120, 122, 125, 127–131, 133,
        165, 167–169
Joseph, 3–6
    abuse of power, 5
    adolescence, 3
    conflicts with brothers, 4–5
    dream interpretation skills, 3–6
    early life, 3
    efficient food crisis management, 4–5
    loyalty to Potiphar, 3–4
    new system of taxation/governance, 5–6

    past family conflicts, 4–5
    in prison, 4
    as vizier of Egypt, 4
Journal of Abnormal Psychology, 23
Jung, Carl, 28, 74

K

Kaiser Wilhelm II
    narcissistic psychopathology, 78
    personality, psychoanalytic
        self-psychology, 79–83
    character of contradictions, 80
    contemporaries, views of, 82–83
    craving for external reassurance, 82
    display of pseudoexcitement or frenzied
        activity, 79
    display of self-certainty, 81
    Reisekaiser or "traveling emperor," 82
    "selfobject" relationships, 80–81
    weakness, 83
    "Wilhelm Proteus," 82
    "political/symbolic leadership," 78
    press and German public opinion, 84–102
    "absolute" monarch, 88
    alliance of England/France/Russia, 93
    Anglo-German naval rivalry, 96
    Anglo-German relations, 84
    Ashanti campaign, 93
    blame on English press, 85
    capacity to grasp/retain information, 94
    communication with Germans, 95
    creation of German fleet, 92
    dependence on public opinion, effects,
        89–90, 98
    effort to prevent publication, 91
    Eulenburg's letter to Bülow, 99–100
    foreign policy, 101–102
    honorary titles, 96
    "Hun" speech, 97
    influence of subjects through press, 89
    influencing press and public
        demonstrations, 92
    Kruger telegram, 99–100
    missionaries, murder in China, 100–101
    "modern monarch,", 86
    pro-English policy, 87
    publication of misinformation, 90
    public condemnation and "nervous
        breakdowns," 89
    Real politik to politics of symbolism, 84
    self-object functions, 88
    symbolic leadership, 95
    "the struggle for the fleet," 92

in psychohistorical perspective, 112–117
  connection between disjointed
      personality and Germans, 115
  extreme behavior to breeding, 112
  hereditary degeneracy, 112–113
  interpretation of Wilhelm's
      psychopathology, 114
  self-pathology, 115–116
  "stigma of nature," 113
symbolic leadership of Germans, 102–111
  absolutism, 107–108
  criticism at Kaiser's methods, 111
  German national unity, 103
  "glorious past," conception of, 105
  historians on "personal regime,"
      108–109
  interview with Ganghofer, 106–107
  lack of self-cohesion, 106
  "modern Kaiser," 103
  narcissistic (self-object) bond, 109
  vulnerability to international insults,
      104–105
Kansas-Nebraska Act, 57, 72
Kennedy, John F., 40
Khomeini, Ayatollah, 40, 133
*Killing in the Name of Identity: A Study of
    Bloody Conflict*, 42
King, Martin Luther, 31–32, 170
Kohut, Heinz
  essay, "On Leadership," 48–49
  examples of theories of leadership, 51–53
  "Forms and Transformations of
      Narcissism," 53
  group self, concept of, 48
  The Interpretation of Dreams, 47
  leader and narcissistically crippled people,
      50–51
  psychoanalytic group cohesion, 47
  submission, 48
  theories of leadership, examples of, 51
  "we-ness," experience of, 48

L
Ladenese Epistle, 120, 126, 131
Langbehn, Julius, 159–160
Leader(s)
  in ancient times
    Alcibiades, 8–11
    Joseph, 3–6
    Plato, 6–8
  charismatic and messianic, 50–51, 53–54,
      97, 162
  illness in leader's life, 38–40

narcissistic, 38, 43
power, 30
psychism, group/history and interface of,
    46
revolutionary ascetic, 37
traits for successful, 126
traits missing in paranoid, 66
Leadership
  family model for, 25, 28
  into *Imago*, 18
    Amenhoteps reign/religious activities,
        18–19
    Bismarck, dream of (Hans Sachs), 23
    life of Henry VIII (Flugel), 21–22
    Napoleon, *see* Napoleon
    political mythology (Lorenz), 18
    Totem and Taboo, 18
  Kohut, Heinz
    essay, "On Leadership," 48–49
    examples of theories of leadership,
        51–53
    leader and narcissistically crippled
        people, 50–51
  paranoid, 153–170
    Ayman al-Zawahiri, 168
    bin Laden, *see* Osama bin Laden
    De Lagarde, Paul, 158–160, 164–165
    Hitler, Adolph, 160
    issues of, 158
    "paranoid gestalt," 153
    Sayyid Qutb, 164–168
    story of Nazi Germany, 158–164
  Plato's theory of, 8
  political, 78, 90, 95
  psychology of (Volkan), 42
  styles, Plato's theory, 6–8
  symbolic, 78, 83, 91, 95, 97, 102–111
    See also Symbolic leadership of
        Germans
  theory of, 32
    Erikson's, 34–36
    Plato's, 8
    psychological theory, 54
*The Leader, the Led, and the Psyche: Essays in
    Psychohistory*, 37
Leading Minds: An Anatomy of Leadership,
    135
League of Nations, 40
Lenin, 37, 52
Life of Washington, 71
Lifton, Robert Jay
  Chinese thought reform, 44
  death symbolism, relevance of, 45

Lifton, Robert Jay (*cont.*)
   ethos of the survivor, 45
   "formulation," 45
   Mao and Chinese cultural revolution, 45
   "psychism," 46
   Revolutionary Immortality, 45
   "shared themes approach," 45
Lincoln, Abraham
   abolitionism, 58, 60
   abolitionists, case of, 67–68
   Declaration of Independence, 57–58, 60,
      62, 70–71
   defensive use of violence, 68
   effect of slavery on white workers, 58–59
   Fugitive Slave Law, 61
   "Holy Crusade" on slavery, 73
   Jacksonian(s), 72
      era, 66
   Lovejoy's death, 67–68
   Missouri Compromise, 58
   opposition to slavery, 57–59
   paranoia, 66, 70
   popular sovereignty, concept of, 62
   racial inequality, 59
   Republican Convention of 1860, 67
   and South, 70–71
   South Carolina Legislature, 72
   speech at State Republican Convention,
      1858, 62–63
      conspiracy argument, 64
      Kansas-Nebraska Bill of 1854, 63
      two distinct parts, 63
   Springfield's Colonization Society, 61
   suspiciousness of 1850s, 69
The Lives of the Noble Grecians and Romans, 8

M
Mao Tse-tung, 45
   revolutionary immortality, 46
   romanticism, 46
Martin Luther, 32, 35
   Augustinian order, 32
   bodily symbols, 35
   public and private, connection between, 35
Mazlish, Bruce
   corresponding processes, 37
   individual *vs.* collective psychology, 36
   The Leader, the Led, and the Psyche:
      Essays in Psychohistory, 37
   "pathographies," 38
   Revolutionary Ascetic, 37
Megalomania, 22

Meinecke, Friedrich (German historian),
   98, 106
Mein Kampf, 52–53, 158, 161
Messianic leaders, 50–51, 53–54, 97, 162
Meyer, Konrad Ferdinand, 13
Milosevic, Slobodan, 43–44
   ethnic-cleansing wars, 43
Missouri Compromise, 58
Modern monarch, 86
   See also Kaiser Wilhelm II
Moses and Monotheism, 25

N
Napoleon
   ambivalence, 20
   life of, 19–20
   Louis, Napoleon's favorite brother, 23–24
   Paoli, 20
   patriotism, 20
Narcissism/narcissistic, 43–44, 53
   bond, 109
   crippled people, 50–51
   disorder, 79
   disturbed adult experiences, 79–80, 117
   injuries, 42, 157–158, 164–165, 167,
      169–170
   leaders, 38, 43
   needs, 49, 79, 109
   organization, 165
   painful experiences, 47
   patient, 76
   personalities, 40
   psychopathology, 78–80, 83, 86, 91,
      115, 117
   rage, 155–156
Narrative identity, 137–138, 142, 145,
   147, 150
Nasser, 167
Nativism, 67, 74–75
Nativist
   movement, 75, 153
   sentiment, 74
Nazi genocidal project, 44
Nazi Germany, 46, 51, 158–164, 168
   excerpt from Wansee conference, 158
Nazi ideology, 159
Neoconservatism, 146
Neuroticism, 138
New Introductory Lectures on Psychoanalysis
   (Freud), 113
"New Light" movement in 1740, 73
Nixon, Richard, 37, 170

O

Obama, Barack, 120, 134, 153
Oedipus complex, 21–22, 28, 37, 139
Office of Strategic Services (OSS), 161
Oligarchy, Plato's theory, 6–8
Ontogeny, 28
Openness to experience, 138–139, 150
Operation Desert Fox, 129
"Ordinary Papyrus," 4
Osama bin Laden, 167–168
  future, 132–134
    9/11 attack, 133
    Feast of Sacrifice sermon, 132
    Pew Trust Global Attitudes survey,
        132–133
    polls and videogames, 132–133
    Ummah Defense (videogame), 133
  mediating cosmic warrior, 128–131
    comparisons, personages of early
        Islamic/contemporary, 130
    epistles, 129–130
    Operation Desert Fox, 129
    pan-Islamic Muslim polity, 131
    relationship to al-Jazeera, 128
    sermon on the holiest day, 129–130
    Taysir Alluni interview, 131
  as a person
    anti-imperial polemics, 122–123
    disgust for Saudi elite, 127
    familial dispossession, effect of, 127
    family, 123
    fundamentalist and terrorist, 121–122
    genres of public political discourse, 122
    "Islamic truth," 126
    Ladenese Epistle, 120, 126, 131
    mother, 124–125
    Nida'ul Islam interview, 124
    risk taker, 125
    Second Gulf war, 126
    US invasion of Lebanon in 1982, 127
    Wahhabi-Salafi model of Islamic
        rules, 125
    Zio-Crusader alliance, 127
  and Qutb, 168–169
  rise of, 52–53
  Saddam Hussein's invasion in Kuwait, 169
Ottoman Empire, collapse of, 85, 131, 157

P

Pahlavi, Mohammad-Reza Shah, 40
Pan-Islamic Muslim polity, 131

Paranoia, 66, 70
Paranoid gestalt, 153–158, 160, 163–164, 167,
        169–170
  annihilation, extreme forms, 154
  French and Russian revolutions, 154
  group, understanding, 156
  ideal state, 154
  imbalance of power, 154
  narcissistic rage, 155
  pride in power, 156
  shame and humiliation, experiences
        of, 154
  weakness or defect, experience of, 156
Paranoid leadership, 153–170
  Ayman al-Zawahiri, 168
  bin Laden, *see* Osama bin Laden
  De Lagarde, Paul, 158–160,
        164–165
  Hitler, Adolph, 160
  issues of, 158
    story of Nazi Germany, 158–164
  paranoid gestalt, *see* Paranoid gestalt
  Sayyid Qutb, 164–168
Pathographies, 17–18, 38
Pathology, 17, 27–28, 34
  See also Psychopathology
Permanent revolution, principle of
        (Trotsky), 46
Personality
  first layer of, 138
    dispositions, 138
    social actor, 138
  second layer, 138
    as motivated agent, 138–139
  third layer, 138–139
    autobiographical author, 138–139
  traits, 40, 138
    dispositional, 150
    See also Traits
Pew Charitable Trusts, 132
  Global Attitudes survey, 132
Phylogeny, 28
Plato, 6–8
  democracy, 7
  despotism, 7
  governmental forms, 6–8
    movement from one form to another,
        6, 8
  oligarchy, 6–7
  psychological basis of leadership, 6
  Republic, 6
  theory of leadership, 8
  tyrant's qualities, 8

Plutarch (first psychohistorian), 8–10
   conflict psychology, 9
   leadership style, 8
   personal characteristics/psychological
      traits, discussion of, 8–9
   platonic conviction of right/wrong, 8
Political leadership, 78, 90, 95
Popular sovereignty, concept of, 62
Post, Jerrold, 38
   effect of health, 40
   illness in leader's life, 38–40
   narcissistic leader and injured group, 38
   "white revolution," 40
Power
   damage to group's sense of, 157
   disparity in power relationships, 156, 160
   experience of, 155–156
   imbalance of, 154
   lack of, 155
   leader's, 30
   of press, 85–86, 88
   pride in, 156
   psychic, 46
   rational and irrational motives, 20
   of self-discipline, 148
   symbolic, 109, 132
   use and abuse of, 5
Protestant alliance, 22
Psychism, 46
Psychoanalysis, 13, 15, 31, 46, 48, 69, 79, 86
Psychobiography, 6, 17, 44
Psychodynamics, 8
Psychohistory/psychohistorical, 5, 9, 50,
      78, 116
   analysis, 50
   investigation of Wilhelm II's leadership, 78
   perspective, 5
      Kaiser in, 112–118
   Plutarch (first psychohistorian), 9
Psychologie de Foules (Le Bon), 29
Psychopathology, 8, 78–80, 83, 86, 91,
      112–115, 117, 138
Psychosexual development in females, 28
Psychotherapy, 138, 142

R
Racism, 59–60, 72
Redemptive narratives in life and culture
   American tales, 141
   generative adults, 141
   generativity, 140
   objective content-analytic procedures, 141
Renshon, Stanley, 40

Clinton presidency, 41
   psychological motivations, 40
Republic, 6
Republic(an)
   aristocratic, 6
   Boer Republic's act, 99
   form of government, 59
   institutions, 58
   political base, 145
   Republican Convention of 1860 (US),
      62, 67
   South African, 93
   virtues, 71
   Weimar, 52
Revolution/revolutionary
   ascetic leaders, 37
   Chinese cultural, 45–46
   Communist, 52
   French, 20–21, 154
   permanent revolution, principle of
      (Trotsky), 46
   Revolutionary Ascetic, 37
   Revolutionary Immortality, 45
   romanticism, 46
   Russian, 16, 154
   'white', 40
Robins, Robert, 40
Roosevelt, Franklin Delano, 39–40
Russian revolution, 16, 154
Russo-Japanese War, 109

S
Saddam Hussein, 120, 126, 133, 139–140,
      150, 169
   Kuwait invasion in 1991, 169
Sadger, Isidor, 13–14, 17–18
Satyagraha, 32
Sayyid Qutb, 164–168
   Ashwak (autobiographical novel), 165
   family, 165
   imprisonment, 167
   influence in jihad, 166
   marriage, 166
   and bin Laden, 169
   paranoid narcissistic organization, 165
   utopian fantasy, 166
Self-pathology, 79–80, 115
Shared themes approach, 45
Shaw, George Bernard, 31, 33
   "professional apprenticeship," 33
Slavery, 57–76
   See also Lincoln, Abraham
Social Justice in Islam, 166

Socrates, 6–7, 9–10
"Spiritual Rappings," 74
Stalin, Joseph, 37, 39–40, 51
"Stigma of Nature," 113
Superego, 28, 38, 50
Surface psychology, 14
Symbolic communication, 109
Symbolic gestures/actions, 95, 97–99
Symbolic immortality, 40
Symbolic leader/leadership, 78, 83, 91, 95, 97
    capacities, 83
    definition, 78
    Wilhelm II, 102–111, 116
Symbolic leadership of Germans, 102–111
    absolutism, 107–108
    criticism at Kaiser's methods, 111
    German national unity, 103
    glorious past, conception of, 105
    historians on "personal regime," 108–109
    interview with Ganghofer, 106–107
    lack of self-cohesion, 106
    "modern Kaiser," 103
    narcissistic (self-object) bond, 109
    vulnerability to international insults,
        104–105
Symbolic power, 109, 132
Symbolism
    bodily, 34
    death, 45
    Real politik to politics of, 84

T
Terrorism, 7, 157
Terrorist attacks of 9/11, 120, 122, 133, 136,
        140, 149–151
Theory(ies)
    conspiracy theory of Lincoln, 64–66
    of inferiority complex (Adler), 114
    of leadership, 32
        Erikson's, 34–36
        Plato's, 8
        psychological, 54
    psychoanalytic, 15, 17, 21, 36–37, 79
    of right of secession (Calhoun), 72
Third World War, 127, 133
*Thomas Woodrow Wilson: A Psychological
       Study*, 25
Traits
    character based personality traits, 40

character traits and ideologies/doctrines,
        correspondence, 37
    dispositional, 138–140
    of extraversion, 139
    important for successful leader, 126
    life narratives and personality, 138
    missing in paranoid leaders, 66
    psychological, 8–9
    psychopathological, 9, 46
Treaty of Brest-Litovsk in 1917, 52
Treaty of Versailles, 27, 157, 160
Turki al-Faisal, 120
Tyrannical government, 6–8

U
Ummah Defense (video game), 133
Uncle Tom's Cabin, 73–74
US invasion
    of Iraq, 136, 139
    of Lebanon in 1982, 127

V
Van den Bruck, Moeller, 159–160
Violence, 5, 53, 68–69, 127, 154, 168
Volkan, Vamik
    crisis, 43
    cultural rituals, 42
    group regression, 43
    psychology of leadership, 42
    "trauma", 42

W
Wahhabi-Salafi model of Islamic rules, 125
Welt politik, 111, 116
West–South alliance, 71
White revolution, 40
*Wilhelm Hohenzollern: The Last of the
       Kaisers*, 113
*Wilhelm II.: Versuch Einer Psychologischen
       Analyse*, 112
Wilson, Woodrow, 27, 39–40
Wittels, Fritz, 14, 16
World Islamic Front, 120
World War I, 52, 111–112, 157, 160
World War II, 53

Z
Zio-Crusader alliance, 121, 127